THE MESOAMERICAN INDIAN LANGUAGES

CAMBRIDGE LANGUAGE SURVEYS

General Editors: W. Sidney Allen, B. Comrie, C. J. Fillmore, E. J. A. Henderson, F. W. Householder, R. Lass, J. Lyons, R. B. Le Page, P. H. Matthews, F. R. Palmer, R. Posner, J. L. M. Trim

This series offers general accounts of all the major language families of the world. Some volumes are organized on a purely genetic basis, others on a geographical basis, whichever yields the most convenient and intelligible grouping in each case. Sometimes, as with the Australian volume, the two in any case coincide.

Each volume compares and contrasts the typological features of the languages it deals with. It also treats the relevant genetic relationships, historical development, and sociolinguistic issues arising from their role and use in the world today. The intended readership is the student of linguistics or general linguist, but no special knowledge of the languages under consideration is assumed. Some volumes also have a wider appeal, like those on Australia and North America, where the future of the languages and their speakers raises important social and political issues.

Already published:
The languages of Australia *R. M. W. Dixon*
The languages of the Soviet Union *Bernard Comrie*

Forthcoming titles include:
Japanese/Korean *M. Shibatani and Ho-min Sohn*
Chinese *J. Norman and Mei Tsu-lin*
S. E. Asia *J. A. Matisoff*
Dravidian *R. E. Asher*
Austronesian *R. Blust*
Afro-Asiatic *R. Hetzron*
North American Indian *W. Chafe*
Slavonic *R. Sussex*
Germanic *R. Lass*
Celtic *D. MacAulay et al.*
Indo-Aryan *C. P. Masica*
Balkans *J. Ellis*
Creole languages *J. Holm*
Romance languages *R. Posner*
Papuan languages of Oceania *W. Foley*

THE MESOAMERICAN
INDIAN LANGUAGES

JORGE A. SUÁREZ

Instituto de Investigaciones Filológicas
Universidad Nacional Autónoma de México

CAMBRIDGE UNIVERSITY PRESS

Cambridge
London   New York   New Rochelle
Melbourne   Sydney

Published by the Press Syndicate of the University of Cambridge
The Pitt Building, Trumpington Street, Cambridge CB2 1RP
32 East 57th Street, New York, NY 10022, USA
296 Beaconsfield Parade, Middle Park, Melbourne 3206, Australia

First published 1983

Filmset in Hong Kong by
Asco Trade Typesetting Ltd
Printed in Great Britain at the
University Press, Cambridge

Library of Congress catalogue card number: 81-21641

British Library Cataloguing in Publication Data

Suárez, Jorge A.
The Mesoamerican Indian languages.–
(Cambridge language surveys)
1. Indians of Central America–Languages
I. Title
497   PM3001

ISBN 0 521 22834 4 hard covers
ISBN 0 521 29669 2 paperback

CONTENTS

ILLUSTRATIONS

MAPS

FIGURES

TABLES

PREFACE

The aim of this book is to offer an overall view of Mesoamerican Indian languages. Although the approach is basically synchronic, in view of the importance of the cultural development of the area before discovery, a historical perspective is adopted in the last three chapters. No previous knowledge of any Mesoamerican language is assumed on the part of the reader, but familiarity with basic linguistic notions and terminology is expected.

The presentation throughout the book is strongly descriptive with little, if any, room for theoretical considerations or generalizations. It has not been the author's intention to give his views on Mesoamerican languages, but to characterize them by adopting a view as neutral as possible. Consequently, except for changes in terminology, the discussion of the data has been kept close to the analyses given in the sources. This procedure runs the risk of a certain heterogeneity in the treatment of the materials, but this seemed preferable to the misinterpretation that might result from a reanalysis of languages which are often known only indirectly from a few descriptions.

The choice of topics dealt with, especially in chapters 5–8, has been largely dictated by the availability of minimally comparable data in the various linguistic families. In some cases important studies have been neglected because they were an almost unique contribution to a certain topic. The distribution of materials has aimed at keeping a balance between characterization of the whole area and a characterization of each linguistic family.

Given the coverage of the book, most of the data used are secondhand and are acknowledged in the sources. While it was considered that for the data in the phonology and morphology chapters global reference to the sources was enough, for the sentences quoted in chapters 7 and 8 precise references are given in the appendix. Whenever no source is indicated the data are from the author's unpublished materials.

An effort has been made to refer in the suggested readings only to published books or papers, but this was not always possible and some references are given to papers read at professional meetings. In case the reader misses some important recent item in the references he should notice that those given here were those actually used for writing the book and that, except for some items known in unpublished form, the author confined himself to works available to the end of 1979.

Thanks are due to Rubén Bonifaz Nuño, director of the Instituto de Investigaciones Filológicas, where this book was written as part of the author's activity at that institution.

Grateful acknowledgment is given to Henry Bradley, Katheryn Josserand, Norman A. McQuown and Mercedes Olivera for permission to quote unpublished materials. A general indebtedness shared by anyone working in this area is due to the members of the Summer Institute of Linguistics and is reflected in the references quoted.

Charles J. Fillmore read an earlier version of the volume and made many detailed and useful suggestions not only as to content but as to presentation and style; most of his remarks were taken into account but, naturally, in no case is he responsible for any deficiencies the book may have. Also various suggestions, especially regarding Mayan languages, were made by Jon Dayley, but again only the author is responsible for the text.

The author is also much indebted to Mrs Penny Carter and Mr Robert Seal for their editing work and for the careful checking of the original to remove inconsistencies and omissions.

This book is dedicated to Norman A. McQuown, a tireless researcher and promoter of research in the field of Mesoamerican Indian languages.

NOTATIONAL CONVENTIONS

-   (1) separates morphemes in examples from Indian languages
  (2) joins English words (in the English literal translation) that translate a single word or morpheme of the Indian language example

=   (1) marks clitics in examples from Indian languages
  (2) separates English words (in the English literal translation) that correspond to different morphemes in the Indian language example

( )=   indicates the English literal translation of a morpheme that, in the Indian language example, has no overt manifestation

X   is used in the English literal translation in the place of a morpheme that cannot be translated separately

Transcriptions are phonemic and use the International Phonetic alphabet; t͡ʃ, ṣ and ẓ are used for the voiceless retroflex affricate, the voiceless retroflex fricative and the voiced retroflex fricative respectively. Slant lines (/ /) are only used in some cases to set off phonemes or words in the phonology chapters.

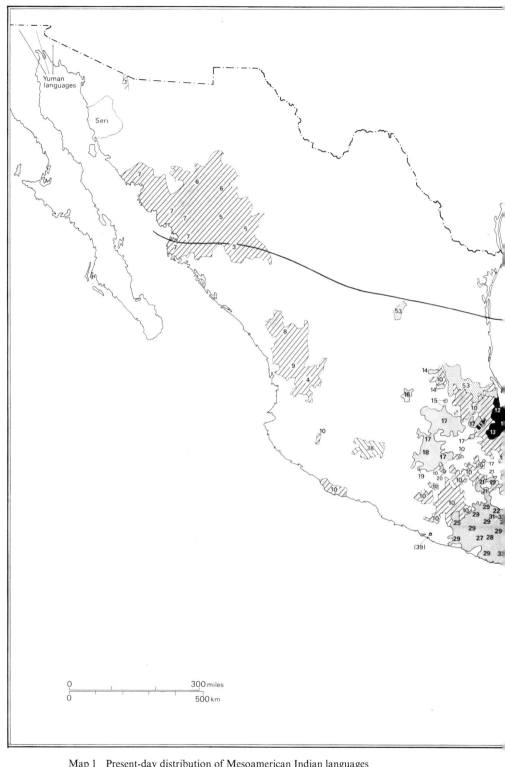

Map 1   Present-day distribution of Mesoamerican Indian languages

ɪ	Uto-Aztecan 1–11	ᴠ	Cuitlatec 39
ɪɪ	Totonac-Tepehua 12–13	ᴠɪ	Tequistlatec-Jicaque 40–43
ɪɪɪ	Otomanguean 14–37	ᴠɪɪ	Huave 44
ɪᴠ	Tarascan 38	ᴠɪɪɪ	Mixe-Zoque 45–52

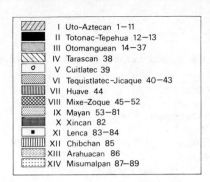

I	Uto-Aztecan	1—11
II	Totonac-Tepehua	12—13
III	Otomanguean	14—37
IV	Tarascan	38
V	Cuitlatec	39
VI	Tequistlatec-Jicaque	40—43
VII	Huave	44
VIII	Mixe-Zoque	45—52
IX	Mayan	53—81
X	Xincan	82
XI	Lenca	83—84
XII	Chibchan	85
XIII	Arahuacan	86
XIV	Misumalpan	87—89

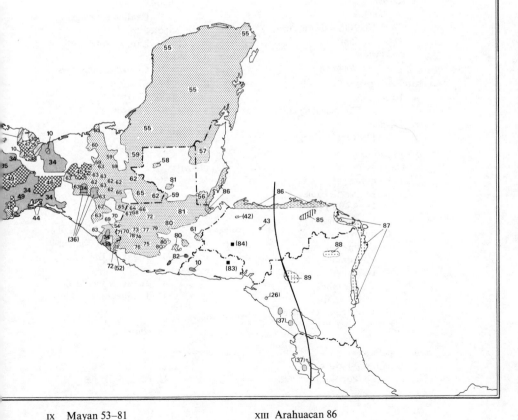

Table 1. *Classification of Mesoamerican Indian languages and index to map 1*

I. UTO-AZTECAN*
(A. Numic)
(B. Tübatulabal)
(C. Hopi)
(D. Takic)
E. Pimic
  (1. Pima-Papago)
  (2. Lower Pima)
  (3. Northern Tepehuán)
  4. Southern Tepehuán
F. Taracahitic
  a. Tarahumara-Varohio
  (5. Tarahumara languages)
  (6. Varohio)
  b. Cahitic
  (7. Yaqui-Mayo)
G. Corachol
  8. Cora
  9. Huichol
H. Aztecan
  a. Nahuatl
  10. Nahuatl languages, Pipil
  b. Pochutec
  11. Pochutec[†]

II. TOTONAC-TEPEHUA
A. Totonacan
  12. Totonac languages
B. Tepehua
  13. Tepehua languages

III. OTOMANGUEAN
A. Otopamean
  a. Pamean
  14. North Pame
  15. South Pame[†]
  16. Chichimec
  b. Otomian
  α. Otomi-Mazahua
  α′. Otomi
  17. Otomi languages
  α″. Mazahua
  18. Mazahua
  β. Matlatzinca-Ocuiltec
  19. Matlatzinca
  20. Ocuiltec
B. Popolocan
  a. Popoloc-Ixcatec
  21. Popoloc languages

22. Chocho
23. Ixcatec
b. Mazatecan
  24. Mazatec languages
C. Subtiaba-Tlapanec
  25. Tlapanec
  26. Subtiaba[†]
D. Amuzgo
  27. Guerrero Amuzgo
  28. Oaxaca Amuzgo
E. Mixtecan
  a. Mixtec
  29. Mixtec languages
  b. Cuicatec
  30. Cuicatec
  c. Trique
  31. Copala Trique
  32. Chicahuaxtla Trique
F. Chatino-Zapotec
  a. Chatino
  33. Chatino languages
  b. Zapotecan
  34. Zapotec languages[‡]
G. Chinantecan
  35. Chinantec languages
H. Chiapanec-Mangue
  36. Chiapanec[†]
  37. Mangue[†]

IV. TARASCAN
  38. Tarascan

V. CUITLATEC
  39. Cuitlatec[†]

VI. TEQUISTLATEC-JICAQUE
A. Tequistlatecan
  40. Coastal (or Lowland or Huamelula) Chontal
  41. Highland Chontal
B. Jicaque
  42. Jicaque from El Palmar[†]
  43. Jicaque from La Flor

VII. HUAVE
  44. Huave

VIII. MIXE-ZOQUE
A. Zoquean
  45. Chiapas Zoque

---

[*] Languages or subgroups in parentheses are outside Mesoamerica.

[†] Extinct language.

[‡] In some classifications of Mesoamerican languages 'Papabuco' is listed either as a distinct Zapotec subgroup or as a further group at the same level as Zapotec and Chatino groups, but Papabuco is simply a Zapotec language that just happened to receive a distinct name in historical sources (cf. Suárez 1972).

[§] A large family; the rest is located in Central and South America.

[**] A large family; the rest is located in South America.

1

The study of Mesoamerican Indian languages

A glance at the chapter references in this book will show that most of the reference works were written within the last fifty years, and consequently any survey of the linguistic work done on the Mesoamerican Indian languages could not fail to stress the great improvement that works published within this period represent over previous studies. In any case, owing to obvious historical reasons, research on these languages does not go back more than four and a half centuries. In spite of this the study of Mesoamerican Indian languages has made a distinct contribution to our linguistic knowledge, and this chapter is devoted to giving an outline of its development.

1.1 The missionary period

Knowledge of Mesoamerican Indian languages began with the first Spaniards who had learned a native language and acted as interpreters, so that the beginnings of the study of these languages may be fixed arbitrarily from the time when, on 13 March 1519, the members of the expedition that would start the conquest of Mexico met Jerónimo de Aguilar, a survivor of a shipwreck who had lived among Mayan speakers and had learned their language. The Spaniards' earliest communication with the Indians was through interpreters and represented only a practical knowledge of the languages. The gathering of systematic knowledge proceeded basically along two lines: descriptions of the languages themselves and the gathering of general information about them. Naturally, information on the languages is to be found in many writings of the epoch; but of special interest is the fact that between 1577 and 1648 the Spanish Crown sent a questionnaire to local authorities which, besides asking for information on geographical, economic, historical and ethnological aspects, also requested details of the languages spoken in the locality: whether there was any general language in use, the name(s) of the language(s), the name of the locality in the local language and its meaning. The answers to this questionnaire constitute the so-called *Relaciones Geográficas* ('Geographical Reports') that are basic for drawing a linguistic map of the area for the period of first contact.

The preparation of descriptions of the languages, on the other hand, was prompted by motivations of religious indoctrination. The conversion of the native population to the Catholic religion was one of the aims of the Spaniards, and it was at the request of the conqueror of Mexico, Hernán Cortez, that the first contingent of Franciscan friars arrived in 1524 to start the task of conversion; they were followed by Dominicans, Augustinians and Jesuits. These regular orders very soon adopted the policy that the conversion effort should be conducted in the native language (cf. chapter 11). To fulfil their tasks the orders needed a much more intimate knowledge of the languages than the rudimentary one sufficient for use as a contact or for trade purposes. They had to teach, preach and take confession in the native languages, and assist the friars to do the same without having to start from scratch. This resulted in an amazing number of *Doctrinas* ('catechisms'), *Confesionarios* ('manuals for confession'), *Sermonarios* ('collections of sermons'), *Artes* ('grammars') and *Vocabularios* ('vocabularies'). In the period from 1524 to 1572 over a hundred were written for ten languages spoken in the Viceroyalty of New Spain (which included only part of present-day Mexico). Many of these works were never printed, circulating only in manuscript; those that were, were printed in New Spain. The friars, especially the Franciscans, were imbued with a humanistic spirit which, among other things, is reflected in the fact that the first bishop of Mexico, Francisco de Zumárraga, introduced the printing press to the New World in 1534, and that the first printed book (1539) was a bilingual catechism in Spanish and Nahuatl. This humanistic spirit was also reflected in the founding of schools for sons of Indian nobility, where Spanish and Latin were taught and religious works were translated into the native languages. The friars were also anxious to familiarize themselves with native cultures, chiefly as a means of preventing the introduction of native beliefs into Catholic religion, and they therefore asked their Indian pupils to write about their cultures. The result was the preservation of a corpus of the language about subjects not related to the Catholic faith (cf. chapter 9).

The grammars written within this period are generally valued only to the extent that they offer raw materials on the respective languages, and are usually lumped together and dismissed as merely latinized descriptions. One should not, however, overlook the fact that they do represent the earliest attempts within the European linguistic tradition at coping with exotic languages. The simple fact of the Spaniards' interest in these languages contrasts sharply with their absolute disregard of foreign languages of the classical Greek and Latin cultures, for example. Of course, the Spaniards were in some ways prepared for their new situation, because of their experience with Arabs and Jews and the problems of conversion they had to face recovering the southern region of Spain from the Arabs. At the time of the conquest of America, Spaniards were very language conscious both about foreign languages and about the assumed superiority of their own. It is important that in 1492 Antonio de Nebrija wrote a Spanish grammar and, when asked by the Queen what use it would be, replied that it would be valuable for teaching Spanish to her new vassals in the same way that she had learned Latin by means of the Latin grammar that he had written years before. It is natural, then, that Nebrija's grammars were taken as a model for writing grammars of unknown languages; indeed, there was hardly any other model, and, as it is repeatedly stated, it is better to have a bad model than no model at all.

Certainly it is not difficult to find instances where the Indian language has been forced into Latin patterns; for example, in the presentation of a full nominal declension for Matlatzinca (Basalenque 1975 [1642]), or in the verbal paradigms of Yucatec presented on the Latin model, showing no awareness of the structure of tenses and modes in the former language (Coronel [1620] in Martínez Hernández 1929). Also, a frequent error to be found in the literature is the assumption that the Indian language has the same parts of speech as Latin. On the other hand, the statement that the language lacked syntax (Carochi (1892 [1645]: 400) is not a unique example), while obviously wrong in absolute terms, is understandable in that the authors were considering as syntax the use of cases and features of agreement proper to Latin, and these patterns were not found in most Indian languages.

However, these grammars were intended as practical aids for learning the language so that in most cases the references to Latin or Spanish were by way of comparison. The practice of inventing declensions for languages not having them was not the most common procedure, but rather the explicit statement that the language lacked declension, or plural, or an article, and so on (cf. Córdova 1886 [1578]: 12). Even in the presentation of verbal paradigms closely matching those of Spanish it is clear that, although they were described as equivalents, the authors were well aware of the differences in structure; this can be seen, for example, by comparing the display of optative paradigms in the first grammar of Nahuatl with the concise statement on its formation in the same grammar (Olmos 1972 [1547]: 77). This practice of giving equivalents for Latin and Spanish forms did not prevent the authors from recognizing and presenting those features that were characteristic of the Indian language; thus Córdova (1886 [1578]: 36–7) states: 'verbs follow, and in order to understand them it has to be noticed that this language (sc. Zapotec) has many different verbs, and among them many which are neither used in our language nor in Latin'. Were friars merely copying Latin structure they could scarcely have described, as they did from the very beginning, the morphological mechanism for transitivity in Nahuatl, for which even a new terminology was coined, for example 'compulsive' (= causative), 'applicative' (= benefactitive). The differences could also be quite marked, like those found in Tarascan in the expressions of location (cf. chapter 6), features remarkably grasped by Gilberti (1898 [1558]: 219) who, summing up the characteristics of the language, points out that one could not simply say 'put it here', but reference had to be made in the verb to the shape of the object, the position it would be in when at rest, and the shape of the place. In some cases the authors not only realized the differences but could deduce the rationale behind the Indian usage, as for example when Carochi (1892 [1645]: 421), after correcting previous descriptions of Nahuatl and stating that in this language locative complements were usually not marked with prepositions, comments that it was not necessary to say 'be in', 'go to', 'pass through' or 'depart from' because the prepositions were already implied in the verbs.

Frequently references to dialect differences are also found in these grammars, and the grammar of Mixtec by Antonio de los Reyes (1890 [1593]) contains an outline of Mixtec dialectology, giving dialect areas and specific indications as to sound differences (cf. the tabulation of these differences in Arana and Swadesh 1965, and the dialect areas plotted in a map by Dahlgren 1954). A quotation from this same work is useful to illuminate another aspect of the friars' attitude toward the Indian languages: 'Notwithstanding the imperfection of this Mixtec language and the defects that may be noted in it characteristic of a barbarous language, most parts of it can be reduced to rules and ordered as an *arte*' (Reyes, Antonio 1890 [1593]: 4). On the one hand the reference to 'imperfections' is a reflection of the concept of 'barbarous' people (this type of unfavourable judgement was never expressed relative to Nahuatl as spoken by the Aztecs – a group that did not impress the Spaniards as barbarous), while it is recognized on the other hand that these languages, even if barbarous, have the basic characteristics of 'true' languages – a remarkable attitude when one realizes that there are still many people who consider Indian languages as 'without grammar' and with 'unarticulated sounds'.

Not all these works are of the same quality: there are clear differences according to the language and to the author, and depending on the part of the language described. As is to be expected for that period, the description and recognition of contrasts are weakest for sounds; in general the friars coped rather well with simple systems like that of the Nahuatl (cf. 3.1.1), and even with those of moderate complexity in the consonants. However, rich vowel systems such as those found in Otomian and Chinantecan languages (cf. 3.1.5) were markedly underdifferentiated, and tones were at most dimly recognized but in no case marked in the orthography. As for grammar, one gets the impression that those languages with tight word structure like Tarascan or Nahuatl were more tractable than those with a more simple structure but which have clitics and particles that interact closely with properly affixal elements.

Most of these grammars were written during the sixteenth and seventeenth centuries, their number and quality decreasing during the eighteenth century, and by the last century very few were produced at all. In spite of this some remarkable contributions are found like the grammar of Nahuatl by Tapia Zenteno (1885 [1753]). This work has the merit of being a description based on the living language, rather than a rehash of older grammars as the tradition became established during the eighteenth century; it contains references to dialect differences, as well as to the non-occurrence in the speech of the Indians of forms given by earlier grammarians. Furthermore, it is probably the first work in which earlier descriptions are criticized because they forced an Indian language into the Latin mould with respect to grammatical categories.

1.2 The nineteenth century

The work by Lorenzo Hervás y Panduro, a Spanish Jesuit who first worked as a missionary in America and was then exiled to Italy, may be considered as the outcome and epitome of the missionary linguistic work and also as marking the beginnings of a new period. In 1784 in Italy, he published part of a larger work, his *Catalogo delle lingue conosciute e notizia della loro affinitá e diversitá* ('Catalogue of the known languages and account of their affinities and diversity'). This work was subsequently reedited in enlarged form in Spanish (Hervás y Panduro 1800–5). In it the author attempted to trace the relationships among human groups on the basis of language affinity. Containing unpublished data that were made available to the author by his missionary colleagues, it concentrates not on description but on enumeration, location and classification of the languages, and constitutes the first survey of Mesoamerican Indian languages. Hervás y Panduro foreshadows the genealogical classification of languages, and for Mesoamerica he recognizes the relationship of Yucatec with the Quichean group (Hervás y Panduro 1800: 304), and reports approvingly the opinion voiced by the Jesuit Andrés Pérez Ribas in 1645 that the languages of the State of Sinaloa (Mexico) had common roots with Nahuatl (Hervás y Panduro 1800: 214–17), this being probably the first suggestion for grouping together part of the Uto-Aztecan languages.

Another important work from this period which builds on the works of the missionaries is the *Mithridates* (Adelung and Vater 1816). Likewise a general work on the languages of the world, it is a compendium of available knowledge containing much geographical and historical data, bibliographies, grammatical sketches, vocabulary lists and the Lord's prayer with grammatical and lexical explanations. Fourteen Mesoamerican languages are treated. The criteria for considering languages related are inconsistent but nonetheless Huastec is added to the group of Mayan languages already suggested by Hervás, and the relationship of Nahuatl with the northwest Uto-Aztecan languages of Mexico is even more clearly proposed than in Hervás.

The volume of the book by Adelung and Vater devoted to Mesoamerican Indian languages was published in the same year as Bopp's book on Indo-European languages which is taken conventionally as the beginning of the type of linguistic comparative work that was to dominate the nineteenth century. Henceforth the study of Mesoamerican Indian languages remained practically outside the mainstream of linguistics, although these languages were to attract attention in general linguistics for their structures, i.e. they were used for typological purposes; on the more restricted level of studies devoted to partial areas, this typological interest was coupled with attempts at classification.

The work of Wilhelm von Humboldt played a leading role in general linguistics, and was probably responsible for the enduring tradition of using Nahuatl as an example of a typical 'incorporating' language, i.e. a language in which words are equivalent to sentences (Humboldt 1960 [1836]: 181–7). Other references to Mesoamerican languages are found in this work: Mixtec is used to exemplify the different values of preposed and postposed adjectives; Huastec and Yucatec are referred to for the use of pronouns with predicative value, and again for Yucatec there is a detailed discussion of pronominal affixes and tense formation in the verb, a lasting theme in Mayan linguistics (Humboldt 1960 [1836]: 279, 283, 388ff.).

The work of one of Humboldt's followers, Heymann Steinthal, later elaborated by Franz Misteli, became one of the standard books on language typology. In it Nahuatl is used as one of the types of incorporating languages (Misteli 1893: 112–35), and it is obvious that the quality of the sketch of that language owes much to the accuracy of its sources, the grammars of the missionaries Molina, Carochi, Olmos and Rincón. It is noteworthy that the friars' remarks on pronunciation were also given full consideration and were correctly interpreted, so that vowel length and other features are included in the transcription, features often ignored in other treatments of Nahuatl, even some done in the present century.

Among the numerous other works on typology, attention should be drawn to that of Friedrich Müller. He gives a classification of Mesoamerican Indian languages based chiefly on Pimentel's work (see below); but the most interesting part of this survey is the series of descriptive sketches that present the sound systems and offer concise characterizations of nouns, pronouns, adjectives, numerals and verbs for less familiar languages like Otomi, Tarascan, Totonac, Matlatzinca, Mixtec, Zapotec and Miskito (Müller 1882: 277–317).

Works on typology rarely presented new data: their sources were still the grammars of missionaries. Furthermore, these were works of wide scope and therefore the treatment of each language or language area was necessarily sketchy. More information can be found in two books devoted exclusively to Mexican Indian languages that are discussed below as final examples of the linguistic activity of the period.

The work of Francisco Pimentel (1874–5) adopts a typological frame and contains much grammatical and lexical data, some of which are taken from unpublished sources. The author discusses at some length the criteria for language classification, taking an intermediate stand between the yardstick of typological similarity and that based on resemblances across vocabulary items. The resulting classification is rather confused, but nevertheless identifies correctly the Mixe and Zoque languages as a single family. Pimentel's book remained for many years a standard reference work.

Of a different sort is the book by Manuel Orozco y Berra (1864). Although the author disclaimed any competence on the problem of language classification, his own work was subsequently as much referred to as Pimentel's. One interesting feature of this classification is that, on the basis of historical documentation and contemporary information, an attempt is made to differentiate languages from dialects. The main contribution of Orozco y Berra's book, however, was its delimitation of the geographic distribution of the languages, an aspect that is discussed at length with much supporting documentation, both ancient and contemporary. The map included in this book constitutes a landmark in the cartographic presentation of Mexican Indian languages.

1.3 The twentieth century

The interest in typology, so characteristic of the nineteenth century, began to decline at the beginning of the present century; and while there are important works like that of Finck (1909) still in that tradition, no Mesoamerican language is included. On the other hand, since the last decade of the nineteenth century, linguists working in this area had returned to gathering material in the field. This, together with the use of improved criteria in language classification and the use of the comparative method in historical studies, differentiates works written in the twentieth century from those of the previous century. In turn the studies made in this period show differences that reflect advances in the development of linguistics as well as an increasing professionalism on the part of the authors.

A premodern period may be considered to extend up until the late 1930s. There are more authors than it is possible to list here, so reference will be made to only a few representative names and works.

Otto Stoll gathered material on several different Mayan languages, and his classification came close to the modern classification in many respects (Stoll 1884). Francisco Belmar published, for the most part, vocabularies of languages such as

Trique (Belmar 1897), Huave, Amuzgo and Highland Chontal, languages which were previously poorly attested or not attested at all; he also worked on the classification of Mexican Indian languages (1905) and identified, albeit rather intuitively, most of the members of the Otomanguean family. His classification, and that of Nicolás León (1900, 1903), were the main sources for the classification by Cyrus Thomas and John R. Swanton (1911) which became standard for several years. The publications on Nahuatl by Franz Boas (1913) and Pablo González Casanova (1922) represented the renewal of the study of the spoken language and the presentation of the data in accurate phonetic transcription. A study of Edward Sapir (1913, 1915, 1914–19) on Uto-Aztecan marked the beginning of systematic comparison and reconstruction of the languages of this area. The publications by Jaime de Angulo (1933) on Chichimec, of Theodor Preuss (1912, 1932) on Cora, and of Leonhard Schultze-Jena (1933, 1935, 1938) on Quiché, Pipil, Tlapanec, Mixtec and Nahuatl are representative of premodern descriptions but are nonetheless very good on the treatment of morphology; in addition, those of Preuss and Schultze-Jena contain extensive bodies of texts. At the end of this period the maps by Othón de Mendizabal and W. Jiménez Moreno (n.d., 1937) represent basic contributions to the delimitation of the preconquest distribution of languages and reflect the state of the classification at a time when little comparative study had been done of these languages.

The modern period began with the activities of linguists schooled in structural linguistics and the consequent rise in the standards of description to a full technical level. At the same time the members of the Summer Institute of Linguistics (or Wycliffe Bible Translators) started their work in Mexico and Guatemala. These missionary–linguists covered almost all the languages of Mesoamerica, and it is from them that we inherit most of the modern studies of these languages. Some trends in their publications are prominent: tonal studies; syntactically oriented descriptions; comparative work (chiefly in Otomanguean); translations of the New Testament; collaboration with national agencies in literacy programmes. It is interesting to note that, with the addition of technical skills, their work represents the modern equivalent of that carried out by Spanish friars, not only in the breadth of its coverage and its results but also in its essentially religious motivation.

It is undeniable that during the present century the knowledge of Mesoamerican languages has kept pace with the quality of linguistic studies elsewhere, yet the many gaps still existing compared with studies in other areas should not be overlooked. Thus, for instance, there is as yet not a single language for which a detailed grammar, an extensive dictionary and a rich collection of texts are available; and there are still languages that represent a distinct subgroup within a family for which there is no adequate sketch of the grammar. Phonology is the branch for which there tends to be most studies, but there have been practically no instrumental phonetic analyses at all. For some important families a full reconstruction of the phonemic system is not yet in print; only recently has grammar been discussed in comparative works, and there are no etymological dictionaries. Dictionaries or vocabularies contain little if any grammatical information; most descriptions of syntax and of derivational morphology are sketchy, and even complex inflectional systems with multiple paradigms have not yet been described in full. There are no in-depth studies of bilingualism, and very little on language attitudes, two very important topics in view of the sociolinguistic characteristics of the area. The linguistic study of old documents has also been very limited. On the practical side (from the point of view of both the beginner and the specialist requiring basic information), general introductory works on single families or subgroups are lacking.

Finally, there is a limitation in the studies of these languages that should not be minimized, namely that in very few cases has more than one linguist studied the same language; in fact one of the traditional reasons for somebody turning his attention to a given language was that no one had studied it before – an understandable situation in view of the fact that languages are many and linguists are few – but a single linguist cannot be expected to cover all aspects of a language with equal competence and accuracy, nor to offer the definitive description of it. Nowadays it is uncommon to find a statement as in Craig (1977: ix) to the effect that the availability of good data on a language was one of the reasons for choosing it for study. But this approach will be necessary if we want to be able to cope with the standards of description concerning scope and depth that are demanded by present-day linguistic theory and practice.

FURTHER READING

There is no extensive treatment of the development of Mesoamerican linguistic studies. Outlines are McQuown 1960b, 1967b in which extensive references to authors and works for all periods may be found. For special reference to linguistic studies in Mexico see Jiménez Moreno 1969.

On the *Relaciones Geográficas* in general, Cline 1972; for the linguistic information they contain, Harvey 1972.

For the cultural background of the Spanish friars see Gibson, C. 1966 (ch. 4); on their linguistic activities, Ricard 1933 (ch. 2); for a positive appraisal of their grammars see Manrique in Basalenque 1975.

On relations with general linguistics, McQuown 1960a. Horne 1966 indicates the place assigned to Mesoamerican languages in the typologies of the nineteenth and twentieth centuries.

Vivó 1941 reproduces the classifications and maps since Orozco y Berra.

Surveys of modern research on genetic classification and comparative work on Mesoamerican languages are to be found in McQuown 1955; Longacre 1967, 1968; Campbell 1979. The history of the classification of individual linguistic families is treated in Longacre 1964 (Otomanguean); Campbell 1977 (Mayan); Lamb 1964, Lastra 1973 (Uto-Aztecan). There are short references for all families in Kaufman 1974a. Grimes, J. 1968 surveys modern descriptive studies on indigenous languages of Latin America.

2

Dialects, languages and linguistic families

The term 'Mesoamerica' is not synonymous with 'Central America', which excludes Mexico but extends as far as Panama, nor with 'Middle America', a more technical, geographical term covering Mexico and Central America. Mesoamerica designates an area that is neither a geographical region nor a political unit, but rather a culture area defined on the basis of common characteristics that were present during preconquest times (cf. chapter 10). In spite of the fact that the conquest produced changes that in more than one sense reshaped the area, there was a certain cultural continuity resulting from the survival of many indigenous groups that had come under the influence of a new but single cultural tradition. From a linguistic point of view the area is rather well defined in the sense that most of the language families found there do not extend beyond its limits.

2.1 The linguistic map

The first step involved in becoming acquainted with a linguistic area is to discover which languages are spoken in it, their geographical location and their classification. This information is given in map 1 and table 1 (above). The linguistic families and subgroups listed follow approximately a north-to-south order. Languages included are for the most part still spoken and the map gives their present-day location, although some which are shown became extinct during the nineteenth or twentieth centuries. By 'extinct' we mean that the language is no longer in common use in a community, although there may still be some speakers. This somewhat contradictory use of 'extinct' is adopted here because it is not always easy to determine whether or not there are some surviving speakers of a language; furthermore, a language known (or in some cases merely remembered) by a few people and not in daily use is not a living language in the commonly accepted sense of the term.

The Mesoamerican culture area *sensu stricto* is delimited on map 1 by the lines that cut across the coastal lines. Languages included south of the area belonged culturally to a transition zone between the Mesoamerican and the South American

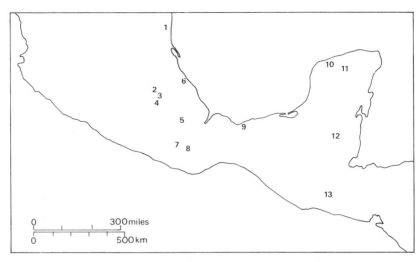

Map 2   Some archaeological sites in Mesoamerica
               1. Tamaulipas   2. Tula   3. Teotihuacan   4. Tenochtitlan
               5. Tehuacán   6. Tajín   7. Tilantongo   8. Monte Albán
               9. La venta   10. Dzibilchaltún   11. Chichen Itzá
               12. Tikal   13. Kaminaljuyú

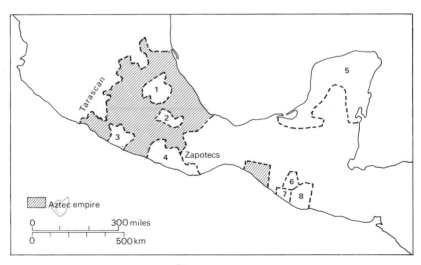

Map 3   Extent of the Aztec empire
        1. Tlaxaca   2. Teotitlan del Camino   3. Yopitzingo
        4. Tataltepec   5. Mayan kingdoms of Yucatan   6. Quiché
        kingdom   7. Tzutuhil kingdom   8. Cakchiquel kingdom

culture areas. To the extent that the information available permits, they will be treated in this volume, but Black Carib, although within Mesoamerica proper, will be excluded because it belongs to a South American linguistic family and further-more because it represents a late arrival (late eighteenth century) to the area. Only languages that belong to a linguistic family with representatives in Mesoamerica proper are included in the table. Reference will be made to some languages beyond the northern limit because most of them belong to the Uto-Aztecan family and so offer contrasting points of reference for the Uto-Aztecan languages within Mesoamerica.

Maps of language distribution at the time of first European contact (see the Further Reading section at the end of this chapter) differ in that indigenous languages, including a number of different languages that are now extinct, cover almost the whole area. On the other hand, the location of the surviving languages was approximately the same as it is today, as is the number of linguistic families. This is owing to the fact that there are no linguistic data on most of the extinct languages and therefore they cannot be classified; consequently it is impossible to determine how many linguistic families may have disappeared.

The classification in table 1 is on three levels: language families (Roman numerals), subgroups within families or within subgroups (letters), and languages (Arabic numerals). The names of languages given in this table are standard ones, but in consulting the bibliography the reader should be prepared to encounter names that end in *-eco* instead of ending in *-ec* as in the table, e.g. 'Pochuteco' instead of 'Pochutec'. The names of language families are also standard, except for Tequistlatec-Jicaque which, as a recently established family, still lacks a name in current usage; also Totonac is frequently used to refer to the whole Totonac-Tepehua family. It can be seen, then, that names of families do not follow a uniform pattern of formation; some have the ending *-an*, whilst others, formed by the juxtaposition of two names, do not in general possess that particular suffix. In this case, however, as in the case of families composed of a single language, the suffix *-an* is sometimes added, e.g. 'Mixe-Zoquean', 'Huavean'. More divergences are found in the names of subgroups, but no attempt has been made to make them uniform as these are the labels in current use among specialists.

Different types of problem are found on all three levels of the classification and will be handled separately starting from the lowest level, that of languages.

2.2 Language vs. dialect

A natural question to ask would be: 'How many languages are spoken in this area?' Unfortunately there is no definitive answer; the most cautious would be: 'Many'. A more risky answer would be: 'Between a hundred and a hundred and ninety'. If the reader turns to the table he can verify that it is not possible to determine the number of languages from it, owing to an inconsistency which should be readily apparent: in many cases after an arabic numeral which supposedly identifies a language, it reads 'X languages' – for example, 'Totonac languages' in II.A.12. This indeterminacy is not owing to an incomplete survey of the area, but derives from the difficulty in drawing the line between dialects of a single language and different languages; the difficulty is not specific to Mesoamerica, it is a general one, and there are no purely linguistic criteria available for making such a decision (and it is doubtful whether they could in fact be devised). Indeed, insofar as the difference is maintained, the technical criteria are the same as those a layman will use: if two persons understand each other when both speak their respective native tongue, they speak the same language. There are two problems with this characterization. On the one hand, it may be the case that both speakers have learned to understand the other's language by repeated exposure to it, to the extent that they are able to carry on a conversation, each using his native language; on the other hand, there are no objective criteria for determining the degree of understanding nor the way it is achieved – gestures and the non-linguistic situation may considerably increase an otherwise low degree of understanding. Furthermore, the determination of mutual intelligibility represents, in most cases, the opinion of a researcher; in other cases it is the opinion of the speakers themselves. While the first procedure is impressionistic, the second is unreliable because in many cases a speaker overrates his comprehension of another linguistic variety or, conversely, cultural prejudices against speakers of other varieties lead him to deny understanding.

To overcome these difficulties a more objective procedure for determining mutual intelligibility is being applied by members of the Summer Institute of Linguistics in the Mexican part of this area. Leaving aside the details, the method consists of the following steps: (1) a text is recorded on tape at each of the points to be tested – the text should not be a traditional tale which may be widely known and allows guesses as to its content; (2) ten questions about the content of the text are formulated in the language variety of each point; (3) the text is then played to ten speakers at each point, including the place of original recording (this is done in order to determine the degree of understanding of one's own dialect when listening to a tape recording and in this way to be able to adjust the results obtained in other places); (4) the answers to the questions are rated as correct or incorrect and averaged for each point. The critical percentage of correct answers which was considered necessary to guarantee adequate understanding was fixed at 80%; in some cases, on the basis of the judgements of linguists who speak one of the varieties and know the area well, the critical percentage was fixed at 70%.

Table 2. *Degree (%) of intelligibility among three Zapotec towns** *(from Egland and Bartholomew 1978: 79)*

	Yatzeche	San Antonio Ocotlán	Tilquiapan
Yatzeche		77	87
San Antonio Ôcotlán	96		59
Tilquiapan	96	67	

*The towns are located in the state of Oaxaca (Mexico), approximately in the centre of the Zapotec area shown on map 1.

The test has various acknowledged difficulties that can introduce errors in the results, one of the most obvious being that people in this area are not used to being subjected to tests. The most important limitation, however, is the test's failure to determine when negative results derive from antagonistic social attitudes or when understanding is the result of the subject's having learned another language, although it is possible to guess at the latter when intelligibility is markedly asymmetrical between two points. In any case it is doubtful that the difficulties could have been overcome given the scale of the test: more than four hundred points were tested.

The problem of language vs. dialect is not automatically resolved once the results of the tests are available since intelligibility is neither symmetrical nor transitive. Speakers at point A can understand speakers at point B better than speakers at point B understand those at A; in turn, speakers at A can understand speakers at point B, and these can understand those at point C; speakers at A and C, however, may not understand each other. Assuming there were no distorting factors at work, table 2 exemplifies this situation with reference to three towns where varieties of Zapotec are spoken. According to these figures, speakers of Yatzeche can understand the variety of Ocotlán, and speakers of Tilquiapan can understand the variety of Yatzeche, but speakers of Tilquiapan and Ocotlán do not understand each other; the intelligibility is mutual between Tilquiapan and Yatzeche, but while speakers of Yatzeche understand speakers of Ocotlán the reverse does not hold. Were this an isolated example it could be given an ad hoc treatment, but cases like this occur frequently over the area. A criterion was therefore needed in order to constitute groups. We will return to this question shortly, but for the moment it should be sufficient to note that the grouping was made so that the lowest possible number of groups was established whereby within each of them there is at least one point – called the centre – whose language is understood by speakers of all the other points within the group at the chosen level of intelligibility. The groups then can be represented showing the different levels of intelligibility by means of contour lines like those found in a relief map.

Fig. 1 reproduces the grouping in the northernmost part of the Mixtec area. The distance between the points is not significant, and only approximate relative position is represented. The numbers indicate the percentage of intelligibility at which speakers of two or more points can be grouped. A line enclosing a single point or a point or group already delimited by a line of higher intelligibility means that, at the percentage indicated, it cannot be further grouped with any other point. The centre is Chazumba.

In this case it can be seen that at a level of 90% intelligibility, only two points – Tonahuixtla and Chazumba – can be grouped; at an 85% level four more points are included – Xayacatlan, Cosoltepec, Tepejillo, Las Palmas – and at an 80% level Petlalcingo is added. This is a high level of intelligibility because for the Mixtec varieties the critical percentage was fixed at 70%. The additional lines indicate that even at a 60% level no other point can be added to this group. Notice that the same is also true for the point called Chigmecatitlan in which the highest score obtained was 38% with Xayacatlan. Naturally the resulting picture varies much from one area to another. Compare fig. 2, which represents another Mixtec area to the south of the former. According to the 70% level there are three groups, but the differences are not as sharp as those in the preceding example. At a 65% level, two of them could be grouped, and going further below the critical percentage, all three.

The number of groups provisionally determined for the cases in which table 1 reads 'X languages' are given in table 3. In relation to the impressionistic judgement a linguist would make in comparing materials from the points classified in different groups, the above seem too many. An apparently unacknowledged limitation of the test is that it does not take into account that in listening to a different linguistic variety, understanding can initially be greatly affected by the diction of a particular speaker. In addition, the listener may, at first exposure, be confused by certain divergent peculiarities to which he can often adjust rapidly. Whatever its shortcomings, however, the method shows with certainty how complex the area is, and gives an approximation of the relative internal diversity for each group. It should be remembered that many of these varieties are spoken in mountainous regions served by bad or non-existent roads. The area of greatest diversity is located in the State of Oaxaca (36,820 sq. miles – compare Portugal with 35,383 sq. miles) where it is estimated that about a hundred mutually unintelligible linguistic varieties may be spoken. Even if this figure were halved, and that would certainly be less than the actual number of varieties, the linguistic fragmentation is impressive.

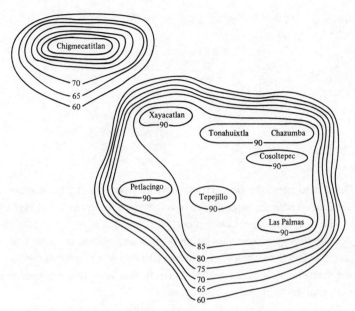

Fig. 1   Language varieties in a Mixtec area
(redrawn from Egland and Bartholomew 1978: 29)

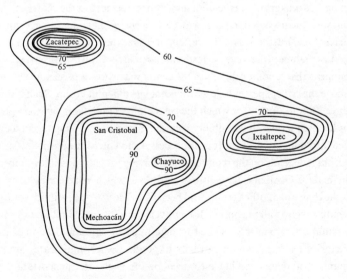

Fig. 2   Language varieties in a Mixtec area

Table 3. *Number of groups within language complexes*

Zapotec	38	Mazatec	6
Mixtec	29	Chatino	5
Nahuatl	19	Popoloc	5
Chinantec	14	Tarahumara	4
Mixe	11	Tepehua	3
Otomi	7	Southern Tepehuán	2
Totonac	7	North Pame	2

One has to stress the fact that no other groupings of these complexes have been determined with the same degree of consistency, objectivity and explicitness.

The label 'language' has been purposely avoided in presenting the above results because these groups cannot be considered languages as the term is usually understood. In fact the dichotomy language vs. dialect was avoided as much as possible in the determination of the groups. Some further elaboration is needed in order to understand what these groups represent.

The fact that speakers at each point within a given group can understand the variety spoken at its centre does not mean that the intelligibility is reciprocal, nor that there is mutual understanding between speakers of two points neither of which is the centre, as is clear from the characterization given above. In the example given in fig. 1, speakers of Xayacatlan understood the next to the centre at an 89% level, but were themselves understood at a 65% level in Chazumba – i.e. below the critical percentage. Furthermore, the variety of Xayacatlan was understood at a 46% level in Las Palmas (the reverse test was not carried out). Moreover, it sometimes happens that a point other than the centre may show a percentage of intelligibility above the critical percentage with a point in a different group. Such is the case in the three Zapotec towns for which the percentages of intelligibility were given: in spite of the high level of intelligibility between Yatzeche and Tilquiapan they are classified into different groups. It is not necessary to enter into the details of why that is so, but it depends on the requirement of having the least possible number of groups. In this case Ocotlán is the centre of a group to which Yatzeche belongs; Tilquiapan is the centre of another group, and because of the way the method works, there is no centre covering all the points. It is convenient to bear in mind that the method is an adaptation of one that is used to determine the optimum number of necessary factories (= centres) that distribute goods (= communicate) among a given number of points, taking into account the costs of transportation (= loss of intelligibility).

In fact the aim of the tests was to determine the number of points for which educational materials needed to be prepared. It is clear that as communication networks (they are presented as such) they are one-sided since they assure communication in one direction only. Notice that the fact that speakers of point A understand those of point B does not imply that they can productively use variety B in order to communicate in it, or with speakers of point C. Therefore the speech of the centres cannot be equated with general dialects; at best they could become one. Rather than seeing these groups as communication networks, it would perhaps be better if they could be considered as groups with a focal point. In many cases the asymmetry in intelligibility is so great that almost certainly learning of a different variety is taking place – an assumption that can be supported in some cases by the fact that the centre is important for commercial or religious reasons.

A different approach to the results of the intelligibility test is possible, but definite conclusions cannot be given, since tests were not made in both directions for all pairs of points, and it was not determined when intelligibility was simply the result of learning another language. Nevertheless an approximate idea of the potential results can be offered.

This approach, like the previous one, also bypasses the language vs. dialect dichotomy and establishes groups within which intelligibility is restricted to certain points. Two types of groups are posited. In one type all the varieties included are mutually intelligible. An example can be found in the northeast area of Nahuatl marked on map 1, the region called Huasteca, in which ten points were tested. There was high intelligibility among the points, whereas there is a sharp decrease in intelligibility between this group and neighbouring varieties. This is a language in the most usual sense, and naturally the grouping agrees with the one made under the previous method. In the other type of grouping the requirement of mutual intelligibility between any pair of points is relaxed; it is sufficient for grouping A, B, C, D that mutual intelligibility exists, pairwise, in chain fashion. Further subtypes can be established according to the number of linking pairs in a group. An example is found in the case (already presented) of the three Zapotec towns Tilquiapan, Yatzeche and San Antonio Ocotlán; according to this method these three would constitute a group, Yatzeche and Tilquiapan being the linking pair.

Although the estimate rests on incomplete evidence it is probable that the number of groups established by the first method discussed could be reduced by at least a third. The interest of the results obtained by the second method would be that, as they presumably derive from closeness of linguistic structure, they would be more in keeping with historical and typological classification based on purely linguistic characteristics.

There is another aspect of the linguistic fragmentation in Mesoamerica that has emerged in cases where enough information is available – in the Tarascan, Tzeltal,

Tzotzil and Quichean languages, for example. In this case, the speech within a given town shows a high degree of uniformity but is set off from that of neighbouring towns by peculiarities which may be phonological, grammatical and lexical. Such varieties have been referred to as 'town dialects', meaning that irrespective of wider groupings the variety in each town constitutes a definite linguistic unit.

Probably connected to this type of situation and to factors that will be dealt with in chapter 10 is the fact that in spite of the fragmentation, there do not seem to be as many cases of irregular developments attributable to borrowing from a different variety as might be expected. Changes may spread across the boundaries established by other changes, but they do so in a regular way and not through the borrowing of individual lexical items that would constitute a radical departure from the developments characteristic of the point. A possible extreme case is found in Huave (a single language with four distinct dialects) in which no single irregularity due to dialect borrowing was found in a list of *c.* 900 forms.

2.3 Language subgroups

The similarities or differences in purely linguistic characteristics among dialects leads to the problem of classification on the next level, subgroupings within a family. On this level intelligibility does not matter – different languages would be unintelligible by definition – but shared characteristics do. When referring to cases like those of Mixtec or Zapotec the discussion will leave the levels of language and dialect undetermined.

It is useful to remember the principles according to which subgroupings are made. Two or more languages may be grouped together if they share the same innovations. For example, the fact that Zapotec languages have changed $*/k^w/$ to /b/ is an innovation that counts positively for subgrouping, whereas the retention of the same protophoneme as $/k^w/$ in the Chatino languages is a neutral feature. This is because common innovations may mean that both languages were formerly the same language or were in close contact, while common retentions may in some cases mean that there was close contact or alternatively, it may simply mean that the languages, without having been in close contact, both failed to innovate. The problem is, however, that innovations can occur independently at two or more points, especially when they represent frequent changes that occur anywhere and at any time, such as the palatalization of a dental consonant before a front vowel. For innovations to be diagnostic there must be a certain number of them or they have to be very specific (i.e. the conditions under which a change took place need to be very complex) or structurally important.

An example of a considerable number of common innovations is found within the Mayan languages in the subgroup called 'Greater Mamean' for which eight phonological innovations are given. An example of a specific innovation is the palatalization of a velar stop before non-back vowels when these are followed by a uvular stop, a change that occurred in some Quichean as in Cakchiquel /kaq/ › /ḳaq/; as noted above, palatalization before a front vowel is a frequent change but this is not true of a change conditioned by an environment including a low vowel and a following uvular stop. Structurally important changes are those that distinguish the Chatino and Zapotec languages: Chatino has developed both long and nasal vowels, while the Zapotec languages have shifted stress to the penultima, have developed sequences of identical vowels with intervening glottal stop and a contrast between strong and weak consonants.

There is, however, a wide margin of disagreement among linguists as to the number of innovations required before they can be considered diagnostic, or what constitutes a significant innovation. It is important to bear this in mind when consulting table 1. The subgroups may not be homogeneous according to the criteria by which they were established. Furthermore, the certainty of subgroupings is in direct relation to the amount of historical work carried out for each family, and this has not been the same for all families. Moreover, for the most part the aspects that were used were phonological and lexical, and little has been done using grammatical criteria. This means that for this area any list of subgroups has to be taken cautiously and regarded as the results of research in progress rather than research completed. Nevertheless there are some characteristics that can be tentatively proposed for each family.

Taking into account the degree of differentiation of the Mayan family, the classification into subgroups is rather elaborate. It should be noticed that on the level of language the actual situation is probably less tidy than table 1 suggests: some of the languages have been recent additions as distinct languages, and some varieties normally considered to constitute different languages are considered as dialects by some specialists. Also some modifications have been proposed – for example to group Huastecan and Yucatecan with Greater Tzeltalan and Greater Kanjobala, or to eliminate altogether the Chujean subgroup. In general, however, it does not seem as though common innovations overlap much, although not in all cases are there many or significant common innovations.

An example of the distribution of common innovations within the Greater Kanjobal group is given in fig. 3. The innovations plotted are phonological and grammatical, but they are not further specified here because what we are interested in is the pattern of distribution. One important characteristic of this pattern is that the lines (isoglosses) representing innovations run parallel to each other except for two of them, and that, with respect to Tzeltal-Tzotzil and Kanjobal-Jacaltec, there is only one instance of overlapping innovation. It is clear that both pairs of

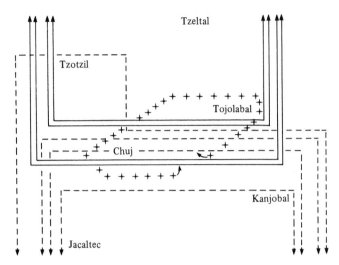

Fig. 3   Pattern of isoglosses in the Greater Kanjobal group
           Arrows point toward innovating areas
           (redrawn from Robertson 1977)

languages constitute two neatly differentiated groups. Tojolabal and Chuj could be considered a transition area, but the situation in general is the closest to a tree pattern that one can expect to find in the subclassification of a family. On the other hand, one point which emerges from the study from which the example was taken is that Tojolabal should be reassigned to the Tzeltal-Tzotzil group, and Chuj to the Kanjobal-Jacaltec group. This depends more on the weighting of the significance of the innovations than on the number of isoglosses delimiting both groups, but since this requires a detailed discussion the reader is referred to the original source.

     Coupled with the predominant tree pattern of the classification of the Mayan family is the fact that most Mayan languages belonging to a group, with the exception of Chortí, are adjacent to each other, or at least no language of another group is in between (compare table 1 with map 1); Huastec and Chicomuceltec, for example, are separated by languages belonging to different families.

     The subclassification of the Uto-Aztecan languages reproduced in table 1 is a cautious one, and only clear subgroups are recognized. More inclusive groups have been suggested – for example, the joining of Aztecan with Corachol – and all of them in turn with the Taracahitic and Pimic groups. But even if those bigger groups were not validated, the fact remains that neighbouring Uto-Aztecan groups seem to be more similar among themselves than they are to other more distant groups. This means that the groups have more or less kept the same relative positions they had at

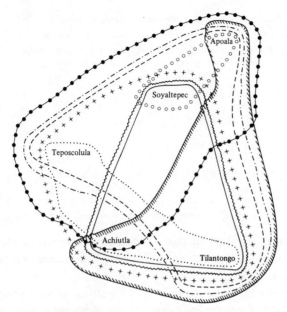

Fig. 4   Patterns of isoglosses in a Mixtec area
Lines enclose innovating areas
(compiled from Bradley and Josserand 1980)

the time of differentiation (with the exception of Southern Tepehuán). No sub-groups are indicated for the Nahuatl languages but there are probably two main ones with smaller subgroups in chain-like relation, i.e. neighbouring groups sharing common features; these groups occupy roughly continuous areas, a situation that agrees with the fact that the extended area in which Nahuatl is found represents a relatively recent expansion.

The situation in Otomanguean is more varied. The higher level of the classification in which eight groups are listed is the most provisional, not in the sense that these groups are not well differentiated, for, on the contrary, they are much more differentiated than the groups from the first level of subgrouping in the other families, but in that more inclusive groups can perhaps be established. On the basis of phonological innovations this does not seem likely since shared innovations overlap a good deal. However, no grammatical data have been taken into account, and this aspect could eventually furnish decisive criteria. On the next level, which is comparable to the first level of classification seen in Uto-Aztecan and Mayan, the picture is different in the various groups.

In the Popolocan group, the Chocho and Popoloc languages could be put

Table 4. *Distribution of innovations in some Mixtec languages*

	Apoala	Soyaltepec	Teposcolula	Achiutla	Tilantongo
———		X		X	X
∿∿∿∿		X		X	X
+ + +		X	X	X	X
– – – –	X	X	X		X
–·–·–·	X	X	X		X
⊔⊔⊔⊔⊔⊔⊔	X			X	X
•–•–•	X	X	X	X	
·········			X	X	X
o o o o	X	X			

together in a separate group from Ixatec, adding a further level to the classification; Mazatec languages, in turn, can be classified internally according to a relatively well-founded tree pattern.

Within Otopamean, the languages of the Otomian group share several innovations that contrast it with the Pamean group; but within the latter the number of common innovations shared by Chichimec and the Pame languages are perhaps not numerous enough to justify the grouping, in which case Chichimec would occupy an intermediate position as an independent branch that shares some characteristics with the Pame languages.

In the Mixtecan group the relationships between the three groups are not clearcut, and some might consider that Mixtec and Cuicatec are more closely related among themselves than any one of them is to Trique. Within the Mixtec group, in turn, the general situation is similar to the one in fig. 4 representing common innovations in an eastern area roughly comparable in size to the Mayan area depicted in fig. 3.

Fig. 4 and table 4 speak for themselves. There is no possibility of classifying these languages using a tree structure. Notice that even if the isoglosses can be ordered chronologically any group delimited by the first ones would be crossed by successive isoglosses, and the possibility of constructing a tree diagram derives from the fact that chronologically successive innovations occur within the groups which share the earlier innovations. In certain cases, where there were a considerable number of isoglosses defining some groups, and just one or two isoglosses cutting across them, a tree classification could be maintained and the disturbing isoglosses interpreted either as independent innovations or as diffusion across already well-delimited groups. However, not even that is possible with the data in fig. 4, since there are only two pairs of innovations (1–2, 4–5) that have the same distribution. Notice too that approximately an equal number of innovations is shared by most pairs of languages and that they decrease progressively (5, 4, 3, 2).

Reference was made before to some characteristics that differentiate Chatino and Zapotec, but it is probable that some languages for which few data are as yet available could represent intermediate links, a situation that could be expected since there are certain innovations that embrace the whole Zapotec area, except for some varieties bordering the Chatino area. Within Zapotec, in turn, the situation is similar to that seen in Mixtec. Specifically it should be noticed that the traditional classification into a northern, a central and a southern group is untenable; some isoglosses cut across the area from north to south, others from east to west; in the east central area isoglosses crisscross each other; in the north they spread fan-like; only in part of the southern area do a considerable number of isoglosses run together to establish a clearcut limit between two groups – a limit which represents not a differentiation *in situ*, but an independent movement of populations into the area.

The two groups of Mixe-Zoque seem clearly differentiated, although the relationships within each subgroup are as yet not explicitly characterized; within Zoquean the innovations have a highly overlapping distribution.

Not enough information about the other families is available, but the first level of the subclassification, e.g. Tepehua and Totonac, or Tequistlatec and Jicaque, involves clearly differentiated groups.

It is not easy to give an objective measure of degrees of differentiation, and table 1 does not attempt to do so; global impressionistic estimates (e.g. that the Chatino-Zapotec languages have an internal differentiation similar to that found in the Romance group) are probably correct but are difficult to make consistently. A more objective but rough measure can be obtained by counting the number of cognates in a list of 100 lexical items – the so called Swadesh 100-item basic list. This list includes glosses for referents (actions, qualities, objects) that are supposed to be named in any language; these words are generally most resistant to borrowing, and there is some evidence that there is a correlation between the number of cognates shared by two languages and the time span during which they have been diverging.

According to this measure, the language families for which computation has been carried out can be arranged in order of decreasing differentiation as follows: Uto-Aztecan (the whole family including languages in northwest Mexico and the United States) 22%, Misumalpan 27%, Mayan 29%, Mixe-Zoque 33%, Totonac-Tepehua 45%, Lenca 54%. Otomanguean has been omitted because no reliable calculation is available for the whole family. However, by way of comparison, within Otopamean the lowest percentage is 34. In other words, a single subgroup has an internal differentiation greater than Totonac-Tepehua and close to that of Mixe-Zoque and

Mayan; by contrast, the highest percentage between the Otopamean group and any of the others is probably around 20. We have chosen, for the sake of simplicity, to refer to the more inclusive groups as a 'family' but Otomanguean is not a family in the usual sense – no standard terminology exists for degrees of differentiation above the language level, and 'hyper-family' or 'stock' might be appropriate terms.

2.4 Language families

Language families are groups of languages that are genetically related, i.e. descendants of a common ancestor. Basically, two or more languages (or groups of languages) are considered genetically related when they show systematic correspondences in form and meaning that cannot be attributed to chance or borrowing. Chance is eliminated by the number of correspondences, borrowing in considering decisive correspondences found in basic vocabulary. Naturally the number of related items and correspondences, as well as their quality, will vary according to the amount of time that has elapsed since the languages began to diverge from the ancestor language. It is inevitable that such relationships will become obscured, and the problem then arises as to what quantity and quality of correspondences is enough to prove that two languages are related – and there is ample room for different viewpoints. However, there is a lowest level on which there is agreement that two languages are related. This level is determined by the possibility of reconstructing a phonemic system that is at least typologically realistic (i.e. known to occur in attested languages) and from which most of the phonemic systems of the descendant languages can be derived; in such cases related languages usually share a fair number of grammatical characteristics. This is the lower limit of relationship represented in table 1. The choice of this criterion is not simply a means of avoiding a problem: it is significant in that it allows us to trace the history of at least part of the linguistic systems and to determine common innovations and make subgroups, and in some cases, to advance hypotheses about the primitive homeland, associated culture and migrations.

There is no doubt that the families recognized in table 1 are families in the above sense, but it could be the case that other more inclusive families are as yet undetected. In fact it was only quite recently that Tlapanec and Paya were proved to belong in the Otomanguean and Chibchan families respectively, and that the relationship between Tequistlatec and Jicaque was demonstrated. However, it is not particularly likely that there are any more cases, with the exception of the assumed relationship of Mayan to Mixe-Zoque and Totonac-Tepehua. (It is possible that Uto-Aztecan may be related to Kiowa-Tanoan, a family located in the United States, but this is outside the scope of this book.) Notice that the internal differentiation of these groups may still leave room for the systematic reconstruction of a relationship at a higher level, as is the case in Otomanguean. In any case, even if these three families turn out not to be relatable on a level of systematic reconstruction, the possibility is strong that they are genetically related on a more distant level.

A special case is Huave, and seemingly cogent evidence was advanced to link it with Otomanguean. However, a typological comparison of grammatical features widespread in Otomanguean showed such a marked difference from the grammatical characteristics in Huave that a relationship on the level of reconstruction seems very unlikely, and indicates that the correspondences produced should be reconsidered; furthermore, the issue is rendered more complex because of the possibility of a relationship between the Huave and Mixe-Zoque languages. Other suggested relationships have a chance of being correct, but on a decidedly remoter level than the ones represented in table 1; such are the relationships of Misumalpan with Chibchan, and of Tequistlatec-Jicaque with the Yuman-Seri group. (Seri is located in the State of Sonora (Mexico); some Yuman languages are found in the Mexican State of North Lower California, but the bulk of the family is in the neighbouring territory of the United States.)

In principle, since the differentiation of languages genetically related is gradual, it could be expected that the possibility of reconstruction would diminish gradually, and this is true within the limits represented in table 1; thus, the possibilities of reconstructing morphology or syntax are much greater for a group like Mixe-Zoque than they are for Otomanguean. In practice, however, there seems to be a breaking point beyond which the possibilities of reconstruction are almost nil. Consequently most proofs of relationship become slim and controversial, an exception being when parallel irregular alternant forms are found in different languages, for example Huatla Mazatec $y^{\eta}a^3$ 'he is carrying it', $t\int^{\eta}a^4$ 'you are carrying it', Tlapanec ha^3-ya^3, $t\int a^2$ with same meanings (superscript numbers indicate tones; see chapter 4). This kind of evidence, however, is not frequently encountered in certain types of morphological structures, nor has it been widely used in discussing distant relationships within Mesoamerica. Repeated proposals linking all Mesoamerican families in chain fashion (but with different arrangements), therefore, remain inconclusive. Furthermore, these assumed distant relationships have proposed links among languages in such a way that they dismember proven linguistic families. Even assuming that they were correct, these relationships have the further limitation that little additional knowledge can be derived from them, the time depth being too great and the evidence too scanty to permit hypotheses about historical developments. A further point of importance justifying the distinction between the classification obtained through the applications of the comparative method and hypotheses of distant relationship, is that within the former classification no language in Mesoamerica except for Uto-Aztecan languages and Paya has ties outside this area.

2.5 Glottochronological results

In Mesoamerican linguistics the hypotheses about distant relationships have gone hand in hand with the method known as glottochronology, although there is no necessary connection between the two. We will therefore restrict the discussion of this method to cases of certain genetic relationship.

Glottochronology is an attempt to calculate quantitatively the time which has elapsed since a language began to differentiate internally, giving rise to two or more descendant languages. Its basic assumption is that the replacement of words in the basic list of 100 items proceeds at a constant rate, 14% of the original list being replaced in a millennium. Therefore, given the percentage of cognates in the list of two languages it is possible by means of a mathematical formula to calculate the time depth of the group. In this way the percentages of cognates (given before as a rough estimate of the degree of differentiation) can be converted into years of separation. The results are as follows: Uto-Aztecan 5100, Misumalpan 4300, Mayan 4100, Mixe-Zoque 3600, Otopamean 3500, Totonac-Tepehua 2600 and Lenca 2000. These figures indicate minimum years of separation, but even with this qualification the results should be taken cautiously. The glottochronology method has been criticized in all of its aspects: the basic assumption, the sample on which the constant rate of replacement was calculated, the estimation of time depths and, in its application to Mesoamerican languages, the fact is that no improvement or revision has been made to meet the criticisms. Nevertheless, it is known that in some cases where there is independent information on the time two groups began to diverge the method has given good results, and there is at least one case in Mesoamerica. It is known by documentary information that the speakers of Isthmus Zapotec migrated not much before the arrival of the Spaniards from a place in the region of Zaachila (to the southwest of the city of Oaxaca in Mexico) to their present-day location in the Isthmus of Tehuantepec toward the Pacific coast; common linguistic innovations between the languages of the two points support this information. Now it is precisely with languages of the region of Zaachila that Isthmus Zapotec shows the greatest percentage of cognates in the basic list, and the time of separation given by the method of glottochronology is 560, which fits well with the documentary information. In other cases, as will be seen in chapter 10, glottochronological figures and archaeological data seem compatible, although this type of correlation is rather uncertain.

To summarize, the figures given by glottochronology cannot be accepted mechanically nor rejected outright, but they should be weighed against other types of evidence.

SOURCES

The distribution of languages within Mexican territory given in map 1 is taken from Olivera, Ortiz and Valverde n.d. (a map based on the census of 1970). For Guatemala the map reproduces the distribution given by Goubaud Carrera 1946. No modern map of language distribution for the region south of Guatemala is available; the locations indicated in the map are taken from different sources that only give approximate distribution of the languages, and this may affect the exactness of the areas marked for Black Carib, Miskito, Paya, Sumu and Pipil. The classifying of the languages in this southern area as 'extinct' has been made according to the information in Campbell 1979 and Kaufman 1974a.

The classification given in Table 1 can be considered standard and many linguists have contributed to it. Points where it departs from other classifications are justified by Rensch 1977, Suárez 1979 (Tlapanec as Otomanguean); Holt 1976 (Paya as Chibchan); Oltrogge 1977 (Tequistlatecan as related to Jicaque). For Huave as Otomanguean, Rensch 1973; as non-Otomanguean, Hollenbach 1978. A recent attempt to prove the relationship of Mayan with Mixe-Zoque is that of Brown and Witkowski 1979.

The results of the intelligibility tests are from Egland and Bartholomew 1978. The second method of grouping discussed is proposed by Hockett 1958: 323–6 (not specifically for Mesoamerica).

Problems of subgrouping: Campbell 1977* (Quichean and Mayan in general); Kaufman 1971a* (Mayan), 1978* (Mayan); Robertson 1977* (Chujean group). Bartholomew 1965 (Otopamean); Bradley and Josserand 1980* (Mixtec languages); Gudschinsky 1958* (Mazatec languages); Hamp 1958* (Popoloc-Ixcatec); Rensch 1973 (Otomanguean); Suárez 1977a (Zapotecan). Campbell and Langacker 1978 (Corachol and Aztecan). Kaufman 1964, Nordell 1962 (Mixe-Zoque).

Glottochronological figures for Uto-Aztecan are from Hale 1958, for Otopamean from Bartholomew 1965, and for the other groups Kaufman 1974a.

FURTHER READING

Sources marked with an asterisk are recommended for the respective topics.

Modern maps with the pre-Hispanic distribution of languages are based on Mendizábal and Jiménez Moreno n.d.; more accessible are Johnson 1940, Longacre 1967; see also Harvey 1972.

For discussions of variation among town dialects: Friedrich 1971a, Hopkins 1970, Campbell 1977.

On intelligibility testing with reference to Mesoamerican languages, see Casad 1974. For the grouping of varieties as communication networks, Grimes, J. 1974.

On genetic classification with a discussion of the problems of subgroupings in Mesoamerican languages, see Longacre 1967.

For some works of linguistic reconstruction for whole families, see Voegelin and Hale 1962, Miller 1967, Langacker 1976 (Uto-Aztecan); Rensch 1976 (Otomanguean).

On glottochronology and distant relationship: Swadesh 1967.

3

Phonology I

The phonemic systems of Mesoamerican languages show considerable diversity with regard to the number of contrasting units, less with regard to the types of contrasting features, and in general they offer few typologically uncommon characteristics.

In the present survey phonemes which occur only in Spanish loanwords will be excluded. There are various reasons for this: (1) these elements constitute relatively recent additions and can be identified as such with certainty, and their exclusion therefore helps to emphasize differences and similarities which are due, insofar as we can determine it, to internal developments of the native systems; (2) even within a single dialect, speakers vary in the use of non-adapted Spanish loanwords, and therefore any listing of these phonemes in a chart would give a false picture of the phenomenon which is basically variable; (3) a phonemic chart including borrowed phonemes might also give a false picture since in many cases there are in fact two coexisting phonemic systems. However, the changes introduced through Spanish loanwords (treated briefly in 3.1.6) will be of interest in relation to some of the topics dealt with in chapter 10.

A few remarks are in order about the way phonemic systems will be represented in charts and the terminology used. Rows representing manners of articulation and columns which represent positions of articulation will be referred to as series and orders respectively. This classification into two dimensions is not altogether accurate – the series in particular do not represent a single dimension of classification – but it serves to render the discussion less cumbersome. When speaking of the number of positions of articulations in reference to stop series affricates will be included but lateral affricates or glottal stop will not. Consonants articulated with closed glottis pushing upwards, as well as vowels with glottal constriction, will be considered glottalized. In vowel systems, when speaking of basic dimensions, reference is made to tongue height, advancement of the tongue and position of the lips.

Table 5. *Distribution of number of consonants in 38 languages*

Number of consonants

	13	14	15	16	17	18	19	20	21	22	23	24	25	26	27	38
Number of languages	1	1	2	3	2	3	3	5	6	1	4	2	1	2	1	1

Table 6. *Distribution of number of basic vowels in 38 languages*

Number of vowels

	3	4	5	6	7	8	9
Number of languages	2	2	14	12	5	1	2

3.1 Phonemic systems

As a general point of comparison for the discussion of individual phonemic systems, tables 5 and 6 give the lower and upper limits of the number of consonants and vowels attested in this area, and the distribution within these limits of a sample of 38 languages. The sample was selected so as to include most linguistic families and well-differentiated branches within the larger families. The Miskito, Misumalpan and Lencan families were excluded because the phonemic analysis that is available is insufficiently reliable. Huave was also excluded because there is the possibility of more than one reasonable analysis of the system and each yields marked differences in the number of phonemes. Cuitlatec, Tarascan and Xincan are each represented in the sample by a single language. The other families are represented in the sample as follows: Totonac-Tepehua: 2, Tequistlatec-Jicaque: 2, Mixe-Zoque: 2, Uto-Aztecan: 5, Mayan: 7, Otomanguean: 17. It is worth noting that a random sample of 84 languages shows a similar distribution.

When reference is made to the relative complexity of a system, it refers primarily to the number of phonemes.

3.1.1 *Uto-Aztecan. Cuitlatec*

The Uto-Aztecan family has the simplest system of consonants found in this area; the Huichol system is reproduced in table 7. This system is not only simple from the point of view of the number of consonants, but also in the number of features in general and per individual phonemes, no more than two being necessary to dif-

Table 7. *Huichol phonemic system*

p	t	ts	k	kʷ	ʔ				
						i	ɨ	u	
		ʐ		h					
							e		
m	n								
		ɾ						a	
w		j							

ferentiate minimally any phoneme from the rest; /n/, for instance, is 'nasal' and 'alveolar', and /k/ can be characterized simply as 'velar'. These characteristics are reflected in the fact that the number of consonants (13) is almost the same as the number of features (12), assuming that the retroflex articulation of the voiced fricative and of the flap is non-distinctive. The vowel system is not complex but there are others that are even simpler in basic dimensions. The syllable patterns are simple too: CV, CVC, CVVC. Huichol has no distinctive stress, but it does have a tonal system, which will be discussed in chapter 4.

Many Nahuatl languages (or dialects) are like Huichol, having only a few more phonemes. The system of the Central Nahuatl languages is: /p t ts tʃ k kʷ ʔ s ʃ m n tɬ l w j i iˑ u uˑ e eˑ a aˑ/, but several Nahuatl languages lack the lateral affricate /tɬ/ and some have shifted /kʷ/ to /b/. In relation to Huichol there are also additional syllable patterns: V, VC, CCV(C), although the number of CC sequences is very restricted. Stress falls regularly on the penultimate syllable in the word; when suffixes are added stress shifts accordingly as in the following example from Texcoco Nahuatl: *ʃiʼtlali* 'sit down!', *ʃimotlaliʼtsino* 'sit down please!'

Other Uto-Aztecan languages outside the limits of Mesoamerica like Yaqui, Tarahumara and Lower Pima differ from Nahuatl mainly in the presence of voice contrast in the stop series, but there are fewer voiced consonants than voiceless ones; there may be five or six vowels, in some languages with long counterparts, and as in Nahuatl stress does not seem to be contrastive but falls on the first or second syllable of the word.

Among the Uto-Aztecan languages considered here, the Tepehuán languages have the system with the most consonants; Northern Tepehuán has twenty-one, and besides a series of voiced stops it has a palatalized order (/t, d, n/), and a contrast of alveolar vs. uvular vibrant (/r/, /R/).

It is interesting to note that compared with the phonemic system reconstructed for proto-Uto-Aztecan –*/p t tʃ k kʷ ʔ s h m n w j i ɨ u o a/ – the systems of the languages which lie within Mesoamerica proper have not changed much with regard to their inventory of phonemes.

The isolated language Cuitlatec has the following phonemic system: /p t tʃ k kʷ ʔ ß ð ɣ ʃ h m n ɬ l w j i ɨ u e o a/. Although it does not exactly match the system of any of the Uto-Aztecan languages mentioned above, it is similar in its number of phonemes and types of contrasts. Notice that the stop series only differs from that of Huichol by having /tʃ/ instead of /ts/, a rather minor difference since both languages have only one affricate; the same comment applies to the contrast /tʃ/ vs. /ʃ/ in Cuitlatec as against /ts/ vs. /z̪/ in Huichol, or to the contrast of voiceless stops vs. voiced fricatives in Cuitlatec compared with the contrast of voiceless vs. voiced stops in Northern Tepehuán. As to the vowels, Northern Tepehuán and Lower Pima have the same system as Cuitlatec. On the other hand, an important difference is that stress in Cuitlatec falls unpredictably on either of the last two syllables in the word; there are few languages in Mesoamerica in which the placement of stress is completely unpredictable.

3.1.2 Mixe-Zoque

Some Zoque languages have a consonant system which is only a little more complex than those of the Uto-Aztecan languages. Copainalá Zoque, for example, has /p t t̪ t̠s̪ tʃ k ʔ s ʃ h m n ɲ l w j/, but Sierra Popoluca adds four voiced stops /b d ɖ g/, another nasal /ŋ/, and a flap /ɾ/; the vowel system in both languages is the common /i ɨ u e o a/. Some Mixe languages have fewer consonants but in at least one, Mixe from El Paraíso, the consonants /p t t̠s̪ k ʔ ş h m n l w j/ are matched by the corresponding palatalized consonants. (This system has been analysed with palatalization considered as a feature of whole words; according to the consonant in which it is marked, its domain varies.) In some Mixe languages, e.g. Totontepec Mixe, the palatalized consonants can be analysed as consonant plus /j/, but in the language from El Paraíso these sequences contrast with palatalized consonants, as in /man̪/ 'his son', /mjahmaʔn/ 'your blanket'.

Mixe languages also have many vowels, and the Totontepec Mixe system (table 8) is among the richest found in Mesoamerica. Mixe languages also have the most complex syllable nuclei. The glottal consonants /ʔ/ and /h/, together with the vowel(s), constitute the nucleus of the syllable yielding the following types: short (V), long (V·), short checked (Vʔ), short aspirated (Vh), long checked (V·ʔ), long aspirated (V·h), rearticulated or interrupted (VʔV), and rearticulated aspirated (VʔVh). As in /ˈtsuʔuhmk/ 'purple' the vowel quality does not change in rearticulated nuclei.

Since there are other languages in Mesoamerica in which glottal consonants are

Table 8. *Totontepec Mixe*
vowels

i	ɨ	u	
e	ə	o	}± length
ɛ		ɔ	
	a		

part of the syllable nucleus it is worth indicating the reasons for this type of analysis in this particular case. In VʔV sequences there is no interruption of phonation; the articulation is a long vowel with partial glottalization, and they differ from Vʔ and Vh sequences only in the portion of the articulation affected by the glottal effect. /ʔ/ and /h/ differ from other consonants in that, like the vowels, they show no systematic restrictions as to which consonant follows, while the rest of the consonants show definite restrictions. In verb paradigms short and long nuclei with or without glottal consonants alternate among themselves, e.g. /ˈmpet/, /ˈpɛhtp/ (forms of the verb meaning 'to go up'); /ˈpɛ·tp/, /ˈnpeʔet/ (forms of the verb meaning 'to sweep'). Furthermore, in two varieties of Mixe, extra long vowels correspond to the long aspirated nuclei of Totontepec Mixe. That is, in these Mixe languages we find the typologically uncommon contrast between short, long and extra long vowels; the following is an example from the variety from El Paraíso: /ʔoj/ 'although', /ʔo·j/ 'he went', /ʔo꞉j/ 'very'.

As for stress, in no language does it seem to serve to differentiate forms that are otherwise identical, although its placement varies from language to language. Mixe from El Paraíso has phrase and clause stress (i.e. there is no word stress); Copainalá Zoque normally has stress on the penultimate syllable of the word, but there are exceptions; Totontepec Mixe has stress on the stem but if affixes are added stress may fall on different syllables within the word; in Sierra Popoluca the placement of stress varies a good deal in different words, but can be predicted by the morphological structure through rather complex rules; finally Sayula Popoluca may have more than one primary stress per word.

3.1.3 *Mayan. Xinca. Totonac-Tepehua*

In Mayan languages a rather different type of phonemic system is found. There are some traits that, with a few exceptions, are found in the whole family: (1) two symmetrical series of voiceless and glottalized stops in at least five orders (/p t ts tʃ k/) plus a glottal stop; (2) at least three fricatives (/s ʃ/ and /h/ or /x/ or /χ/); (3) at least two nasals (/m n/); (4) two semivowels (/w j/); (5) a

Table 9. *Aguacatec phonemic system*

p	t	t͟s	t͜ʃ	t͜ʃ̣	ḳ	k	q	ʔ
bʔ	tʔ	t͟sʔ	t͜ʃʔ	t͜ʃ̣ʔ	ḳʔ	kʔ	qʔ	
		s	ʃ	ṣ			χ	
m	n							
	l							
	ɾ							
w			j					

Vowels:

$$\left. \begin{array}{ccc} i & & u \\ e & & o \\ & a & \end{array} \right\} \pm \text{length}$$

minimum of five vowels (/i u e o a/). But there are languages with a greater number of consonants like Aguacatec (table 9). It is typical of most Mayan languages that /p/ is matched by /bʔ/ instead of /pʔ/ as in the Aguacatec system, but Yucatec has both /pʔ/ and /bʔ/. /bʔ/ is a phoneme with several variants such as bilabial implosive, preglottalized bilabial and glottalized labial nasal.

Stop consonant systems in other languages can be obtained by subtracting the retroflex order (Cakchiquel), the palatalized velars (Teco), retroflex order and palatalized velars (Pocomchí), retroflex order, palatalized velars and uvulars (Yucatec). In fricatives the maximum is /s ʃ x h/, as in Yucatec. Some languages add another nasal: Yucatec /ɲ/, and Jacaltec /ŋ/; some languages as Cakchiquel lack /ɾ/. Languages like Tzeltal have the same basic vowel system as Aguacatec but without long vowels while others, like Chol, have six vowels without the contrast of length. The most divergent language is Huastec which has labiovelars (/kʷ kʔʷ/), no glottalized partner for /p/, and neither /l/ nor /ɾ/.

The typical syllable patterns in Mayan languages are CVC and CV, and in some languages CVʔVC also occurs. There are some initial consonant clusters but their composition is extremely restricted because most of them originate in prefixes that have lost the vowel. Some languages, e.g. Aguacatec, may have initial consonant clusters with up to four consonants and final ones with up to three.

In some languages stress is phonologically conditioned. In Aguacatec, for example, it falls on the last syllable with a long vowel, if there is one, otherwise it falls on the final syllable; in Chol, on the other hand, it falls on the last syllable if this ends in a consonant, otherwise on the penultimate syllable; in other languages, such as Jacaltec, it falls on the stem and consequently on different syllables within the word.

Compared with the systems of the daughter languages, the system reconstructed for proto-Mayan – */p ṭ t t͟s t͜ʃ k q ʔ bʔ ṭʔ tʔ t͟sʔ t͜ʃʔ kʔ qʔ s

Table 10. *Coastal Chontal phonemic system*

p	t	t̡	t͡s	t͡ʃ	k	ʔ			
pφ'			t͡s'	t͡ʃ'	k'				
f			s	ʃ	x		i	u	
β	ð				ɣ		e	o	± length
	n̩							a	
m	n			ɲ					
m'	n'			ɲ'					
	t͡ɬ'								
	ɫ	ɫ̰							
	l	l̰							
	l'								
	ɾ								
	r								
w̥				j̊					
w				j					
w'									

ʃ x h m n l ɾ w j i u e o a i· u· e· o· a·/ – shows a remarkable stability in the series, most changes having affected the number of contrasting orders, which have usually been reduced.

Xinca and Tepehua are typologically very similar to Mayan languages. Xinca has /p t t͡s t͡ʃ k/, Tepehua /p t t͡s t͡ʃ k q/, and in both these stops are matched by glottalized ones; the rest of the consonant systems are similar to the most simple Mayan systems, with the addition of a contrast of voice in laterals (/ɫ l/). Xinca has six vowels, both short and long; Tepehua three (/i u a/) also both short and long or checked by /ʔ/. The Totonac system is similar to that of Tepehua but includes an affricate lateral and lacks the glottalized series; in some of the languages, e.g. Papantla Totonac, the three vowels, both short and long, can occur glottalized. Stress in Xinca is as in Mayan Chol (see above); in Totonac it generally falls on any of the last two syllables of the word.

3.1.4 *Tequistlatec-Jicaque. Tarascan*

Glottalized consonants also occur in Tequistlatec-Jicaque, but in patterns which are rather different from those of the Mayan languages. The system of Coastal Chontal, the one with the most consonants reported in Mesoamerica, is given in table 10.

There are two obvious differences from the Mayan systems regarding glottalized sounds: they do not form a symmetrical series with the stops, and the contrasts · occur in nasals, laterals and semivowels. Notice also the presence of voice contrast in fricatives, nasals, laterals and semivowels. This system is not only the most complex with regard to the number of consonants; the subsystems of laterals, nasals and semivowels are also the most complex in this area. Compared with the Huichol system, the difference is seen not only in the number of consonants but also in the ratio of features needed to specify the phonemes with the number of phonemes; in the case of Coastal Chontal seventeen features would be required, i.e. less than half the number of consonants; consequently the characterization of each consonant is more complex. It was noted that /k/ in Huichol could be characterized simply as velar, whereas /k/ in Coastal Chontal is velar, plain (i.e. non-glottalized) and stop.

In Coastal Chontal a single vowel can constitute a whole syllable; other types of syllables may have up to three consonants before the vowel and one or two consonants at the end. Consonant clusters show definite restrictions on possible sequences, so in three consonant clusters the occurring combinations are sk'w, ʃk'w, skw, ʃkw. More than one primary stress may occur in a word as in ˈpatse̱ˈduj, 'he is doing it'.

In the other branch of the family, Jicaque has a less rich system lacking contrast in voice or glottalization of the nasals, laterals and semivowels, having no flap or trill and only a small number of orders; it does, however, offer the only example in Mesoamerican of a triple contrast of simple vs. glottalized vs. aspirated stops: /p t k t̠s̠ pʰ tʰ kʰ tsʰ p' t' k' t̠s̠'/.

Tarascan resembles Jicaque in having aspirated stops, although it has no series of glottalized consonants; in other respects the system is a common one: /p t ts tʃ k pʰ tʰ ts̠ʰ tʃʰ k s ʃ x r ɾ m n w j i ɨ u e o a/. The placement of stress is not predictable; it falls, in general, on any of the first two syllables in the word.

3.1.5 Otomanguean

The greatest internal diversity of phonemic systems is to be found within the Otomanguean family. This is to be expected since, as stated in chapter 2, it is the family whose members have been diverging for the longest period of time within Mesoamerica. There are, however, other reasons for this situation. The system reconstructed for proto-Otomanguean is: */t k kʷ ʔ s h n w j i u e a/ (plus tones); such a system is close to the lowest limit for the number of consonants in any attested phonemic system; therefore, if changes other than a simple reassignment of allophones were to occur, they were in all probability directed toward creating more consonants (and vowels). Besides, the system is reconstructed with a basic CV syllable pattern which could be preceded and followed by glottal, palatal or nasal elements; these elements fused or conditioned the nuclear consonants and vowels producing new orders and series of different types and with varying symmetry. It is hardly surprising, therefore, that the number

Table 11. *Cuicatec phonemic system*

	t	t͡s	k	kʷ	ʔ			
β	ð							
	s			h		i		u
m	n					e		
	l					ɛ		ɔ
	ɾ						a	
	j							

± length and/or nasality

Table 12. *Peñoles Mixtec phonemic system*

p	t	t͡ʃ	k	kʷ				
ᵐb	ⁿd	ᶮd͡ʒ	ᵑg	ᵑgʷ				
f	s	ʃ		h				
β	ð	ʒ			i	ɨ		u
m	n	ɲ			e			o
	l					a		
	r							

± nasality

of consonants may vary from fourteen to thirty; the number of vowels from four to nine; that orders vary from three to seven; that some languages may have only two fricatives and others twelve; that a language may have vowels contrasting only in the basic dimensions while others have both long and nasal vowels. Considerable diversity also exists in syllable patterns, and, as will be discussed in 4.2, in the tonal system.

Since it is the one with the least number of consonants, the system of Cuicatec (table 11) comes rather close to the protosystem. It should be clear that the comments made in relation to Huichol apply to the Cuicatec system too. Syllable patterns are equally simple: V, CV, CVʔ, and there are only few infrequent consonant clusters at the beginning of the syllable.

The Cuicatec system is not typical of the Mixtecan group; in fact its three subgroups have rather different phonemic systems. Chicahuaxtla Trique, like Cuicatec, lacks a labial stop and also has only one series of stops, although it has twenty-four consonants with contrast of voice in fricatives and of length in nasals, laterals and semivowels. In turn, Mixtec languages characteristically have a series of prenasalized stops, and contrast of voice in fricatives is also common. The system of Peñoles Mixtec (table 12) is standard for the group. The prenasalized phonemes could be interpreted as sequences of a nasal plus stop, e.g. /ᵐb/ as /mp/, but as these would be the only consonant clusters in the language and always belong to a single syllable, their analysis as unit phonemes seems preferable. In the vowel system there are long vowels too, but because of tone patterns (cf. 4.2) they are analysed as two vowels.

Amuzgo resembles the Mixtec languages in having a series of prenasalized stops (although the phonemic realization may be different) and like Cuicatec it lacks /p/ (in fact in most Mixtec languages /p/ may occur in just a couple of native words). It differs more in the syllable patterns and syllable types; syllables can be checked only by /ʔ/, but at the beginning up to four consonants may occur, and there is a type of syllable called a 'controlled' syllable and another called a 'ballistic' syllable (marked with a stress on the vowel), as for example /ʃiõ²¹/ 'crab', /síõ¹³/ 'humming bird'. The terms of 'controlled' and 'ballistic' themselves provide a reasonably clear picture of these syllable types but, with considerable exaggeration, ballistic syllables could be said to be hiccoughed.

The Popolocan group, like Mixtecan, shows marked variation in its phonemic systems. Huautla Mazatec, for example, has a consonant system slightly more complex than the Cuicatec system with sixteen consonants; Chocho, on the other hand, has twenty-three. The differences occur among the fricatives: Huautla Mazatec has /s ʃ h/, Chocho has /ɸ θ s ʃ ʂ x ß ð z ʒ ʐ ɣ/. Differences are also found in the number of vowels: Huautla Mazatec has four (/i e o a/), while Chiquihuitlan Mazatec has six (/i u e o ɛ a/); in both languages, nasalized vowels also occur, and there are groups of two and three vowels. Consonant groups are more frequent than in Mixtecan but possible combinations are highly restricted. In Tlacoyalco Popoloc, in which any given clusters may have up to three consonants, one of these must be either /ʔ/, /h/ or /n/. However, there are again differences, even in closely related languages; Huautla Mazatec has open syllables only, but may have initial clusters with /h/ or /ʔ/ as the first or second member i.e. Ch, hC, Cʔ, ʔC; Chiquihuitlan Mazatec, on the other hand, has syllables closed by /h/ or /ʔ/ but with initial clusters with only /h/ or /ʔ/ as the first member.

The Chinantecan, Otopamean, Zapotecan and Subtiaba-Tlapanec branches can be roughly characterized as having contrast of voice at least in stops, but there are many differences of detail and peculiarities within each group, and even between single languages within a group. We will therefore quote only the Zapotec system in full, although we shall mention some of the features found in other groups.

Zapotec languages are usually analysed as having a contrast of strong vs. weak consonants in almost all series, but in the absence of instrumental data it is difficult to know whether the contrast is really one of fortis vs. lenis articulation or whether it is simply a contrast of voice in the stops, voice or length in the fricatives, or of length or point of articulation in laterals and nasals (strong laterals and nasals are dental in some languages, weak ones alveolar). Table 13 gives the Guelavia Zapotec

Table 13. *Guelavia Zapotec phonemic system*

p̲	t	t̲s	t̲ʃ	t̲ʃ	k̲	ʔ				
p	t	ts	tʃ	tʃ	k			i ɨ u		
		s̲	ʃ̲	s̲				e o		
		s	ʃ	s̠				a		
m̲	n̲									
m	n									
	l̲									
	l									
w			j							

phonemic system which can be considered average for this group of languages (strong consonants are underlined). Within Otomanguean this type of system has the greatest number of consonants. It is also typical of Zapotec languages that the glottal stop belongs to the syllable nucleus, originating checked and rearticulated nuclei; in some languages, for example Zapotec of Guevea de Humboldt, there are also aspirated syllable nuclei. Nasal and long vowels are, in general, absent, but they occur in the closely related Chatino group. Some Zapotec languages, like Isthmus Zapotec, have open syllables only, but in many languages the final vowel in the word has dropped, producing checked syllables in which practically any consonant can occur. Initial consonant clusters may have two or three members, but their combinations are rather restricted (in most cases one of the consonants is /w/ or /j/); several languages have dropped the vowel from some prefixes thereby considerably increasing the number and types of initial consonant clusters.

Chinantec languages have contrasting voiced stops and fricatives; oral vowels are matched by nasal and/or long vowels, and in some languages there is contrast of rounding as in the following system from Quiotepec Chinantec: /i y ɯ u e ɤ o a/. At least two Chinantec languages, Usila and Palantla, have a contrast between controlled and ballistic syllables, but unlike Amuzgo this contrast is found only in stressed syllables. The syllable patterns are those most typical for Otomanguean: only a glottal can end a syllable, and the combinations permitted in initial clusters are very restricted. These are similar in the various languages; Lalana Chinantec, for instance, has clusters beginning with /k/, /g/ or /h/ and followed by /y/ or /w/, and clusters beginning with a glottal followed by a nasal, lateral or semivowel.

Otopamean languages do not show many peculiarities in the consonant system compared with those already discussed, except that the voiced series in general is

Table 14. *Phonemes in
Indian languages due to
Spanish influence*

p	t		k
ⓑ	ⓓ		ⓖ
ⓕ	s		ⓧ
m	n	ⓙ	
	ⓛ		
	ⓒ		
	ⓡ		

made up of obstruents rather than stops, i.e. the phonemes have stop and fricative allophones. The vowel systems are of the complex type in their basic dimensions and there are nasal vowels too, although fewer nasal vowels than oral ones; Mazahua has /i ɨ u e ə o ɛ ɔ a ĩ ũ ẽ ə̃ õ ã/. On the other hand, Otopamean languages stand in sharp contrast to the other Otomanguean languages by virtue of the consonant clusters that occur closing a syllable. Even initial clusters show many more combinations than in other Otomanguean languages, only Chatino being similar to the other Otomanguean languages in this respect; final clusters also permit a large number of combinations and sequences with as many as four consonants; the following are examples from Northern Pame: *ŋhjŏst²²* 'put it down!', *nl²ospt²* 'their houses', *wa²a²habmpt* 'he asks them', *iŋgja²okŋ²n* 'rest yourselves!'

3.1.6 *Elements due to Spanish influence*

Changes in the types of phonemic systems caused by the introduction of unassimilated Spanish loans can be briefly summarized. Table 14 is a partial chart of a consonant system in which contrasting elements due to Spanish influence have been circled. Many languages in Mesoamerica that previously lacked these phonemes now have them, and in addition, many languages have new consonant clusters with a stop or fricative plus lateral or flap, e.g. /pl/, /gr/. Some languages have also added syllables ending in a consonant to their inventories of syllable patterns.

The changes produced in the vowel systems are less noticeable because either the indigenous languages had a Spanish-type system (/i u e o a/) or they had a richer one; few languages had a smaller number of vowels than Spanish. The appearance of vowel clusters like /ia/, /io/, /ei/, etc. is more common. Moreover, the common native pattern of phonologically predictable stress is disrupted by the unpredictable stress of Spanish loanwords.

3.2 **Phonological processes**

The term 'phonological processes' is often used in conjunction with the study of morphophonemics. However, this would entail consideration of diverse and complicated phenomena that would be inappropriate in this volume. Here the term will be used only to refer to those cases in which a change in otherwise contrasting phonemes occurs regularly when morphemes and/or words are put together, irrespective of the particular morphological elements that are combined. In this restricted sense, phonological processes are not very important in many languages in Mesoamerica. There are cases like the Mixtec languages where no change of this type occurs in segmental phonemes (although, as will be discussed in 4.2, there are comparable changes in tones); in other languages there may be some regular changes but the conditions under which they occur only affect a few elements. Thus in Huautla Mazatec there is regular contraction of vowels which occurs only when suffixes indicating person are added to noun or verb stems.

Phonological processes are important in Mixe-Zoque languages, in Coastal Chontal and, to a lesser extent, in Totonac and the Uto-Aztecan languages outside Mesoamerica proper (although they are also prominent in certain Uto-Aztecan languages not treated here). Sierra Popoluca, a Mixe-Zoque language, for example, has the following processes: vowel lengthening, vowel shortening, doubling of vowels, glottal insertion, sonorization, palatalization and assimilation of position of articulation. Coastal Chontal has assimilation, dissimilation, epenthesis, elision, palatalization, glottalization and devoicing. Examples will be given of the most important processes.

Metathesis, a regular process in Mixe-Zoque, occurs in Copainalá Zoque when morphemes ending in /j/ are followed by morphemes beginning with labials, velars or glottal stops; notice the resultant forms when the stems *tih-* 'arrive' and *poj-* 'run' are followed by the suffix *-pa* 'continuative aspect': *tih-pa* 'he arrives', *po-pja* 'he is running'. Metathesis also occurs between nasals, laterals or semivowels and a following glottal stop, for instance: *ʔune* 'child', *kom* 'post'; with the locative suffix *-ʔaŋi* these yield *ʔune-ʔaŋi* 'to the child', *koʔm-aŋi* 'to the post'.

Reduction of consonant clusters is again extensive in Copainalá Zoque, for example: *wiht-* 'walk' with *-pa*, *witpa* 'he walks'; *ʔuhk-* 'drink' plus suffix *-kuj*, *ʔuhkuj* 'a drink'. Akin to this process is consonant loss as in Northern Totonac, where the final glottal stop is lost when a morpheme is added: *tlan'kaʔ* 'big', *tlanka-tiˈxiʔ* 'a wide road'. Vowel loss also occurs in Northern Totonac in the sequences lV, jV when they are followed by a morpheme beginning with /n/: *maqta·ji-ˈma* 'he is helping', but *maqta·j-ˈnan* 'he helps'.

Consonant epenthesis is attested in Coastal Chontal when a word ends in a vowel and the next word begins with a consonant; in this case /x/ is added at the end of the first word; for example, *ˈɬtepa* 'bit me', but *ˈɬtepax ˈmiḻa* 'a dog bit me'.

In other types of process the change does not involve a whole phoneme but rather a feature of it. In Sierra Popoluca palatalization of an alveolar consonant is caused by a preceding palatal consonant: *tukpa* 'be cutting', *iɲ-* '2nd person sg.', *iɲṭukpa* 'you are cutting it'. In Coastal Chontal glottalization occurs when the glottal stop would follow a voiceless continuant; in this case the voiceless continuant is glottalized; compare *mu'ḷi* 'boy' and *imoɬ* 'sheep' when pluralized by /ʔ/: *mu'ḷiʔ* 'boys', *imoɬʔ* 'sheep (pl.)'. Assimilation involving the point of articulation of nasal consonants is widespread; for example in Copainalá Zoque: *an-* '1 st sg.', *an-'tukpa* 'I am cutting it', *am-puj* 'my foot', *aŋ-'watpa* 'I do it'. In Sierra Popoluca sonorization of voiceless consonants takes place when morphemes ending in a vowel and a voiceless stop are followed by a suffix or word which begins with a vowel: *huˑt* 'where?', *iʔɲiʃ* 'you saw it', *'huudiʔɲiʃ* 'where did you see it?' This sequence also exemplifies the process of a long vowel becoming a double vowel when followed by a voiced consonant if the next morpheme or word begins with a vowel.

In Northern Totonac vowel lengthening occurs when a word with a final short vowel becomes phrase medial: *taˑ'ta* 'grandfather', *taˑ'ta-ʔaɬ* 'the grandfather went away'. In Sierra Popoluca vowel shortening takes place in suffixes beginning with a consonant: *'joˑʃ-'aˑp* 'he works', *'joˑʃ-'ap-ṭim* 'he works too'.

Vowel harmony – as a living process – affects some suffixes in the Mayan and Mixe-Zoque languages, and in Tarascan and Huave, but it is more general in Mazahua. In this language the root vowel determines the stem vowel in bisyllabic stems; if any one of /i ɨ e ə ĩ ẽ ə̃ ã/ is the root vowel, the stem vowel is the same, e.g. *'pe¹se* 'to end', *'mə¹ʃə* 'turkey'; if the root vowel is /ɛ/ the stem vowel is /i/, e.g. *'pɛhpi* 'to work'; and if the root vowel is any one of /a u o ɔ õ ũ/ the stem vowel is /i/, e.g. *'ba¹²ʃi* 'broom', *'ʃɔ¹²mi* 'night'.

SOURCES AND FURTHER READING
See chapter 4.

4

Phonology II

In chapter 3 the discussion focussed on whole phonemic systems within language groups. In section 4.1, attention is turned to classes of phonemes and their occurrence across linguistic families. The quantitative statements in this section refer to a sample of eighty-four languages. Section 4.2 deals with tone systems.

4.1 Distribution of phonemic characteristics

4.1.1 *Consonants*

The Aguacatec system given in table 9 exemplifies the maximum number of orders of stops in this area, namely nine; the minimum is three (/p t k/), but this is only attested in Otomi of Tenango de Doria and (depending on the analysis) in Yaitepec Chatino; most languages add one or two orders of affricates (/ts̪/, /tʃ/), two in fact being more common. An additional order, represented by the retroflex (/tʃ/), is less common; it only occurs in ten languages belonging to the Mayan, Zapotecan and Popolocan languages. The absence of a labial stop is characteristic of a few Otomanguean languages; uvular stops are only found in Mayan, Totonac-Tepehua and, marginally, in North Pame.

Labiovelars are common, being possessed by a third of the languages in the sample belonging to five different families. Labial stops with modification of rounding occur in Cora (/pʷ/) and Yaqui (/bʷ/). Palatalization as a feature affecting all members of a consonant system was exemplified with Mixe from El Paraíso. Except for languages such as this, where palatalized consonants contrast with sequences Cj, linguists may differ in their analysis of the same language as to whether the consonant is palatalized or a sequence Cj. Nevertheless, palatalized dentals may be said to occur in some Otomanguean languages, Coastal Chontal and Uto-Aztecan languages; palatalized velars are uncommon (some Mayan languages) and only Amuzgo has both /tʲ/ and /kʲ/. Contrast between the dental and alveolar stop (/t̪ t/) is attested only in Tlacoyalco Popoloc, and the affricate /tʳ/ in contrast with /t t̪s t̪ʃ t̪ʃ/ occurs in San Vicente Coyotepec Popoloc.

The greatest number of orders generally occurs in the stop series, and within these, in the voiceless series, although there are a few exceptions such as Lalana Chinantec which has more voiced stops than voiceless ones (/p t k b d d̪z d̪ʒ g/) and Chocho which has a labial fricative not matched by a stop.

Only a few languages – Huave and Tarascan, both Tepehuán languages – lack the glottal stop completely, but in several languages it only occurs as part of the syllable nucleus.

The greatest number of orders in the fricatives (six) has already been exemplified with Chocho in 3.1.5. All languages have at least two fricatives, one being alveolar or alveopalatal, and the other velar, uvular or glottal. Between the two extremes there are various combinations of fricatives; the different types of fricatives ordered according to decreasing frequency are /h ʃ x χ ʂ f θ/, the last only occurring in three languages in contrast with /s/ or /ʃ/.

The maximum number of contrasting stop series is the triple one of Jicaque; Mixtec of San Miguel El Grande also has three series of stops but these are voiceless, prenasalized and voiced. A single series is found in fourteen languages, half of which are Otomanguean, the remainder belonging to the Uto-Aztecan, Totonac-Tepehua, Mixe-Zoque and Cuitlatec families. Other languages have two series of stops, one of which is voiceless; the other may be aspirated as in Tarascan, prenasalized as in Mixtec languages, Amuzgo and Huave, glottalized as in Mayan, Xinca, Lenca, Tequistlatec-Jicaque and Tepehua, or voiced as in Otomanguean and Uto-Aztecan. In chapter 3 attention was called to the fact in several languages the voiced series, having both stop and fricative allophones, was a series of obstruents. Contrast of voice in fricatives only occurs in some Otomanguean languages, and contrasts of voice in both stops and fricatives, as in Quiotepec Chinantec (/t d s ð k g x ɣ/), are exceptional.

All languages have /m n/ except Rincon Zapotec which lacks /m/ (in other Zapotec languages /m/ may occur in a few native words). A palatal nasal is common (twenty-four languages); much less frequent is the velar nasal. Only ten languages have /m n ŋ/, and there are only five languages that have /m n ɲ ŋ/. The only example of /mʷ/ is found in Cora. Contrasts of length in nasals occur in Chicahuaxtla Trique and (depending on the analysis) in Zapotecan languages; glottalized and voiceless nasals are only found in Tequistlatecan. A syllabic nasal occurs in Amuzgo, but always in non-final syllables, for example /n̩¹lká²/ 'candle'. Quiotepec Chinantec also has a syllabic nasal with the further peculiarity that it can constitute a whole word together with glottals and modification of length, and that more than one syllabic nasal may occur in sequence; for example: /mʔ¹/ 'ant', /m·²³/ 'sandal', /hmʔ³/ 'tomato', /ʔm·³mʔ⁴/ 'you (pl.) pinch', /m·⁴²mʔmʔ²⁴/ 'we (excl.)

pinch'; notice that there is no vowel phonetically, and these words are pronounced with closed lips throughout.

Only two languages in the sample, Totontepec Mixe and Huastec, do not have either a lateral or a vibrant. Fifteen languages lack a contrast between lateral and vibrant, those having only a vibrant being in the minority (five languages); Tarascan has no lateral, but has /r ɾ/. Languages without vibrants may have two laterals, e.g. Cuicatec (/ɬ l/) and Nahuatl (/tɬ l/). Most languages have at least /l/ and /ɾ/, and a dozen have /r/ as well. The most complex system of laterals was exemplified with Coastal Chontal (table 10). Contrast of alveolar (or dental) vs. palatal lateral is rare (besides Tequitlatecan languages, North Pame and Chatino languages) as is the presence of a uvular trill, e.g. in Southern Tepehuán and in some Zapotec languages, in which a labialized uvular trill also occurs (e.g. Yatzachi Zapotec). Two languages, Amuzgo and Isthmus Zapotec, have a bilabial trill (in Amuzgo it is prenasalized and syllabic) which is found in a single word: Amuzgo ʃaˈmbʳ¹, Isthmus Zapotec ʃambʳ, both meaning 'ant lion'.

4.1.2 *Vowels*

Three vowel systems, both in Totonac and Tepehua, have /i u a/; four vowel systems are found in Huautla Mazatec and in Nahuatl languages, both having /i e o a/. These systems can equally well be represented with a /u/ instead of /o/; the choice of the symbol depends on the frequency of allophone [o] compared with allophone [u]. The most frequent five-vowel system has /i u e o a/, with only Huichol having /i ɨ u e a/, and North Pame /i a e ɛ a/. Six-vowel systems all have /i ɨ u e o a/. In seven-vowel systems, two, Chicahuaxtla Trique and Matlatzinca, have /i ɨ u e ə o a/; Amuzgo lacks the central vowels but has an additional degree of height (/i u e o ɛ ɔ a/). Quiotepec Chinantec seems to be the only example of an eight-vowel system with contrast of rounding in both front and back vowels: /i y ɯ u e ɤ o a/. A similar nine-vowel system (/i ɨ u e ə o ɛ ɔ a/) is found in Totontepec Mixe and in Mazahua. As this summary shows (cf. also table 6), most systems have three degrees of height, and those with four degrees (assuming that /a/ is considered phonemically different in height from /ɛ/ and /ɔ/) are relatively uncommon. A contrast of front vs. central vs. back in high vowels is common, but a contrast of rounding independent of front vs. back is not.

In chapter 3 systems with long and/or nasal vowels were exemplified; some general characteristics will now be considered. With occasional exceptions, such as a dialect of Mam and a Zoque language (Ostuacan Zoque), nasal vowels occur only in Otomanguean languages, and, as is common typologically, they are less numerous than oral vowels; Temoaya Otomi, for example, has nine oral vowels and only three nasal vowels. Furthermore, oral and nasal vowels do not usually contrast when they are in contact with nasal consonants. A further characteristic of nasal vowels is that they usually contrast in one syllable per word, the stressed or the final one, depending on the language; in fact, in most languages nasalization may be considered a feature of the word since when the contrasting syllable has a nasal vowel nasality extends backwards (forward in North Pame and Ostuacan Zoque) through vowels and consonants with the exception of the stops. For example Tlapanec /nĩ²raʔ²ũ¹/ [nĩ²r̃ãʔ²ũ¹] 'you were seated', /jo³hõ³/ [jõ³h̃õ³] 'mosquito'. A Chinantec language, that of Palantla, shows a typologically unique contrast between oral vowels and two degrees of nasal vowels, e.g. /ʔe³²/, /ʔẽ³²/, /ʔẽ̃³²/, forms of the verbs meaning 'leach', 'count', and 'chase' respectively; the second word has a vowel which is slightly nasal, the third one which is strongly nasal.

Length in vowels is more common than nasality in terms of language families; it occurs in all families except Cuitlatec and Tarascan. This feature also differs from nasality in that long and short vowels are usually equally distributed. Copala Trique constitutes the only example in the area (elsewhere it is not unusual) of a system with a larger number of long vowels than short ones; the vowels are /i u a i· u· e· o· a·/; furthermore, long vowels have a higher frequency of occurrence than short vowels.

In Otomanguean languages long vowels, like nasal ones, contrast in a particular syllable in the word, whereas in other languages long vowels can occur in different syllables, and there can be more than one per word as in the following examples from Classical Nahuatl: /tla·katekolo·tl/ 'demon', /niktʃi·wa/ 'I do it', /mitsto·ka·jo·ti/ 'he named you'.

Tlacoyalco Popoloc and Eastern Popoloc have a feature analysed as stress, and which is manifested by vowel and consonant length. Each word has either a long consonant or a long vowel, as in these examples from Tlacoyalco Popoloc: /t̯h·ao³/ 'wet', /to·²e¹/ 'hole'; when the long element is a consonant it is usually the last in the word, and the length is shifted when a suffix containing a consonant is added, e.g. /di¹k·õ²/ 'I see', but /di¹ko²ʃ·ĩ/ 'I see with (something)'.

4.1.3 *Other phonemic characteristics*

In the survey of phonemic systems in chapter 3 no mention was made of units higher than the syllable, but units such as phonological words, phonological phrases and phonological sentences – marked variously by special consonant or vowel allophones, differences in stress and in syllable timing and intonation – are attested in most languages for which adequate analysis is available.

Finally, there are some phonological phenomena that may be considered an aspect of 'register'. Since their recognition depends for the most part on fine-grained

1   2   3   12   13   21   23   32   31   323

Fig. 5   Tlapanec tones

analysis which has not yet been carried out on all languages, they may prove to be much more common than they appear at present. Some examples follow.

In Coatzospan Mixtec there is a difference between women's and men's speech; before /e/ or /i/ men have /t/ and /d/, women have /tʃ/ and /dʒ/ respectively. A difference between normal speech and baby talk occurs in Huichol: /t ts z̢ ʈ n/ in normal speech corresponds to /t̪ tʃ ʂ ~ z ~ s ɲ/. Also, in Jicaltepec Mixtec there is a 'diminutive style' in which /p/ is substituted for /kʷ/, and /tʃ/ for /ʃ/. We also find the use of continuous lip rounding coupled with oversoft voice and loose articulation in Jicaltepec Mixtec as a rhetorical style; falsetto voice in voiced sounds is used in Huichol to express excitement, while in Totontepec Mixe a breathy quality is used to express excitement or emphasis, and laryngealization for apology or supplication.

4.2   Tone systems

Tone systems can be classified by various features, and the order in which these are presented below is not necessarily significant. Attention is called to the way tones are indicated: a raised '1' represents the highest tone in a system and successively higher numbers indicate progressively lower tones; this notation is the reverse of the one employed in other areas, but since it has been predominantly used in Mesoamerican linguistics it is followed here. Tones are marked after the syllables possessing them, and two or more numbers on the same syllable indicate a combination of the respective simple tones.

4.2.1   *Types of tone systems*

Most Mesoamerican tone systems are of the type called 'register systems' or systems of levels. What is contrastive in this type of system is the relative height of pitches that fall into a number of levels such as high, mid, low; when changes in the height of a pitch are significant they can be identified by their beginning and ending pitches with a sequence of two or more level tones. This can be represented in a kind of musical staff notation as in fig. 5 which represents the tones of Tlapanec. When the vowel is long and has the same tone throughout it is as if the same tone occurred in sequence, but since there is no reason to analyse the long vowels as geminates

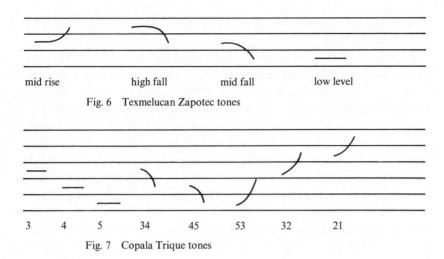

mid rise   high fall   mid fall   low level

Fig. 6   Texmelucan Zapotec tones

3   4   5   34   45   53   32   21

Fig. 7   Copala Trique tones

(combinations of tones can occur in a short syllable) a single tone is said to occur, as in /dã·²/ 'pot'.

In 'contour systems', on the other hand, it is the configuration or profile of the pitches that is significant (rise, fall, level, rise-fall, for example), in which case the beginning or ending points of changing pitches cannot be identified with level tones. Differences in relative height occur frequently within a contour and it is necessary to distinguish between, for example, high rise and mid rise. One of the systems that seems to be more the contour type comes from Texmelucan Zapotec; the tones can be represented as in fig. 6. Notice that if the tones were represented as level tones, each one would have to be marked with two numbers with the exception of the fourth; the first three cannot be differentiated by relative height (only the direction of the glide has to be specified), and if we marked the tones as 21, 12, 23, 3, then tones 2 and 1 would occur only in combinations.

Another system that can be analysed, at least partially, as a contour system is that of Copala Trique; the tones can be represented as in fig. 7. The first three tones represented are level, and the following three glides can be analysed as a combination of two of the level tones, but in the last two glides the higher pitches cannot be identified with any level tone so that what seems contrastive are the rises which are kept apart by relative height. This system may be considered of mixed type.

There are several systems in Mesoamerica with high and low tones which in addition have either a rise or a fall glide (more rarely both); these systems are usually analysed as three- (or four-) tone systems, i.e. as contour types. These systems will be represented here as two-tone systems plus one or two combinations, i.e. 1, 2, 12 and/or 21.

Some languages have a type of tone system called the 'terrace system'. There are two varieties, one with 'downstepped' and the other with 'upstepped' terrace tones. Coatzospan Mixtec exemplifies the former. This language has two tones, high and low, occurring also in combinations high–low, low–high; furthermore, when morphemes or words are put together, and after the occurrence of a high tone, successive high tones may be lowered without becoming confused with low tones; that is, there is a change in key that continues until there is a pause. This process may occur more than once in a sequence, the tones being downstepped progressively each time the process takes place. This effect is associated with particular morphemes or words.

In the following example the exclamation mark denotes the lowering of following tones: $di^1o^1\text{-}ko^1!\ tu^{?1}tu^1!\ vi^1i^1!\ lu^{?1}ku^1$ 'I want crazy cold paper'. Represented by lines on different levels the tonal profile is as follows:

```
 – – –
    – –
     – –
       – –
```

Notice that this lowering effect cannot occur immediately after a pause since it always occurs after a high tone.

The other variety of terrace system is found in Acatlán Mixtec. This language has three tones (high, mid, low) and an upstepped high tone, marked by 1^+, that is higher than a preceding high tone or another preceding upstepped tone, those being the only two environments in which it occurs. If more than one upstepped tone occurs in a sequence the pitches become progressively higher. An example is: $ma^{3'}ne^1e^1te^{1+}\ sa^{1+'}k^wa^1a^1\ {}'?i^{1+}da^{1+}$ 'he will not skin the deer the day after tomorrow'; if the relative pitches of that sequence are represented by lines on different levels, the profile is as follows:

```
                    –
                   –
                 – – –
                  –
               – –

               –
```

As the diagram indicates, a high tone is level with a preceding upstepped tone.

It may be noticed that the two systems are analysed in different ways. In the first case the change in key is interpreted as a process that affects a sequence of tones; in the second case, an additional tone is posited that conditions the height of following tones.

4.2.2 Number of tones

As will be obvious from the previous examples, tone systems also differ in the number of tones; the smallest number is naturally two, the largest, in register systems, is five. There are as yet only two languages in Mesoamerica that are known to have a five-tone system, Usila Chinantec and Chicahuaxtla Trique (although the latter may be considered a mixed type); both languages also have some combinations of the five tones. Examples from Usila Chinantec showing the five tones contrasting before a following mid tone are: $o^1\eta i^3$ 'thread', $a^2 l\acute{o}^3$ 'leather', $a^3 l\acute{o}^3$ 'this one', $\tilde{u}^4 k\acute{u}^3$ 'grain of corn', $\tilde{u}^5 k\acute{u}^3$ 'world'.

Four-tone systems are a little more common, being found in the Popolocan group, in Lealao Chinantec, in Yaitepec Chatino and in Mixtec from San Antonio Atatlauhca.

Three-tone systems are the most common, and are attested in Zapotecan, Chinantecan, Mixtecan, Popolocan, Tlapanec and Amuzgo.

Systems of two tones plus a combination of them are typical of Otopamean languages. North Pame and South Pame have high, low and high–low, but Mezquital Otomi has high, low and low–high; Isthmus Zapotec is of the same type, but Mitla Zapotec has high, low, high–low and low–high. Matlatzinca and Chichimec, instead, have two tones, but without the combinations; outside the Otomanguean family this is the only type of system found, and is attested in Huichol, Huave of San Mateo, Yucatec, Tzotzil of San Bartolo and Uspantec.

There is another difference between systems with three tones or more and two-tone systems besides the mere difference in number of tones. In two-tone systems, forms differentiated only by tones, such as Yucatec $ma^1 ko^{\eta 2}$ 'man', $ma^2 ko^{\eta 2}$ 'cover', are very rare; in the other systems with more tones, they serve to differentiate a large number of lexical items which would be otherwise identical and, in addition, to indicate different grammatical categories. Examples from Chiquihuitlan Mazatec (a language with four tones): $t\int a^1$ 'I talk', $t\int a^2$ 'difficult', $t\int a^3$ 'his hand', $t\int a^4$ 'he talks'.

4.2.3 Combinations of tones

As was mentioned earlier, tones can occur in combinations; different systems, however, have different possibilities. In Tlapanec all the possible combinations of two tones occur along with a three-tone combination. In other systems there are restrictions that can be exemplified with the following four Chinantec three-tone languages. Lalana allows 23, 32, and 31; Sochiapan has 13, 21, 32; Palantla 12, 13, 31; Tepetotutla has all possible combinations except 13. On the other hand, in a language like Huautla Mazatec single tones and combinations of tones can occur in any syllable irrespective of whether it has a simple or complex nucleus, as in $ni^3 sa^{34}$ 'waterjug', $la^4 hao^4$ 'stone', $'si^{43} k^{\eta} ia^{43}$ 'I paint', $va^{43} ntia^{423}$ 'I travel'. On the other hand, in Mixtec of San Miguel el Grande a combination of two tones can only occur in a syllable with a long vowel which is tonally equivalent to a two-syllable sequence and is therefore represented with a geminate vowel, e.g. [ke·²] /ke²e²/ 'eat'.

4.2.4 *Domain of tone, and stress*

The possibility of tones being contrastive in one or another syllable within the word (or word plus clitics) may be termed the domain in which tones are contrastive, and this is yet another dimension along which languages differ. The polar types can be exemplified with North Pame where only the stressed syllable carries contrastive tone, as in *monʔŏ²ɛhɛʔ* 'my path', *nambo¹²* 'block', and with Huautla Mazatec in which every syllable carries contrastive tone, as in *siʔ¹kʔo¹vha³ya³tʔa⁴³* 'he changes his mind'. There are intermediate types; in Palantla Chinantec, for example, tones are contrastive on any syllable except those that are poststressed, as in *guˇ¹tiŏ³¹niw* 'you go confess (it)' (ˇ marks controlled stress).

The domain of tone in a given system is independent of the number of tones in a system. Yaitepec Chatino has four tones (plus combinations) contrastive only on the stressed (last) syllable: *kwiyaʔ¹* 'soap', *huʔwa²³* 'pile', while Northern Tepehuán has two tones contrasting on any syllable: *o²na¹i¹kɨ²ɗɨ²* 'with salt', *a²i¹ɲi²* 'it is broken'.

A further difference in the domain of tone is found in Huichol and Mazahua. Tones are contrastive on every syllable except on the last two in Huichol and on the final one in Mazahua. In the final syllables of the phonological sentence the inherent lexical tones are cancelled by tones belonging to the intonational system. In the following example from Huichol, / ´ / and / ` / mark lexical tones (high and low), raised numbers the intonational contour: *jàáwì + kámí + maa²na⁴ #* 'look, there is a coyote!' (the plus sign and the double cross mark phonological features that are not relevant here); were the word *jàáwì* 'coyote' used as a whole exclamatory sentence, its inherent low tones would be replaced by an intonational contour: *jaa¹wɨ⁴ #* 'a coyote!'. Systems similar but more complicated as regards the domain of tone are found in Otomi languages.

In various places mention was made of stress in systems with tones, and a variety of conditions governing stress placement is found to be similar to those in systems without tones.

In Huichol and Tlapanec stress is determined by tones and by the structure of the syllable. In Tlapanec, for example, in a bisyllabic word with low–high tones the second syllable is prominent; if tones are high–low the first syllable is more prominent; if both syllables have the same tone and the second syllable is long both are heard as equally stressed; and so on. In North Pame, as exemplified, the stressed syllable is the one carrying contrastive tone; in Chicahuaxtla Trique stress falls on the final syllable in the word, i.e. it is not contrastive as to position, but marks the end of the word. In Mixtec languages stress usually falls on the first syllable of the root (which is normally bisyllabic) but it remains invariable when affixes are added so that its placement varies within the word.

4.2.5 *Tone sandhi*

Tone systems may differ through the presence or absence of tone sandhi or, as it is also called in Mesoamerican linguistics, tone perturbation. Tone sandhi is the tonal correlate of the phonological processes discussed in 3.2, and therefore represents changes in tones when morphemes and/or words are combined, and like the other phonological processes it is a mechanical one. In contrast with the function of tones in manifesting grammatical categories or in differentiating words, the change of tone does not in this case manifest or differentiate meanings.

Languages with no tone sandhi or in which it occurs exceptionally are the Chinantec language, Tlapanec and Yucatec; those in which tone sandhi does occur are Northern Tepehuán, Huave and, notably, Mixtec and Zapotec languages. Closely related languages may differ in this respect: Huautla Mazatec, for example, lacks tone sandhi yet Soyaltepec Mazatec has an extensive system.

Although the rules of tone sandhi are generally regular in each language they are rather complex and numerous (sixteen are needed to cover the system in Ayutla Mixtec). We will therefore only exemplify the basic characteristics of the systems and those which differ more obviously from language to language.

In the rules for tone sandhi, morphemes and/or words fall into different classes which are largely arbitrary. That is, membership is determined by listing. In addition, words and/or morphemes are classified according to their basic tone patterns (in the most simple case, the pattern a form has when uttered in isolation) and by the changes they cause and/or undergo. For example, in Jicaltepec Mixtec, the word meaning 'people' has as its basic tones high–high, $'ɲi^1wi^1$; in the sequence $'du^1wa^2$ $'ɲi^2wi^2$ 'the people fell' the basic tones have been replaced by two mid tones because the first word has a high–mid tone pattern. If, however, the first word has low–mid tones, the changes are to low–mid as in $'de^3ku^2$ $'ɲi^3wi^2$ 'the people are sitting'. When the first word has the same tone pattern as that of the last example, but the second word has mid–mid basic tones, e.g. $'to^{ʔ2}o^2$ 'town father', then these change to low–low as in $'tě^3da^2$ $'to^{ʔ3}o^3$ 'the town father's store'. In $'wa^3ta^3$ $'ɲi^2wi^1$ 'people lie' it can be seen that after a word with low–low tones the changes are to mid–high, whereas in $'tʃa^{ʔ3}nu^3$ $'ɲi^1wi^1$ 'the people are old' the basic tones remain unaltered; that is so because $'wa^3ta^3$ and $'tʃa^{ʔ3}nu^3$, in spite of sharing the same tone pattern, belong to different arbitrary classes regarding the sandhi effect they produce.

In the foregoing examples the changes in tone always occurred in the second word of a sequence; they were examples of progressive perturbation. When the perturbed tones occur before the conditioning tones it is a case of regressive perturbation, and there are cases in which the changes are in both directions. Notice, finally, that in this language certain tone patterns, e.g. low–high, are never changed when second in a sequence.

The tone patterns that determine classes, the specific changes produced and the direction of perturbation are all dimensions along which languages may differ. For example, in another Mixtec language, that from San Miguel el Grande, tone perturbation is progressive only, and the changes are always to higher tones. A different type of conditioning appears in this Mixtec language: the segmental shape of morphemes may also determine classes in sandhi rules. In a class of morphemes with mid–low basic pattern, if they have a CV^2CV^3 shape they change to CV^2CV^1, and if they have a $CV^{?2}CV^3$ shape they change to $CV^{?1}CV^3$ after a certain class of morphemes.

In the previous examples only phonological features were elements that delimited classes in sandhi rules; in other cases the syntactic construction may be the determining factor. In the following examples from San Esteban Atatlauhca Mixtec – $^2\vartheta^2ng^2\ nd\vartheta^3b\vartheta^4$ 'another egg' and $u^2ku^2\ nd\vartheta^1b\vartheta^1$ (literally) 'egg mountain' – the basic tones of the word $nd\vartheta^2b\vartheta^4$ 'egg' undergo different changes (in spite of the common mid–mid tone pattern of the first words) because the second sequence is a construction of a special type which actually means 'the place where eggs are to be had'. In other languages the grammatical class of a word may also be a determining factor.

There may be differences among languages as to the domain in which sandhi rules operate. In Acatlan Mixtec, rules apply to continuous morphemes within a word or across word boundaries. For example, $'vi^2u^2$ 'corn plant' and $'sa^2ku^2$ 'few' are affected in the final tone by the same rule in the sequences $'vi^2u^3\ 'k^wa^2ti^2$ 'small corn plants' and $'sa^2ku^3te^2$ 'few of them', in spite of the fact that in the first case the conditioning morpheme belongs to a different word, while in the second it is a suffix. In Soyaltepec Mazatec, on the other hand, morphemes of a certain class only change the tone of another morpheme within the same word, while morphemes of a different class only affect tones of a different word.

4.2.6 *Whistled speech*

Several tone languages – some Mazatec, Chinantec and Zapotec languages – also have a system of whistled speech. The Huautla Mazatec system is sketched here.

Tones of words as well as word stress and sentence rhythm of normal speech are reproduced in whistle. Since tones are differentiated in normal speech by relative pitch, in whistled speech the key on which their relative height will be significant is established by the first speaker; the key may be higher or lower depending on distance, but if one speaker leaves the key that has been established, misunderstanding may arise.

As there are many words and phrases that have identical tone sequences, and which in normal speech are distinguished segmentally, ambiguities can arise, although these are normally eliminated by the context.

It should be noted that an interchange using whistled speech may be a real conversation with a beginning and an end, not just an occasional call or warning; there are specimens quoted of thirteen sentences being whistled, and examples have been heard lasting up to three minutes. Also an interchange which begins with whistled speech when the speakers are at a considerable distance from each other may continue in normal speech when they get closer. A detail of sociolinguistic interest is that whistled speech is understood by women, but only men use it actively.

Whistled speech has also been reported in non-tonal languages, for example in Tepehua. Naturally, in these cases what is reproduced is not lexical tones but intonation. A further difference is that, in the Tepehua system at least, changes in tongue position, as well as changes in lip tension and contour, are used to reproduce, in modified form, vowels and consonants.

SOURCES

Aguacatec: McArthur and McArthur 1956. *Amuzgo*: Bauernschmidt 1965*. *Cakchiquel*: Grimes, L. 1968. *Chatino*: (*Tataltepec*) Pride, L. 1963; (*Yaitepec*) McKaughan 1954. *Chinantec*: (*Lalana*) Rensch and Rensch 1966*; (*Palantla*) Merrifield 1963; (*Quiotepec*) Robbins 1961*, 1968*, 1975; (*Sochiapan*) Foris, D. 1973; (*Tepetotutla*) Westley 1971; (*Usila*) Skinner 1962. *Chocho*: Mock 1977. *Chol*: Aulie and Aulie 1978. *Chontal*: (*Coastal*) Waterhouse 1962, Waterhouse and Morrison 1950; (*Highland*) Turner 1967a. *Cora*: McMahon 1967. *Cuicatec*: Needham and Davis 1946. *Cuitlatec*: Escalante 1962. *Huastec*: Larsen and Pike 1949. *Huave*: Pike, K. and Warkentin 1961, Suárez 1975. *Huichol*: Grimes, J. 1955, 1959*. *Jacaltec*: Day 1973a. *Jicaque*: Fleming and Dennis 1977. *Lenca*: Campbell 1976a. *Mam*: Canger 1969. *Matlatzinca*: Cazés 1967, Coronado Suzán et al. 1974, Escalante 1977. *Mazahua*: Amador Hernández 1976, Pike, E. 1951*, Spotts 1953. *Mazatec*: (*Chiquihuitlan*) Jamieson, A. 1977a*, 1977b*; (*Huautla*) Cowan 1948*, Pike, K. 1948*, Pike, K. and Pike, E. 1947*, Pike E. 1967*; (*Soyaltepec*) Pike, E. 1956. *Mixe*: (*Coatlan*) Hoogshagen 1959; (*El Paraíso*) Van Haitsma and Van Haitsma 1976; (*Totontepec*) Crawford 1963*. *Mixtec*: (*Acatlan*) Pike, E. and Wistrand 1974*; (*Ayutla*) Pankratz and Pike 1967; (*Coatzospan*) Pike, E. and Small 1974*; (*Jicaltepec*) Bradley 1970; (*Peñoles*) Daly 1973, 1977; (*San Esteban Atatlauhca*) Mak 1953*; (*San Miguel el Grande*) Pike, K. 1948*. *Nahuatl*: (*Classical*) Andrews, J. 1975, Newman 1967; (*Mecayapan*) Law 1955; (*Milpa Alta*) Whorf 1946; (*Zacapoaxtla*) Robinson 1969*, 1970. *Otomi*: (*Mezquital*) Wallis 1968*; (*Temoaya*) Andrews, H. 1949; (*Tenango de Doria*) Blight and Pike 1976. *Pame*: (*North*) Gibson, L. 1956*; (*South*) Manrique 1967. *Pokomchi*: Mayers 1960. *Popoloc*: (*Coyotepec*) Barrera and Dakin 1978; (*Eastern*) Karlstrom and Pike 1968*; (*Tlacoyalco*) Stark and Machin 1977*. *Popoluca*: (*Sierra*) Elson 1960, 1967;

(*Sayula*) Clark 1961. *Tarascan*: Foster 1969, Friedrich 1971b*. *Teco*: Kaufman 1969. *Tepehua*: Bower and Hollenbach 1967. *Tepehuán*: (*Northern*) Bascom 1959*; (*Southern*) Willet 1978. *Totonac*: (*Northern*) McQuown 1940; (*Papantla*) Aschmann 1956. *Trique*: (*Chicahuaxtla*) Longacre 1952*; (*Copala*) Hollenbach 1977*. *Tzeltal*: Kaufman 1971b*. *Yaqui*: Lindenfeld 1973. *Yucatec*: Blair 1979, McQuown 1967a, Pike, K. 1946. *Zapotec*: (*Choapan*) Lyman and Lyman 1977*; (*Guelavia*) Jones and Knudson 1977; (*Isthmus*) Pickett 1960, 1967; (*Texmelucan*) Speck 1978. *Zoque*: (*Copainalá*) Wonderly 1951b*.

FURTHER READING

The sources asterisked are recommended either because of the detail of the analysis and/or because of the analytical framework.

For general surveys of Mesoamerican phonemic systems (with different emphasis): Escalante 1975, Kaufman 1973; see also Hockett 1955.

Pike, E. 1976 discusses the most important characteristics found in this area within phonological units higher than the phoneme.

A typology of phonemic systems within a linguistic family (Uto-Aztecan) is offered by Voegelin and Hale 1962.

Some references to typological peculiarities of some of these systems in relation to consonant clusters are found in Greenberg 1978.

On tone systems Pike, K. 1948 is a basic treatment and deals in detail with two systems of Mesoamerican languages. Fromkin (ed.) 1978 is a more recent and fuller treatment of tone languages, but references to languages of this area are few. For divergent analyses of a tone system see the source for Mezquital Otomi and the references quoted therein; also Bernard 1974. For different interpretations of terrace tone systems see Pike, K. 1970, Clements 1979. On multiple stress systems, see Pike, E. 1974a.

The influence of Spanish on an indigenous phonemic system is exemplified in almost all descriptions; of special interest are Fries and Pike 1949, Wonderly 1946, Law 1961, Clark 1977.

5

Morphology I

Differences in the morphology of various languages are inevitably many and complex, and a detailed comparison of even two languages would require an extensive treatment. Nonetheless it is possible to characterize morphological patterns broadly in relation to complexity of word structure, richness of morphological devices, categories expressed morphologically and types of morphemes or of morpheme processes. In relation to word classes the discussion in this chapter will be restricted to major word classes – roughly those comparable to English nouns, verbs and adjectives – and more details will be given in the chapters on syntax.

5.1 Word structure

Although morphology is concerned with the structure and formation of words it will be convenient in some cases to take into account the forms called clitics. Clitics cannot occur flanked by pauses but show characteristics – that may vary from language to language – which set them aside from free forms (words) and bound forms (bound roots or stems, and affixes).

In some cases formulas of position classes of elements will be presented; in conjunction with information about the elements occurring in each position, these formulas give an approximate idea of a given system's potential for building words and of the complexity a word may have. It should be borne in mind, however, that a formula showing, for instance, position classes A B C indicates only that some elements of class A occur before some element of class B, and some elements of class B before some of class C; it may be the case that not all elements of A occur before elements in B, and that elements of classes A and C do not co-occur.

5.1.1 *Otomanguean languages*

Simple morphological systems are found in Otomanguean. Jicaltepec Mixtec, for instance, has the following position classes in the verb:

Transitive–Aspect–ROOT–Person

This scheme represents the upper limit of morphemes a verb may have, root and aspect being the only positions which have to be filled obligatorily. There are four prefixes that indicate transitivity: 'transitivizer', 'intransitivizer', 'causative' and 'iterative' which, as one would expect, only occur with certain roots. Person (of subject) is expressed by suffixes for certain persons only; in most cases person is expressed by enclitics, and when there is a pronominal or nominal subject the enclitic may be dropped. Compare the following two constructions:

$$'ka^3na^3 \quad =na^3 \; 'ku^{\eta 1}w\tilde{o}^2$$
be-calling   she   your-sister
$$'ka^3na^3 \quad 'ku^{\eta 1}w\tilde{o}^2$$
be-calling   your-sister

both have the same meaning. Aspect (incompletive, completive and continuative) is not always strictly speaking a prefix because in a class of verbs it is indicated by a change of consonant and tone, as in $'k^wi^1so^1$ (incompletive), $'ti^1so^2$ (completive), $'di^1so^2$ (continuative) 'to carry'; and since the pattern of Mixtec roots is CVCV the first consonant is simultaneously part of the root. Moreover, in another class of verbs completive and continuative aspects are differentiated by tone; in yet another class incompletive and completive aspects have the same form; only in one class of verbs is the completive really a prefix, as in $'t\int a^1\text{-}'ko^1o^1$ 'be located'.

The structure of nouns in Jicaltepec Mixtec is equally simple: only some persons (denoting possessor) are indicated by suffixes; for others, enclitics are used. There are four nominal prefixes (not very productive), two marking nouns that designate animals and trees, the fourth being a nominalizer. Words belonging to other classes are monomorphemic. Owing to the simple morphology, word classes can only be imperfectly characterized by morphological criteria; verbs are inflected for tense, but only some statives and nouns are inflected for person. ('Statives' are predicative forms having the meaning of quality or state; morphologically they have fewer inflectional categories than verbs, usually lacking tense – aspect. 'Adjectives', on the other hand, cannot constitute a predicate by themselves. However in some languages the difference between the two is not consistently maintained and both terms refer to predicative classes.) The basic classification of words has to be done on a syntactic basis. Nominal, stative and verbal roots show little overlap in their membership, and since there is practically no mechanism for changing the major class of a root or stem, this yields a characteristic organization of the vocabulary: it is composed mainly of unrelated words most of which contain only one morpheme.

On the other hand, this system contains the basics of a more complex one. The verb, as indicated above, is the nucleus of a verb phrase in which the other elements are clitics and words that occur in fixed relative orders. Moreover, person suffixes and clitics may be attached to elements other than the verb in the verbal phrase as in $yu^{\eta 3}wi^1 \; \int \tilde{a}^1\tilde{a}^1 =\eta a^3$ be-afraid very she 'she is very afraid', $me^3ku^2 \; \int \tilde{a}^1i^2$ spotted

Table 15. *Positional classes in the Choapan Zapotec verb*

Negation–Aspectual/Temporal–Aspect/Mode–Transitive–ROOT–Modifier–Modifier–		
'still'	'too much'	'also'
'already'	'early'	'more'
'just'		'with'
'right away'		
'later'		
'in the future'		

Modifier–	Modifier–Plural–Person of subject–Person of object
'much'	'more'
'always'	'before'
'momentarily'	'better'
'as much as'	'with'
'not very'	'just'

very = I 'I am dusty'. Thus little change is needed in order for the clitics to become affixes and for the modifying words to become at first clitics and then affixes; such processes have already partially taken place in other Mixtec languages. These clitics and words express temporal ('still', 'just now'), aspectual ('completed') and modal ('let's') meanings, as well as notion of manner ('quickly'), number ('plural'), negation, etc. The following is an example of a verb with three clitics:

$$t\int a^3 = \qquad ni^1 = \qquad t\int a^1\text{-}{}'ku^3 da^3 \qquad\qquad = ra^1$$

a-while-ago   completed   completive = sit-down   he

'he has already sat down'

Verb structures similar to the verbal phrase of Jicaltepec Mixtec are found in the Zapotec group, although the degree of complexity varies from language to language depending on the point reached by the process of clitic fusion. Table 15 reproduces the positional classes in Choapan Zapotec; for each position, with the exception of Aspect/Mode, the meaning of the elements filling it is given within single quotation marks. In the Aspect/Mode position the following distinctions are made: imperative, impersonal, infinitive and indicative; within indicative, in turn, continuative, completive, intentive and incompletive are distinguished, and within the first three aspects, repetitive and movement can be expressed. Notice that in the second and fourth suffix positions the meanings 'with' and 'more' recur, and are manifested by the same morpheme respectively, a fact which suggests that they retain some characteristics of enclitics (an affix would not normally be expected to occur in different positions with the same meaning).

This system allows words of considerable complexity, e.g.:

bi-ne-k-ibi-rɛɛ-le-jaka-bi-n   (*gjaʔ*)
negative = still = incompletive = wash = also = with = plural = he = it   (soap)
'they also have not yet washed it with (soap)'

Nonetheless it is not yet a morphologically rich system. It retains some of the basic characteristics we saw in Mixtec that are almost general in Otomanguean: absence of a productive mechanism of compounding, greatly limited possibilities for changing the major class of a root, and a noun morphology largely reduced to marking person of possessor. Note also in the formula for the Choapan Zapotec verb that in the modifier positions the meanings are not homogeneous, in contrast with those in the position labelled Aspectual/Temporal; that is, they do not constitute a series of options along a single dimension, a characteristic which would make them more similar to an inflectional system; on the contrary, they seem to constitute a system of loose adverbial modifiers which are in fact restricted in occurrence by the choice of elements in the Aspect/Mode and Aspectual/Temporal positions.

The different categories of aspect have for the most part a fused form in Choapan Zapotec, and this is typical of the Otopamean, Chinantecan and Tlapanec groups. This characteristic yields a different type of word structure. In Palantla Chinantec, for instance, there are not many more position classes in the verb than there are in Jicaltepec Mixtec; these are:

Negation–Aspect–Tense–Movement–STEM

In the position labelled 'stem' the following categories may be expressed in fused form: aspect, repetitive, transitive, person of subject, gender of subject and of object, number of subject or number of object. The markers for these categories may be tone, stress, change in vowel quality or quantity and infixation. Some examples are: *je³* 'it floated' (inanimate, intransitive, completive, third person), *jé²* 'he floated it' (inanimate, transitive, completive, third person), *já²* 'he floated' (animate, intransitive, completive, third person). The peculiarity of this type of system is that, although there may be few sequential elements (or even only one), as many obligatory categories may nevertheless be expressed as in more complex morphological systems (see below).

Word classes in Otomanguean languages are in general the same as those in Mixtec, i.e. verbs, statives and nouns, or instead of statives there may be a class of adjectives as in Mazatecan.

5.1.2 *Uto-Aztecan*

Some Uto-Aztecan languages – Classical Nahuatl, Huichol, Cora – have rich morphologies and complex words. This is exemplified by Classical Nahuatl (the

Nahuatl language of the sixteenth and seventeenth centuries preserved in writing). The position classes are as follows, although the listing may be incomplete:

> Tense/Mode–Person of subject–Person of object–Plural of object–
> Directional–Indefinite subject–Reflexive–Indefinite object–
> STEM–Transitive–Causative–Indirective–Voice–Connector–
> Auxiliary 1–Tense/Aspect–Auxiliary 2–Plural of subject

The complexity of the system derives from: (1) the number of compatible positions; (2) the obligatory character of several positions in many constructions; (3) the number of elements in certain classes; (4) the productivity of most morphemes; (5) the possibilities of compounding within the stem.

As for compatibility of positions, in certain causative constructions up to four prefixes indicating person are possible:

> *ni-mits̲-te·-t̲la-maki·-lti·-s*
> I = you = him = it = give = causative = future
> 'I shall persuade somebody to give it to you'

him > someone
it > something

In this word the marking of 'causative' is obligatory as would be the marking of 'indirective' in verbs with two objects as in *ni-te-tla-kow-i-a* I = him = it = buy = indirective = present 'I buy it for someone' (cf. *ni-tla-kow-a* 'I buy it'); notice that the prefixes marking indefinite animate and inanimate objects are obligatory too, because no definite objects are marked, and in the corresponding construction the marking of reflexive is also obligatory.

In addition to the above there is a frequently used 'honorific' (form of respect) category that is manifested by augmenting the transitivity marking. Thus, if the verb is intransitive or transitive, the honorific form is shown by marking the verb as reflexive and causative (or indirective); if the verb is causative, by marking it as indirective and reflexive; and if the verb is reflexive, by the addition of a special morpheme. In the following examples the first in each pair is the neutral form, the second one the honorific form:

> *ki-wi·ka*
> (he)-it = carry = (present)
> 'he is carrying it'
> *ki-mo-wi·ki-li-a*
> (he)-it = reflexive = carry = indirective = present
>
> *ti-mo-tlalo-a*
> you = reflexive = run = present
> 'you are running'

ti-mo-tlalo-ṯsino-a
you = reflexive = run = honorific = present

In most positions not many alternative elements can occur: thus, in the first position, either 'past' or 'imperative' occurs; there are only two directionals; the positions of Auxiliary 2 and of Plural of subject are filled by only one morpheme each. More possibilities are found in the position for Tense/Aspect where present, past, remote past, future, imperfect, conditional and imperative are distinguished. On the other hand, in Auxiliary 1, the class contains around eighteen frequently used verbal roots rendered as 'come to', 'go to', 'come (do)ing', 'keep (do)ing', 'be able to', etc. The element occurring in the Auxiliary 2 position is the verb root *neki* 'want to', used as freely as the English equivalent, and which has the uncommon peculiarity of being added to an inflected form, i.e. a full word, as in the following example:

> *ni-ki-n-ṭḷa-kʷal-ti-s-neki*
> I = him = plural = it = eat = causative = future = want-to
> 'I want to feed them'

compare *nikinṭḷakʷaltis* 'I will feed them'. This characteristic does not make a phrase out of that sequence; it is a single word as indicated by the fact that there is only one stress falling on the next to last syllable (... *'neki*); besides, the construction exists with two words as in *nineki nikinṭḷakʷaltis* 'I want to feed them'.

Stem formation, in turn, has the following possibilities: (1) Reduplication, as in *wiʔ-wi·tek* 'to hit repeatedly' (cf. *wi·tek* 'to hit'). (2) Compounding of noun plus verb (incorporation), the noun having the value of direct object as in *kʷaw-akia* tree = put-into-a-hole 'to plant a tree', of instrument as in *ṭḷe-waṯsa* fire = dry 'to roast', or of location as in *kal-aki* house = enter 'to enter into a house'; in some cases it is possible to incorporate two nouns as in *iʃ-ṭḷa·l-te·mi* face = dirt = fill 'to fill (somebody) at the face with dirt' (= 'to blind (somebody) by throwing dirt in his face'). (3) Compounding of two verb stems, as in *kʷalan-ka-itta* be-angry = connector = to-look 'to look in an angry mood'. The various mechanisms of stem formation can be combined among themselves and with other derivational elements as in the following:

> *mo-jaw-tʃi-tʃi·ʷ-ti-wiṯs*
> reflexive = war = reduplication = make = connector = to-fall
> (i.e. quickly) 'to get ready quickly for war'

> *kʷalan-ka-iṯs-ti-nemi*
> be-angry = connector = look = connector = live
> 'to go around looking angrily' (= 'to be in perpetual enemity')

Noun morphology is complex too. Most nouns when singular and unpossessed are marked by an 'absolutive' suffix, e.g. *kal-li* 'house'; they may be inflected for person of possessor as *no-kal* 'my house', or for person of subject as *ni-t̪aka* 'I (am a) man', or for both as *ti-n-a·wi* you = my = aunt 'you are my aunt'. Nouns also inflect for plural (*kojo·-me⁹* 'coyotes' cf. *kojo·-t̪* 'coyote') and may have forms that express diminution, endearment or augmentation (equivalent to honorifics in verbs), e.g. *to·to·-pil* 'little bird' (*to·to·-t̪* 'bird'). There are suffixes that, unusually for Mesoamerica, productively derive nouns from other nouns, e.g. *aka-t̪* 'reed', *aka-wa* 'the one who has reeds', *aka-t̪a* 'place where reeds grow abundantly'. An extensive number of noun roots are equivalent to locative suffixes, e.g. *kal-pan* 'in the interior of the house', *kal-tek* 'against the house'. Compounds of two nouns such as *kʷaw-ewa-t̪* tree = skin = absolutive 'treebark' are commonplace; compounds of three nouns like *a-kal-jaka-t̪* 'water = house = point = absolutive 'prow' are not uncommon, and in poetry and religious writings compounds of more elements can be found.

Verbs can be derived from nouns and vice versa. There are not many such suffixes, but those that exist are extremely productive. Verbs derived from nouns are, for example, *te-tia* 'to become hard as stone' (*te-t̪* 'stone'), *te-kal-tia* 'to build a house for someone' (*kal-li* 'house, *te-* 'indefinite animate object'). Examples of nouns derived from verbs are: *kʷi·ka-ni* 'singer' (*kʷika* 'sing'), *miki-lis-t̪i* 'death' (*miki* 'die'). Many of these forms are verbal nouns and a good deal of verb morphology can be carried over to the nouns, e.g.

> *mo-te·-t̪a-po·polwi-lia-ni*
> reflexive = animate-indefinite-object = inanimate-indefinite-object =
> forgive = indirective = nominalizer
> 'the one who forgives somebody something'
> *no-t̪a-po·polwi-l-o·-ka*
> my = inanimate-indefinite-object = forgive = indirective = passive =
> nominalizer
> 'my being forgiven by somebody'

Because of the productivity of all the word-formation devices, most Classical vocabulary is organized into extensive word families – a lexical structure opposite to that found in Otomanguean languages. A rather modest example of a word family (most probably incomplete) is the following one based on the noun *te·-t̪* 'stone':

> *te-ti* 'to harden like a stone', *te-ti-lis-t̪i* 'hardness', *te-ti-lia* 'to harden' (transitive), *te-ʃal-li* 'whetstone', *te-ton-tli* 'small stone', *te-wi-t̪i* 'pointed stone', *te-kal-li* 'house made of stone', *te-apas-t̪i*

'heap of stones', *te-nami-t̪* 'fortified wall', *te-t̪a* 'place full of stones', *te-yo* 'stony'

From the survey above the morphological characteristics of nouns and verbs should be clear. In addition, there is also a class of adjectives derived from nouns and verbs (there is no class of adjectival roots), e.g. *teti-k* 'hard' derived from the verb *tetia* 'to become hard' (in turn derived from *te-t̪* 'stone'), *soki-tik* 'wet' derived from the noun *soki-t̪* 'mud'.

Present-day Nahuatl languages have preserved the basic devices found in the Classical language, although some derivative elements have been lost, and the rest are used much more parsimoniously, especially compounding and derivation from one major class to another. Other Uto-Aztecan languages outside Mesoamerica (Yaqui, Tarahumara, Varohio) are simpler than Classical Nahuatl but still more complex than Mixtec languages.

5.1.3   *Totonac-Tepehua and Mixe-Zoque*

The morphological system of Totonac-Tepehua and the Mixe-Zoque languages is similar to that sketched above for Classical Nahuatl, although, naturally, there are numerous differences in detail. In fact, Totonac is more complex than Nahuatl; the number of positional classes is greater – they have not yet been fully detailed, but they probably exceed those of Classical Nahuatl by at least one-third in both prefixes and suffixes. The number of affixes is greater too; there are, for example, three partially overlapping sets of classifying prefixes, each with approximately thirty members occurring with nouns, numerals and verbs (cf. 6.4), in addition to a large number of affixes having adverbial meaning or the value of auxiliary verbs. The Tense/Aspect system makes more distinctions than the one in Nahuatl; not only are person of subject, object and indirect object marked in the verb, but also instrument, accompaniment, location and action toward or away from someone. Verbs can be derived from nouns and nouns derived from verbs or from other nouns. Only compounding seems less extensive than in Classical Nahuatl. Verbs and nouns form the major word classes; the words that by their meanings are equivalent to adjectives are morphologically nouns. The following word, not necessarily in common use, gives an idea of the possibilities afforded by the system:

> *a-k-ma-ʔaksta-ʔaqapi·-tʃaqa·-ni-qu·-kam-putu-ma·-w*
> imperfect = we = causative = reflexive = ear = wash = indirective = (him) = (it) = terminative = reflexive = desiderative = progressive-imperfective = we
> ['him' and 'it' are within parentheses since these persons have no

overt manifestation, but these are the positions where other persons
would be expressed]
'we were wanting to make him finish washing his ears'

Mixe-Zoque languages also have a rich morphology. In terms of the number of
positions within the verb, Copainalá Zoque comes closer to Totonac than to
Nahuatl; it has four positional classes of prefix which express (a) negative, (b)
person of subject and object, (c) reciprocal, and (d) various types of transitivity. The
stem then follows with many possibilities of compounding of verbal roots (up to
three), a productive system of noun incorporation, and extensions of the stem by
adverbial and aspectual suffixes; then follow eleven positional classes that express
modal, aspectual, temporal, locative, subordinating and interrogative meanings.
Most classes, however, have only one or two members, and the actual combinations
that occur within the stem are more idiomatic than in Classical Nahuatl or Totonac,
i.e. constituent morphemes are easily identified but the resulting meanings are not
usually predictable.

In Mixe-Zoque noun morphology, too, is rich. Besides person of possessor and
person of subject there is a system of cases; plural, as well as some adverbial
meanings, is marked, e.g. *pɨn-eh-mah* man-like = still 'still like a man'; the latter
belong to a set of suffixes which also express meanings like 'just', 'interrogation', 'it
is said', 'already', and can be attached to any major word class.

Other languages in the Zoquean group, e.g. Sierra Popoluca, are slightly simpler
than Copainalá Zoque, and the Mixean languages, although similar in outline, are
simpler still.

5.1.4 *Tarascan and Mayan*

Neither Tarascan nor Mayan have words as complex as those found in Classical
Nahuatl, Totonac or Mixe-Zoque, but, in different ways, both have a rich
morphology.

In Tarascan there is no compounding, but there is extensive root reduplication.
Although words with up to twelve morphemes can occur, commonly they have no
more than five or six. On the other hand, Tarascan is the language with the largest
inventory of affixes (all in fact suffixes); there are more than 160 frequently used
affixes, so most words are polymorphemic. The relative positions in the verb are as
follows:

Root–Adverbial–Spatial–Voice–Adverbial–Aspect–Tense–Person–
Number–Mode

While there are both verbal and nominal roots, on the word level many nouns and most adjectives are derived from verbal roots or stems. Verbs, in turn, can be derived from nouns with the meaning 'to be X'. The marking of person within the verb is rather restricted, but the system of modes, aspects and tenses is the richest reported for this area. Nouns and adjectives may inflect for case, and nouns for person of possessor.

More characteristic of the language than the type of word structure are the meanings expressed. Predominating are those referring to location or space (cf. 6.1.3) and, owing to the derivational devices of the languages, elements with locative meaning occur not only in verbs but also in nouns and adjectives.

Mayan languages have rather simple words. Aspect (or tense) and mode (both very simple systems), person of subject and, when transitive, of object too, and plural of person are marked in the verb; furthermore there may be approximately five classes of relative positions filled by derivational elements, most of them also indicating transitivity. However, few, if any, of the affixes express adverbial meanings or the type of meaning commonly associated with auxiliary verbs. Nouns may be inflected for person of possessor and of subject; compounding in nouns is extensive.

Derivational elements are many and very productive. They can change the major class of a stem or change the subclass of verbs (intransitive, transitive, bitransitive, causative, passive). As a result, the vocabulary, like that of Nahuatl, is organized into rich word families whose members show a high degree of predictability.

Word classes are usually verbs, statives, adjectives and nouns. There are roots of double or triple membership and roots requiring a stem-formative element in order to belong to a definite class.

A characteristic of Mayan languages are the clitics and free forms, especially those in the verb, that belong to the same classes as affixes owing to their possibilities of occurrence; consequently in some analyses the level of word is skipped and the description is made in terms of morphemes and phrases.

5.1.5 *Other families*
The remaining language families can be characterized briefly by reference to those already discussed.

Cuitlatec, Miskito and Huave have a reduced morphological apparatus, comparable to the one found in Mixtec languages. Huave, for instance, may have up to three prefixes and three or four suffixes, but these rarely occur together. The obligatory categories are person of subject and tense (a simple system of present, past and future); other categories are reflexive, transitive and indefinite subject. The only inflectional category within nouns is person of possessor. There is reduplication but no compounding, and there are two nominalizing prefixes.

Tequistlatec languages have a more complex morphology than Mixtec languages but words do not normally contain as many morphemes as they do in Choapan Zapotec. In Coastal Chontal verb suffixes fall into twelve positional classes, several of which contain only a single member; the only obligatory positions are aspect–mode and person. Nouns may inflect for person of possessor or subject, number, definiteness and location; some affixes derive nouns from verbs.

5.2 Types of morphemes

The formulas for positional classes give partial information about an aspect of morphology not explicitly treated, namely types of morphemes as prefixes or suffixes; this aspect is better handled across language families.

There is only one language, Tarascan, that is exclusively suffixing. Coastal Chontal (but not Highland Chontal) comes near to being so in the verb, in which, except for a single prefix indicating first person singular, all affixes are suffixed. In nouns, however, there are more prefixes than suffixes. Most other languages have both prefixes and suffixes; some of them, like the Mixe-Zoque languages, have more suffixes than prefixes; others, e.g. Huichol and Totonac, have approximately an equal number of prefixes and suffixes; a language like Palantla Chinantec can be considered as having only prefixes unless some of the changes which manifest categories (in fused form) as vowel length or quality are analysed as suffixes.

Some infixes are found in Huave, Miskito, Tlapanec and in a few Mayan languages; e.g. Huave *-ndok* 'to fish', *ando-ro-k* 'there is fishing'. Infixes are more common in Chatino, Otopamean, Chinantecan, and the Mixe-Zoque languages, all of which have the infixed element as a palatal phoneme (/i/ or /j/) resulting historically from a process of metathesis which represents the same phonological process mentioned for Copainalá Zoque in 3.2; compare the examples given there with the following: *pata* 'mat', *p-j-ata* 'his mat'; the difference is that in the present case the infix has a grammatical value and never occurs in the original position (i.e. there is no *j-pata*). As in the case of metathesis, the infix resulted in the palatalization of the preceding consonant in Copainalá Zoque, as in t̠*atah* 'his father' (*tatah* 'father').

Vowel alternation is uncommon. Some languages, e.g. Tarascan, Tlapanec and some Chinantec languages, offer a few examples, but to find vowel alternation as a productive morphological procedure we must look to Huave, in which /i/ indicates 'diminutive' as against /a/ or /o/; an example from the dialect of San Meteo is *akot/akit* 'to scrape'.

Nasality and vowel length are frequent manifestations of grammatical categories in Chinantec languages and in Tlapanec. In the latter, for instance, a lengthened vowel regularly indicates 'animate gender' (e.g. *miʔ²ʃa¹/ miʔ²ʃa·¹* 'white').

Consonant alternation is found in Totonac with the same meaning as vowel alternation in Huave; in the Northern variety, for example, there is a prefix which, along with /s/ or /ts/, indicates augmentative, but which with /ʃ/, /ɬ/, /tʃ/ indicates diminutive as in ʃ-*mu'lut* 'a large bow', *s-mu'lut* 'a small arch'. In Papantla Totonac the device is more extensive and involves the interchange (among the consonants) of the following sets: (1) /s/ /ʃ/ /ɬ/, (2) /tʃ/ /ts/ /tɬ/, (3) /k/ /q/; the meanings expressed are: intensity, endearment, augmentative, diminutive; in this case the phenomenon is probably better grouped with those mentioned in 4.1.3.

Consonant alternation (in some cases change of a feature) marking morphological categories either partially or totally is extensive in Otopamean and Zapotec languages. Note the following examples from Choapan Zapotec in which the alternating consonants are in bold type; *r-***g***ibi-biˀ* 'she washes', *u-***d***ibi-biˀ* 'she washed', **k***ibi-biˀ* 'she is washing'; in the first two examples aspect is indicated by a prefix and a change in the first consonant of the root; in the third example aspect is indicated by a change of consonant only.

The first two examples are instances of what may be called double marking of a category, common in Mesoamerican languages; some examples follow. In Mazahua, person is marked simultaneously by the bold-type prefixes and suffixes in the forms **ro**-'*pɛph*-**khɔ** 'I worked', **go**-'*pɛph*-**khe** 'you worked', **o**-'*pɛph*-**hnu** 'he worked'. In Coastal Chontal, plural is sometimes marked by a suffix and an infix, and in Classical Nahuatl, by reduplication and a suffix. The Totonac word quoted in 5.1.3 contains two instances of double marking (for 'we' and for 'reflexive'). Some of the elements listed under Aspect in table 15 (5.1.1) are obligatorily accompanied by an element in the first modifier position as in **la**-*razu*-**te**-*biˀyao* 'she bathes *right away*'. In Mixe-Zoque languages there is a rather extensive class of prefixes and suffixes that go in pairs; e.g. in Mixe from El Paraíso: **ko**·-*iʒ*-**iy** 'to look into' (-*iz*- is an alternant form of *ˀihʃ* 'to see').

In no case does tone seem to be the only marker through which a category is manifested in a language. The typical role of tone in the expression of a grammatical category is parallel to that of consonant alternation in the above example from Choapan Zapotec. In some cases the category is manifested by segmental material, in others by both segmental material and change of tone, and finally, by tone alone; examine the following pairs of forms in Tlapanec: $ni^2ga^1hna^{·3}/ni^2ga^1hnu^{·3}$ 'you went out'/'he went out', $ni^2hri^1jã^{·21}/ni^2hri^1ja^{·3}$ 'you escaped'/'he escaped', $ni^3ba^3ji^{·1}/ni^3ba^3ji^{·3}$ 'you moved'/'he moved'.

Reduplication is well represented in Uto-Aztecan, Mayan, the Mixe-Zoque languages, and in Huave and Tarascan, but it is absent from Tequistlatec, Totonac and the Otomanguean languages. The most common type of reduplication concerns the first CV of the element, sometimes with subtypes as to length of the vowel and addition or suppression of a following glottal stop; e.g. (from Classical Nahuatl) *kojo·tɬ* 'coyote', *ko·-kojo-ʔ* 'coyotes'. Reduplication expresses plurality, intensity of action and repeated action (at different times or upon different objects); e.g. (from Classical Nahuatl) (*te·ṭa-)maka* 'to give (something to somebody)', (*te·ṭa-)maʔ-maka* 'to give (something) to each (person)'; *weṭska* 'to laugh', *we-weṭska* 'to laugh a lot'; (*ṭa-)teki* 'to cut (something)', (*ṭa-)te·-teki* 'to slice (something) up'. Another type of reduplication occurs in Sierra Popoluca; in this case what is reduplicated is the final VC(C) as in *pʔuqʔ* 'to belch', *pʔuqʔ-uqʔ* 'to growl (of the stomach)'.

Suppletive roots are found in considerable numbers (not merely as a sporadic phenomenon like *go/went* in English) in some Uto-Aztecan languages, e.g. Cora, Huichol, Varohio (but not in Nahuatl), and in some Otomanguean languages, e.g. Tlapanec and Chinantec languages. The category expressed by suppletive roots is number of subject in intransitive verbs and number of object in transitive verbs; the following examples are from Huichol: *-mi¹e²* (sg.)/*-hu¹u²* (pl.) 'to go'; *-mi²e²* (sg.)/*-kʷi²i²* (pl.) 'to kill'. In some cases the root is the only marker of number as in Tlapanec *ni²ri¹ja·³ ṭsu²wã²* 'I pulled out the thorn', *ni²gu¹wi¹ ṭsu²wã²* 'I pulled out the thorns'; in other cases plurality may also be marked by inflection, e.g. (again from Tlapanec) *ni²ʃi¹ja·³ ʃti¹la³* 'I killed the chicken', *ni²gu¹dĩ·¹ ʃti¹la³* 'I killed the chickens' (*-ĩ·* is a regular marker of third person animate plural). Note that these suppletive roots are not the result of a single root having been split by phonological change; they represent historically different roots, probably synonymous, which also differed as to individual vs. collective contrast in the subject or object, as in the English *kill* vs. *exterminate*.

The references to stress in chapter 3 clearly imply that placement of stress can hardly be a marker of a grammatical category; only in Coastal Chontal are there some cases in which a shift of stress is the marker for plural in nouns, e.g. *a'tajgiʔ* 'word', *ataj'giʔ* 'words'.

SOURCES

Chinantec: (*Palantla*) Merrifield 1968. *Chontal:* (*Coastal*) Waterhouse 1962, 1967; (*Highland*) Turner 1971. *Cora:* Preuss 1932. *Cuitlatec:* Escalante 1962. *Huave:* Stairs and Hollenbach 1969, Suárez 1975. *Huichol:* Grimes, J. 1964. *Mazahua:* Amador Hernández 1976. *Miskito:* Heath 1913, Thaeler n.d. *Mixe:* (*El Paraíso*) Van Haitsma and Van Haitsma 1976. *Mixtec:* (*Jicaltepec*) Bradley 1970. *Nahuatl:* (*Classical*) Andrews, J. 1975, Carochi 1892, Newman 1967, Schoembs 1949. *Popoluca:* (*Sierra*) Elson 1960. *Tarascan:* Foster 1969, Friedrich 1971c. *Tlapanec:* Suárez n.d. *Totonac:* (*Northern*) McQuown 1940, Reid et al. 1968; (*Papantla*) Aschmann 1973. *Zapotec:* (*Choapan*) Lyman 1964. *Zoque:* (*Copainalá*) Wonderly 1951c, d, 1952a.

FURTHER READING

As stated at the end of chapter 1, the morphology of very few Mesoamerican languages has been fully described. For Classical Nahuatl Newman 1967 is a synthesizing but clear presentation; the changes in what may be the modern Nahuatl languages which are most closely related to Classical Nahuatl are discussed in Lastra de Suárez 1980a. For the rather similar morphology of other modern Nahuatl languages see Whorf 1946, Law 1958, Langacker (ed.) 1979.

The only source for Totonac morphology is the detailed but unpublished description in McQuown 1940.

For Mixe-Zoque languages, the most thorough sources are those indicated for Sierra Popoluca and for Copainalá Zoque.

For Mayan languages, see Kaufman 1971b (Tzeltal), one of the few descriptions of a Mesoamerican language that is explicit as to productivity of derivational elements; also, Blair 1979 (Yucatec), Day 1973a (Jacaltec).

Merrifield 1968 describes in a certain amount of detail the verb morphology of Palantla Chinantec; Robbins 1968 on Quiotepec Chinantec concentrates on noun morphology. For Zapotec languages, besides the source indicated for Choapan Zapotec, see Pickett 1953, 1955 (Isthmus Zapotec), Butler 1980 (Yatzachi Zapotec), Speck 1978 (Texmelucan Zapotec). Mazatec morphology presents an unusual number (for an Otomanguean language) of compound verbs and is discussed at length in Pike, K. 1948.

The problems posed by the analysis of clitics and suffixes in a Mixtec language are dealt with in Pike, K. 1949.

For the fusional type of Otomi morphology see Echegoyen Gleason 1979 (Highland Otomi) and Wallis 1964 (Mezquital Otomi). Examples of suppletion (Tlapanec) are given in Schultze-Jena 1938 (the phonemic transcription is defective but does not much affect the presentation). Double marking of categories is dealt with in Longacre 1959 (Chicahuaxtla Trique), in Wallis 1956 (Mezquital Otomi) and in Suárez n.d. (Tlapanec). For the grammatical role of tone, besides the sources quoted for Palantla Chinantec and Jicaltepec Mixtec, see Beebe 1974 (Eastern Popoloca), Jamieson, C. 1976 (Chiquihuitlan Mazatec), Robbins 1968 (Quiotepec Chinantec).

The description of Tarascan by Foster 1969 deals *in extenso* with morphology but is difficult to follow; for a clearer partial description see Friedrich 1971c.

For Huave it is interesting to compare the description of the verbs by Stairs and Hollenbach 1969 with the restatement by Matthews 1972; for a paradigmatic presentation of the data see Stairs Kreger and Scharfe de Stairs 1981.

For a better idea of the complex morphological systems it is valuable to examine the few extensive dictionaries available, e.g. Molina 1970 (Classical Nahuatl), Gilberti 1901 (Old Tarascan), McLaughlin 1975 (Tzotzil), Aschmann 1973 (Papantla Totonac), Barrera Vásquez (ed.) 1980 (Yucatec). Also useful are analytical dictionaries that give inventories of roots and affixes, e.g. Swadesh 1969 (Old Tarascan), Swadesh and Sancho 1966 (Classical Nahuatl).

6

Morphology II

6.1 Categories in verbs

In chapter 5 the survey of morphological systems focussed chiefly on the form of words. In the present chapter attention is turned to the categories expressed.

6.1.1 *Aspect, tense, mode, negation*

The discussion of these categories will focus first of all on those that are expressed obligatorily, and, owing to lack of pertinent information, will mainly be restricted to those categories which are expressed morphologically. The reader should bear in mind, however, that these categories are usually supplemented by particles and/or auxiliary verbs and by adverbs, all of which form part of the total system of a language for expressing these notions.

Some languages have a tense system, others an aspectual one; still others have both aspect and tense, and there are languages in which tense and aspect combine to form a mixed system; it is even fairly common for mode not to form a clearly separate system from tense – aspect.

Simple tense systems are found in Mayan languages. Jacaltec, for instance, marks past and non-past. Past is used for completed events in the past; non-past is used to refer to a present event *sensu stricto*, to a habitual or repetitive event, to a present event that started in the past (i.e. I have been doing . . . for X time already), to events contemporaneous with other past or future events (i.e. (I did/will do something) while doing . . .), and, in combination with a suffix which has other values, it refers to future events. This morphological system is supplemented by a verbal phrase formed with one of three particles and a tenseless verb that express progressive aspect (*laŋan hawaji* progressive you-sleep 'you are sleeping'), subsequent event (*şul naχ* **kat jilni** *naχ* 'he arrived, *and then he saw* it'), or previous event (**lahwi jilni** *na şul naχ* '*after he saw it*, he arrived').

Other Mayan languages with basically the same number of categories mark different categories. In Mam there are also two tenses, future and non-future, the first only referring to future events, the second to events happening at any time (including future). There is also a series of preposed adverbs (some actually fused with the verb) that, unlike the construction in Jacaltec, go with a verb inflected for tense. Among those that co-occur with non-future two are more inflection-like and refer to recent or distant past; e.g. **ma** *t͡ʃin-t͡ʃʔx-on* recent past/I-wash = non-future 'I just washed', **o** *t͡ʃin-t͡ʃʔx-on* distant-past/I-wash = non-future 'I washed (not today')'.

A more elaborate system of temporal values is found in Otopamean languages. Chichimec, for instance, distinguishes a present (*e¹ha¹* 'I drink') that covers durative, continuative and habitual values, an immediate past (*u¹ha¹* 'I drank (e.g. a few moments ago)'), a recent past (*ku¹ha¹* 'I drank (e.g. this morning)'), an anterior past (*tu¹ha¹* 'I drank (e.g. yesterday or before)'), a future (*ga¹ha¹* 'I will drink'), a relative tense of simultaneous event (*ra¹ha¹* 'while drinking'), and a potential (*nu¹ha¹* 'I would drink').

Coastal Chontal, by contrast, has a system which is basically aspectual. As would be expected, aspectual values that are expressed with a single tense in the above systems appear differentiated here. The aspects are: progressive (*'xoo-***i** 'he is crying'), continuative (*'pats̱ena-***wa** 'he is going on doing'), habitual (*'muʃ-***maa** 'he smokes (as a habit)'), incomplete (*'kwaj-***mʔa** 'he will arrive'), incomplete movational (*siŋ-***ta** 'he will go to see'), and punctual (*t͡ʃupɸʔk'oj-***pa** 'he entered in').

Totonac and Tarascan languages have both aspect and tense. Both have a morphologically simple system and a compound one. The richest system is that of Tarascan with thirteen tense – aspects. Present, future, past, past perfect and imperfect are distinguished for tense, e.g. *'pa-***a**-*ti* 'he will take', *'khwi-ʃ-kʰa* 'you slept'; within most of these tenses, however, aspect differences as to durative and habitual are made, e.g. present durative (*pʰa'merekware-***ʃa**-*ka* 'it hurts me'), present habitual (*xa'ni-***sin**-*ti* 'it rains (e.g. this year)'), future durative (*xi'rina-***ʃam**-*kani* 'I will continue to look for it'), imperfect durative (*a'ta-***an**-*ti* 'he was hitting him'), imperfect habitual (*'t͡ʃonarʈi-***siraan**-*ki* 'I used to be afraid'). Furthermore, in Tarascan there is a system of six modes – indicative, subjunctive, clarificational, infinitive, imperative, emphatic – and the tense and aspect categories are combined with three of the modes (indicative, subjunctive, clarificational). As for the values of the modes, subjunctive is subordinate although it also has a desiderative value; clarificational is used in questions and answers as in *'ne 'kamaam-***pi** 'who brought it?', *'xi 'kamaam-***pi**-*ni* 'I brought it'. The infinitive is a subordinate mode but is also used as narrative in main sentences. The emphatic indicates speaker's reaction of pleasure, annoyance or wonderment (*pʰa'mekwaʈ-***kʰa** 'how it hurts!').

The combinations of tense – aspect and mode occurring in Tarascan are rather unusual for Mesoamerican languages, although they are also found in Southern Tepehuán. A more common situation is that of Coastal Chontal where the aspects

listed above are mutually exclusive with the mode system which includes three
imperatives (simple imperative, movational imperative, i.e. 'go do!', and polite
imperative, i.e. 'please do!'), exhortative and subjunctive (used in subordinate
sentences). Furthermore, the exhortative has the same form as the incompletive
aspect. This lack of a special form for exhortative is rather common; in Tlapanec,
for instance, the exhortative and the future tense have the same form. Note that,
compared to many languages where only imperative and exhortative are differentiated, the system of Coastal Chontal makes many mode distinctions.

In discussing the Jacaltec tense system, it was mentioned that non-past is used for
events contemporaneous with past events; this use of a given tense as a relative tense
can be considered aspectual, and is found in other languages. Tlapanec, for instance, has three tenses which, in main clauses, have clear values of present, future
and past. When the verb in the main clause is inflected for past, however, the verb in
the subordinate clause is inflected for present to indicate a contemporaneous event,
and for future to indicate a subsequent event, as in the following examples:

ni^3-$nda^{?3}e^{?2}$ ma^3-ce^3 $ru^{?1}kho^3$
past=ask-he-me   future=buy-I   that
'he asked me to buy that'

ni^2-$nu^1hngo^{.3}$ na^3-$\int ma^3ta^1$ bu^1ro^3
past=go-by-he   present=pull-he   donkey
'he went by pulling the donkey'

With verbs that have in their meanings the feature 'volition', as in the first example,
the verb of the subordinate clause will always be inflected for future. On the other
hand, in conditional clauses, past may have a value of completed event in the future
as in the following example:

$\int i^1$ $ne^{?2}kho^2$ $ri^1ge^{?3}$ ma^3-$ha^3j\tilde{u}^{12}$
if past=eat-I   this   future=die-I
'if I eat this I will die'

In these uses these morphemes can be equated with incompletive, completive and
durative aspects. Tlapanec also has the potential to refer to future with a feature of
eventuality or doubt, so it is more mode-like.

In Nahuatl languages there is a system where tense and mode categories are not
clearly separated: present, past and past perfect seem exclusively temporal; counter-
factual and conditional are modal; imperfect, however, may be temporal (past
value), aspectual (continuative value) and modal (value of unfulfilled event); future

is temporal (like future proper), modal (used in polite forms and as potential) and aspectual (future with regard to a past event, or, as in Tlapanec, with regard to any temporal value when depending on a verb of volition).

The categories of tense, aspect and mode appear to be more intermingled still in Isthmus Zapotec. Habitual, completive and progressive as aspectual refer to present or to future events, although the completive form is also used as imperative; future and perfect are tenses, referring only to future and past events respectively; potential is modal and is used as exhortative and in subordinate clauses, though it may have temporal value when used just for future; subjunctive is modal too and is used as desiderative, except with negation when it is used as negative completive; compare the following examples:

ɲa-*pa*   *tobi*
subjunctive = have   one
'I wish I had one'

ke   ɲu-*ni-be-ni*
negation   subjunctive = do = he = it
'he did not do it'

Since in other aspect – tenses of Isthmus Zapotec the negative proclitic is simply added to the inflected verb for the particular category, the negative completive is skewed as to the form – meaning relationship, and this is also the case for other languages.

Copainalá Zoque marks inflectionally only incompletive and completive aspects, and imperative and exhortative modes. However, negation of completive aspect is expressed by the imperative inflection with a negative prefix, while negation of incompletive aspect and of imperative is expressed by auxiliaries and the inflected verb with a special suffix; the forms are as follows:

min-u   'he came'   *ha-min*-i   'he did not come'   *min*-i   'come!'
min-ba   'he comes'   *haʔn min-i*   'he does not come'   *ʔuj min-i*   'do not come!'

Again, in Tlapanec where tense and negation are manifested in fused form for present (*ciᵍᵘ* 'I am not sleeping') and past (*taᵍᵘ* 'I did not sleep'), they have separate manifestation for future (*ma³-ʃaᵍᵘ* future = negative = sleep 'I will not sleep'), a form also used as negative imperative, e.g.:

a³-t-ja²hũ²
imperative = 2nd-person = work
'work!'

ma^3-$\int a^1$-t-$ja^2h\tilde{u}^2$
future = negation = 2nd-person = work
'you will not work' or 'do not work!'

Similarly, in Jacaltec the suffix for imperative (*waj*-**an** 'sleep!') is not used in a negative imperative, which is expressed by a preposed particle inflected for non-past and second person (*'mat∫at∫ waji* 'don't sleep!'). In Chichimec, in turn, negation is manifested by a prefix mutually exclusive with the tense prefixes, and consequently no tense distinctions are made in the negative; for all the tenses listed above, except future, the negative prefix and the suffix -*mehe* are added, as in su^1-ha^1-me^2he^2 'I do (did) not drink'; for future negative a particle is added: $si^{?2}an^1 su^1ha^1$-me^2he^2 'I will not drink'.

Modes in their basic uses may be characterized as reflecting attitudes of the speaker toward the events referred to in a clause, but modes may also be used in subordinate clauses where their basic values are weakened or effaced completely. There are some languages in Mesoamerica in which this use, according to the grammatical structure and/or function of the clause, seems to be basic for a category that is labelled 'mode'. Examples will be given in 7.4 for the primary and secondary modes of Mixe-Zoque languages, and in 8.3 for the contrast between independent and subordinate modes of Huave.

As stated at the beginning of this section, the categories which have been discussed are those that are obligatory; some languages, however, also have optional affixes in the verb used for expressing the same types of meaning. A good example is Copainalá Zoque, a language which only obligatorily marks either completive or incompletive aspect, but which in addition has seven suffixes with aspectual values such as continuative, frequentative, intentive, repetitive, etc. These suffixes are compatible with the inflectional ones as in $ma\eta$-$d\tilde{t}^?$-u (he) = go = intentive = completive 'he intended to go'. It is convenient to stress again that these elements do not constitute an inflectional system like the one in Tarascan or Coastal Chontal, and a language like Totonac with a tense – aspect system of ten categories has approximately ten optional affixes with temporal and aspectual meaning.

Differences among the systems clearly derive from the general type of each system (i.e. temporal or aspectual or mixed), the number and meaning of categories in each of them, and the optional or obligatory character of categories. Even taking these differences into account, categories with the same label may not correspond to each other perfectly. This can be exemplified with the category called 'repetitive', which is in general an optative category, although it can be considered inflectional in Tlapanec and Chinantec, among the languages discussed here. Copainalá Zoque (Coastal Chontal is similar) has repetitive aspect, but the repetition of the action may be done by the same or a different actor. A form like *min*-**ge?t**-*u*, therefore, will be translated, according to context, as 'he came again' or 'he also came'. This difference is expressed by different affixes in Northern Totonac: *tʃiwi·nam-***pala**-*'quɬ* 'they spoke again', **ha**·-*ktʃiwi·'nan* 'I also spoke'; the category expressed in the first example would probably be considered 'repetitive' but it only partially matches the Zoque category. These different meanings are also expressed in Tlapanec, but, unlike Totonac, when the action is repeated by a different actor an additional word is used equivalent to English *also*; if the actor is the same, the repetitive aspect is used, as in *ma³du·²* (*i²ʃi¹*) 'I will sow (maize) again' (repetitive is marked by lengthening of the stem vowel). Repetitive aspect, however, adds the meaning 'home' (or 'own town' or 'place where one is living for a time') when used with verbs of motion, as in *ni³taʔ³a·²* 'I entered (into my own house)' (repetitive is marked by change of the stem vowel; compare *ni³toʔ³o²* 'I entered (into a place where I do not live)'. Finally, with some verbs repetitive aspect indicates that an action is performed again on the same object, the actor being either the same or different, cf. *ne³ce³* 'I bought it' and *ni³ci·³* 'I bought it second hand' (repetitive).

6.1.2 *Person*

The category of person is not general at the morphological level. It was seen (5.1.1) that in Jicaltepec Mixtec, person was in some cases expressed by a suffix, but in others it was expressed by an enclitic that could be omitted if there was a free subject (in San Miguel el Grande Mixtec the omission of the clitic or suffix is obligatory when there is a free subject). In Yaqui, person is not expressed at all in the verb; in the clause *nee oʔoota bitʃak* I man saw 'I saw the man', the only indication of person is the pronoun *nee*; in other cases person of subject is expressed by a clitic, but it is attached to a word other than the verb, e.g. *batoi-mak = ne nokpea* people = with I speak-want 'I feel like talking to people'. Tarascan is similar; enclitics that mark subject and object can be attached to the verb, but the usual enclitic position is with the first word in the clause, whether or not this is the verb; in addition there is some marking of person within the verb.

Other languages mark at least one person in the verb. In Huave it is always person of subject. In Coastal Chontal there is a class of intransitive verbs in which person is not marked, but otherwise the person marked may be subject, object or indirect object, depending on the type of transitivity, e.g. *ɬ-teʼa* 'I fell', *ɬ-kopɸʼkiʃpa* '(he) rubbed me', *ɬ-pajpa* '(he) gave (it) to me' (in the last two examples the subject 'he' and the object 'it' are not expressed within the verb but in the context which is omitted here).

In (Classical) Nahuatl two persons may be marked. (Cases like that exemplified in 5.1.2 with four persons can be disregarded here since two of them necessarily have to be 'unspecified third person' (animate and inanimate).) A set of forms always marks subject, a different set always marks object as in the following:

> *ni-meni* 'I live'   *ni-mit̯s-tijas* 'I will kill you'
> *ti-meni* 'you live'   *ti-met̯ʃ-tijas* 'you will kill me'

Possessor in nouns is marked by still another set, as in *no-kal* 'my house', *mo-kal* 'your house'.

Most Mayan languages have instead so-called ergative systems. Subjects of intransitive verbs, of statives and of nouns are marked by the same set of forms that marks the object in transitive verbs, while the subject of transitive verbs and possessor in nouns is marked by a different set of forms; examples from Tzeltal are: *k-al* 'I say (it)' (third person in this case is not marked), *k-oˀtan* 'my heart', *winik-on* 'I (am) a man', *tal-on* 'I came', *a-mah-on* 'he hits me' (*a-* is 3rd person subject). Person marking in some Mayan languages, however, is not consistently ergative; the marking changes according to aspect, mode, use of auxiliaries and use in main or subordinate clauses; in Jacaltec, for instance, in certain types of subordinate clauses the subject of intransitives is marked like the subjects of main clause transitives. The properties of these ergative systems seem to be purely formal, that is, different marking (as in the Tzeltal examples meaning 'I say it' and 'I came') does not seem to imply a difference as to the agent character of the subject, and nor does the identity of the form 'I came' and 'he hits me' imply a common meaning beyond that of first person singular.

In other languages, e.g. Tlapanec, the relationship among forms that indicate person in intransitive and transitive verbs (and in nouns too) becomes quite complex, since both subject and object are marked to some extent in transitive verbs, sometimes in fused form, although the marking of the object is more explicit, i.e. less ambiguous; furthermore, there are various sets of endings in intransitive and transitive verbs and in nouns. Such systems – Tlapanec is not an isolated example, and Huautla Mazatec and Chocho offer different varieties – do not accord with either the Nahuatl or the Mayan systems, although they do seem to show traces of ergativity.

Special marking of person for reflexive is rare, but is found in Cora and Huichol; the following verbs from Cora are reflexive (although this fact is not reflected in the English translation): *na-n-saupe* 'I am resting', *pa-a-saupa* 'rest!'; the prefixes in first position indicate the subject and those in the second reflexive object. In Classical Nahuatl, and some modern Nahuatl languages, there is a special form for first person as reflexive object, other persons being marked by another form; the latter is used for any person in other modern Nahuatl languages, so that the special form is simply a marker of a reflexive verb. This system is common in other languages that mark reflexive verbs.

Finally, Tlapanec has a category that strictly speaking does not belong to that of person but which is marked in conjunction with third person singular or plural. When neither the subject, in an intransitive clause, nor the object, in a transitive clause, is represented by a free constituent (roughly within the same clause), then a third person subject or object verb has a different person inflection. Thus, 'Peter went to town' is *niꞌꝺ³kha³ peꞌdro³ ʃwã²hẽ²* 'went Peter town', but if the answer to a question like 'what did Peter do?' is 'went to town' then the sentence is *niꞌꝺ³khe·³ ʃwã²hẽ²*.

No mention has been made of the specific categories of person because these are the same as those that are expressed in the pronominal systems treated in 6.2.

6.1.3 *Direction, motion, location*

The marking of directional, motional and locative meanings within the verb is not usually obligatory in the sense that all verbs should be marked for them; it does, however, occur frequently, and in certain constructions in some languages it is obligatory. It is, in any case, widespread across linguistic families.

Direction and motion frequently go together but not always; location also shows various possibilities of combination with these two categories. While reference to location of the speaker (as point of reference) is commonly found in different languages, they differ greatly in the degree of elaboration of these notions.

A two way contrast, 'moving toward the speaker' vs. 'moving away from the speaker' is found in Coastal Chontal, e.g. *wiꞌk-waj* 'to come to look at' vs. *wiꞌk-iʃ* 'to go to look at'. In addition there is a set of stem-forming suffixes that indicate place and direction, e.g. 'up', 'down', 'out of'; an example is: *tʃog-apɸꞌi-* 'to throw (water) on someone' (cf. *tʃog-* 'to spill').

In Northern Totonac, location and movement appear disassociated. Two affixes indicate location with reference to the speaker, as in *pa·stak-'tʃa* 'there he learned', *min-tʃa-'ta* 'he already came from there', *ꞌu·-'wi* 'here it is'. Two other suffixes indicate motion without specifying direction or location; one of them indicates only motion, the other indicates 'moving toward some point and returning', e.g. *ʃlakaɬka·-ti·ɬa-kaꞌna* 'you were coming (or: going) along crossing yourself' (the verb root means 'to cross oneself', so that a more literal translation would be 'you crossed yourself while coming (or: going)'), *k-ki·-'laɬ* 'I went (and returned)', *ʃ-ki·-tʃin* 'he used to arrive here (and leave again)'. There is also a prefix that indicates action performed in passing.

Northern Totonac also has a set of prefixes that indicates location, position and shape (cf. 5.1.3). With transitive verbs they refer to characteristics of the object, with intransitive verbs they refer to the place where the event takes place. Several of these prefixes refer to parts of the body such as 'head' (= 'top'), 'foot' (= 'lower part'). Some examples are: **ka·**-*tʃa'qa·j* 'he washes (a horizontal surface such as a floor)', *k*-**laqa**-*tʃa'qa·j* 'I wash (a flat bounded surface such as the face of something)', **qa·**-*tʃa'qa·j* 'he washes (the external vertical sides)', *k*-**pu**-*tʃa'qa·j* 'I wash (inside it)'. Examples with intransitive verbs from Papantla Totonac are: **aq**-*p'un* 'to sprout (on the top)', **tu·**-*p'un* 'to sprout (from the lower part of the trunk, like a banana tree)'. Some of these prefixes could be considered as instances of noun incorporation (but not as object) since they are partially or totally similar to nouns. Many of the prefixes, however, are not related to a noun, although some of them also occur as prefixes with nouns, as with Papantla Totonac *aq*- 'relative to the head' in *aq-ʃa·qa* 'head'.

Tarascan also has a system of directionals in which notions of 'going' vs. 'coming', 'in passing' are expressed as well as 'home', 'not at home', 'upon arrival (at home)', 'before departure (from home)'. There is also a set of about thirty-five suffixes that refer to location and shape, some of which refer principally to body parts. This system resembles that of Totonac although its use is more pervasive. Some roots are used exclusively or predominantly with one of the suffixes, and in many cases their use is obligatory. They are used in transferred meanings not only within physical domains but also within psychological domains, and they occur in combinations. The following examples contain the suffix -*tsi*- or -*ts*ʰi- that makes primary reference to the head: *etsa*-*ts*i-*ni* 'to spread it out over one's head', *tʃakin*-*ts*ʰi 'messy haired', *ts*ʰ*eh*-*ts*i-*ni* 'to measure a hat', *ts*ʰ*irih*-*ts*i-*ni* 'to fill on the top surface', *uandah*-*ts*i-*kpini* 'to speak to the head of others' (i.e. 'to preach'); in addition the affix may refer to the roof of a house, to the cover of a pot, to roots, shoots that emerge from the ground, etc. Other affixes make reference, for instance, to the nose or a protruding object, the face or a flat surface, the mouth, or the opening of an orifice.

Elaborated systems of directionals and locatives, but whose meanings differ from those above, are found in Cora and Huichol. Cora, for instance, differentiates 'toward' vs. 'away' (from the speaker), but also 'toward' vs. 'away' (from a given goal), 'circular motion', 'across a surface and toward the speaker', 'downhill', 'uphill', 'downriver', 'upstream', 'off towards an extreme point' and 'in a circuit'. This system is accompanied by a set of over sixty deictic particles and adverbs that add various dimensions of meanings such as 'near' vs. 'far', 'inside' vs. 'outside' (a given area) – with several refinements – 'beneath' vs. 'in' vs. 'up on top of a slope', and various river-oriented notions.

Some Mayan languages, e.g. Mam, also have a fairly elaborate system of directionals if, in addition to affixes, clitics and auxiliary verbs are taken into account. In other languages the notions most commonly expressed are likewise directional notions; in some languages the elements are affixes, in others they are clitics, but compared with the previous systems they are rather simple, and contrast location near the speaker vs. location away from the speaker with or without concomitant indication of movement. Language families with this type of system are Nahuatl, Mayan, Popolocan, Southern Tepehuán, Zapotecan and Chinantecan. In the last two (at least in some languages) 'coming' vs. 'going' is indicated, although these categories are part of the inflectional system; compare the following forms from Choapan Zapotec:

> *r-gapa* 'I pat'   *ra-gapa* 'I go to pat'
> *wa-gapa* 'I will pat'   *tse-tapa* 'I will go to pat'

The expression of direction is fused with that of aspect, which is obligatory in the verb. In Highland Otomi, on the other hand, it is the notion of location that is part of the inflectional system of tense and mode; the meanings expressed are 'there at some distance from the speaker' and 'above' vs. 'below' (referring to the level at which the speaker is speaking).

Note that there are some languages in which these types of meanings are not expressed within the verb, e.g. Cuitlatec, Huave, Miskito, Mixtec languages and Tlapanec. The expression of these notions by other means may also be rather restricted. This is the case in Tlapanec. Some of the meanings mentioned can be expressed by different verbal roots (cf. 6.4), others like 'going' and 'coming' are expressed by verbal phrases as in English, but for most of them recourse would have to be taken to periphrasis – cumbersome and unusual for the language.

6.1.4 *Transitivity*

Transitivity is not, from a semantic point of view, a verbal category like, for example, aspect or person, but owing to the place it has in the verbal systems of many Mesoamerican languages it is almost an inflectional category; on the other hand, the marking of verbs as 'instrumental' can be considered as a type of transitivity.

All languages have verbs that are inherently intransitive or transitive and are consequently not marked as such. But the English system, where many verbs can be either intransitive or transitive (e.g. *I am eating, I am eating meat*) is the exception in most Mesoamerican languages; in Tlapanec, for instance, these English sentences would be translated as $na^2kwe^{\eta 1}\underline{t}so^2$ 'I am eating' and $na^{\eta 2}kho^2 \int u^2wi^2$ 'I am eating meat', that is, the verb $na^2kwe^{\eta 1}\underline{t}so^1$ cannot take an object, and $na^{\eta 2}kho^2$ used without an object would still refer to an object (contained in the preceding context or in the actual situation) and would be translated as 'I am eating it'.

In 5.1.2 we referred to the obligatory character of the markers for indirective and causative in Classical Nahuatl; in addition, the verbal derivational morphemes in Mayan languages always mark the verb for transitivity; some of these morphemes only mark transitivity. For example, Tzeltal *toh* 'to pay for' is transitive, and can be converted into the intransitive *tohomah* 'to pay an assessment', and then back into the transitive *tohomahtaj*. In 5.1.4 mention was made of (neutral) roots that required the addition of an affix to become a stem with definite transitivity capable of being inflected for aspect and/or categories. These types of root are found in Mayan and Nahuatl, and are particularly common in Totonac. The following is an example from Northern Totonac: *-ţsi·q-* 'hide' is a neutral root; with prefix *ta-* it becomes an intransitive stem, *ta-ţsi·q* 'to hide (oneself)'; with the prefix *ma·-* it becomes a transitive stem, *ma·-ţsi·q* 'to hide (something)'. Compare the functioning of these prefixes with roots which are inherently transitive or intransitive, such as *sta·-* 'sell (something)', *ta-şţa·-* 'to get sold'; *pupu-* 'boil', *ma·-pupu-* 'boil' (transitive).

The types of transitivity marked in different languages are not always the same. In most Otomanguean languages only the categories of transitive and intransitive are marked morphologically; in Uto-Aztecan languages, Totonac, Mayan, Mixe-Zoque and Otomian languages, indirective (or bitransitive or benefactitive) and causative are also marked. Copainalá Zoque, for example, has causative and causative – associative as in *maŋ-* 'to go', *jah-maŋ-* 'to cause to go', *ni-ma-* 'to take away' (i.e. 'to cause to go along with the subject'). Instrumental is more common, and it occurs in Totonac, in several Otomanguean languages and in Mixe-Zoque languages.

6.2 Pronominal systems

Pronominal systems will be considered here according to the categories expressed, the types of pronouns and the relation in form between them.

The basic categories of pronouns (and of person affixes in nouns and verbs) refer to the speaker, the addressee and somebody who is neither speaker nor addressee (first, second and third person in traditional terminology). All systems make these differences although formally third person is frequently expressed not by a pronoun but by a demonstrative. In South Pame only singular categories have a pronominal form, and in some Chinantec languages like Palantla Chinantec there is no pronoun for third person plural. Languages like Nahuatl and Totonac differentiate only the three singular and the three plural persons; a considerable number of languages – Sierra Popoluca, many Mayan languages, Tlapanec – add a difference between first person plural exclusive (i.e. the addressee is excluded from 'we') and first person plural inclusive (i.e. the addressee is included in 'we'). To these distinctions, Huave of San Mateo del Mar adds a distinction of first dual inclusive ('I and you') and a

Table 16. *Mazahua personal pronouns*

$nuts^{\gamma}g\mathfrak{o}$	'I'	$nuts^{\gamma}gebi$	'you and he/she'
$nutsge$	'you (sg.)'	$nuts^{\gamma}g\mathfrak{o}hi$	'I and you and he/she/they'
$nuhnu$	'he'	$nutsg\mathfrak{o}hme$	'I and they'
$nuhna$	'she'	$nutsgehi$	'you (pl.)'
$nuts^{\gamma}g\mathfrak{o}bi$	'I and you'	$nuhjo$	'they (males)'
$nuts^{\gamma}g\mathfrak{o}be$	'I and he/she'	$nuhja$	'they (females)'

Table 17. *Chocho third person pronouns*

$soa^{21}\int\tilde{a}^3$	'she/he (a child)'	$soa^{21}ni^1$	'he/she (devotional)'
$soa^{21}ri^1$	'he (a boy)'; 'it (a wild animal)'	$soa^{21}ba^2$	'it (domestic animal)'
		$soa^{21}ru^3$	'it (a fruit)'
$soa^{21}t\int i^1$	'she (a girl)'	$soa^{21}nda^3$	'it (a wooden object)'
$soa^{21}ga^1$	'he (a close adult friend of same age)'	$soa^{21}ga^3$	'it (an object)'
$soa^{21}nu^2$	'she (a close adult friend of same age)'		
$soa^{21}ri^3$	'he/she (respectful)'		

second dual ('you and he/she'), and Mazahua further differentiates a first dual exclusive ('I and he/she') and a third dual ('they two'). This Mazahua system (also found in Otomian languages) is the most complex reported in this area regarding distinctions of grammatical person, and is given in table 16.

It can be seen that this system adds a further dimension in the third person, namely gender. This category is still further elaborated in some Mixtec, Zapotec and Popoloc languages. Chocho, for instance, makes the gender distinctions shown in table 17. It should be noted that this type of gender system conforms more closely to objective reality than the largely arbitrary systems of French and German, for example.

However, not all distinctions made in the Chocho system are gender distinctions; degree of respect also appears, a distinction that is also made in second person: $g\tilde{a}^2\tilde{a}^2$ 'you (respectful)', $soa^{21}ia^2$ 'you (familiar)'. This dimension is naturally the same as that discussed under the label 'honorific' in connection with verbal inflection in Classical Nahuatl (cf. 5.1.2); some modern Nahuatl languages, e.g. that spoken in Zacapoaxtla, distinguish up to four degrees of respect in second person pronouns; the following forms are ordered according to increasing respect: *teh*, *tehwa*, *tehwatsin*, *tehwapoltsin*. These Nahuatl forms resemble those of Chocho in that they are differentiated by means of different affixes, but in some languages the use of plural instead of singular forms for expressing respect is attested. In Eastern Popoloc, first plural inclusive is used as the form of respect for second person singular; in Chiquihuitlan Mazatec first person plural exclusive is used for first singular, and second plural for second singular; in Varohio plural forms are used for singular ones.

Distinct forms according to the sex of the speaker are found in Chicahuaxtla Trique and Diuxi Mixtec. In the latter, the difference intersects with the formal–familiar distinction as well as with gender of the referent in third person. Thus, whereas an adult man uses *ndo$^{?2}o^1$* as second person familar form, an adult woman uses *yo$^{?2}o^1$* in the same case; again, a male speaker uses *me^{2}es^1* as third person referring to another male adult or to a male child, but a female speaker uses *me^{2}te^1* referring to a male adult and *me^{2}i^1* for a male child.

Reference has been made only to personal pronouns, and a language like Nahuatl has only this series; other languages, however, e.g. Tarascan, have personal and possessive pronouns. Some Mayan languages have personal and reflexive pronouns, and others such as Palantla Chinantec have personal, reflexive and possessive pronouns. These series are frequently built on different roots, as in the following example from Palantla Chinantec: *hni^2* 'I', *njéw^3* 'myself', *kjew^3* 'mine'; this does not necessarily indicate that different pronominal roots had once existed, but probably reflects a situation like that in Totonac in which possessive pronouns are in fact the noun that means 'property' inflected for person of possessor, and reflexive pronouns are the inflected forms of the noun that means 'body' (in the same function Miskito uses the noun that means 'flesh'). Totonac also has a pronominal series that indicates 'X alone', for example *'ki·kstu* 'I alone', *mi·kstu* 'you alone'; Coastal Chontal has a similar series but with a reflexive meaning too, e.g. *'aj'tu'wa* 'myself alone'.

Case differences are attested in Miskito (e.g. *ja* 'I', *ai* 'me') and Chatino; Coatzospan Mixtec also has different pronominal forms for subject and object, but only in clitics and only for some persons.

Although it is doubtful whether differences of relation in form among pronouns of a single series reflect differences in synchronic meaning, they may reflect a difference that existed at the time the system was constituted. Systems like that of English in which forms are unrelated are uncommon, the closest to it being the Huichol system which is: *ne^{1}e^2* 'I', *$^?$e^{2}e^{2}ki^{2}i^2* 'you (sg.)', *$^?$i^{2}ja^1* 'he/she/they', *ta^{1}a^{2}me^2* 'we', *ze^{1}e^{2}me^2* 'you (pl.)'. Otherwise there are two general types of system. First, Otomanguean languages, and some Mayan languages, have personal pronouns built on a root (presumably deictic), as can be seen in the Mazahua system (table 16) in which the root is *nuts-*, and in the following Tlapanec pronouns: *i^{2}khũ·^{1}* 'I', *i^{2}khã·^{1}* 'you (sg.)', *i^{2}kha·^{23}* 'he/she', *i^{2}khã·^{1} = lo$^{?1}$* 'we (inclusive)', *i^{2}khã·^{1} = ʃo$^{?3}$*

'we (exclusive)' $i^2kh\tilde{a}^{\cdot 1} = la^{\eta 2}$ 'you (pl.)', $i^2kh\tilde{i}^{\cdot 23}$ 'they'. In these cases the root is inflected for person like a noun or verb; compare the following forms from Tlapanec: $na^2hng\tilde{u}^{\cdot 21}$ 'I am drunk', $na^2hng\tilde{a}^{\cdot 21}$ 'you are drunk', $na^2hnga^{\cdot 3}$ 'he is drunk', $na^2hng\tilde{a}^{\cdot 21} = lo^{\eta 1}$ 'we (inclusive) are drunk', $na^2hng\tilde{a}^{\cdot 21} = \int o^{\eta 3}$ 'we (exclusive) are drunk', $na^2hng\tilde{a}^{\cdot 21} = la^{\eta 2}$ 'you (pl.) are drunk', $na^2hng\tilde{i}^{\cdot 12}$ 'they are drunk'. Note that in this system first person plural inclusive and first person plural exclusive are built on the forms of second singular, whereas in the Mazahua system they are built on the forms of the first singular.

In the second type, which is more widely represented over linguistic families – Totonac, Nahuatl, Zoque, Miskito, Tequistlatec – singular persons are represented by different roots, but plural persons are represented by morphologically plural forms built on the singular ones. Note the system of Northern Totonac: $^\eta a' kit$ 'I', $'wi\int$ 'you (sg.)' $'wa$ 'he/she', $^\eta a'k$-in 'we', $wi'\int$-in 'you (pl.)', wa-$'nin$ 'they' (-in, -nin are suffixes which also mark plural in nouns). In this system, first plural is built onto the first singular form, although in Nahuatl it is built on second singular, and there is a different root for second plural.

In most cases, forms of personal pronouns show partial or total identity with affixes that mark person in nouns and/or verbs, as in the Tlapanec example above, but it is interesting to note that, although it does not represent a change in category, in Coastal Chontal the pronoun forms are totally unrelated to affixes that manifest person in nouns and verbs.

6.3 Categories in nouns

6.3.1 *Person*

Person of possessor is the category most commonly marked in nouns, and if clitics are taken into account, it is probably general.

Nouns are very frequently classified as obligatorily possessed, optionally possessed and unpossessable. Nouns referring to parts of the body, personal belongings (e.g. clothes) and kin usually fall into the class of obligatorily possessed, but in Tlapanec, for instance, only kin terms are obligatorily possessed, and in Classical Nahuatl probably any noun could occur, at least in quotation form, as unpossessed, and, in this case, marked with the absolutive suffix. The class of nouns that never occurs possessed seems to be determined by largely non-linguistic factors; nouns that are usually unpossessable are those referring to natural phenomena such as the sun, the wind, a river, etc. In some cases there may be a cultural reason for their assignment to this class; in Tlapanec the noun meaning 'steambath' is unpossessable, and in fact steambaths are not individually owned where the language is spoken.

Some Mayan languages (e.g. Mam) mark nouns which are usually possessed when they occur unpossessed but, unlike Nahuatl, there is more than one suffix that indicates an unpossessed noun, and they show semantic consistency. For example: *-jpʔəx* is added to nouns that refer to parts of the body, relatives, and some pieces of clothing or jewellery, as in *tsii-jpʔəx* 'mouth' (cf. *n-tsii* 'my mouth'); *-pʔx* is suffixed to nouns that refer to edibles as in *loʔ-pʔx* 'fruit' (cf. *n-loʔ* 'my fruit'); and *-x* is suffixed to nouns that refer to pieces of clothing or personal belongings in general, as in *kamis-x* 'shirt' (cf. *n-kamis* 'my shirt'). In this language some of the nouns that are optionally possessed also have a special marker when possessed, e.g. *sata* 'cotton', *nsaatan* 'my cotton'. The marking for possessed and unpossessed nouns is fairly typical of Mayan languages, and in some of them it allows distinctions to be made, as in the following two possessed nouns of Jacaltec: *w-etʃel* 'photo of me', *w-etʃel-e* 'my photo of somebody else' (*we-* '1st person', *-e* is a marker for possession when no definite possessor is indicated).

A further distinction found in relation to possession is that between inherent vs. occasional possession (or inalienable vs. alienable possession). In Nahuatl, for instance, inherent possession is marked by the suffix *-jo*, and contrasts arise as in Texcoco Nahuatl *no-naka* 'my meat', *no-naka-jo* 'my flesh'; a similar distinction is found in some Mayan languages and in Totonac.

Some languages have more than one pattern for marking person of possessor, and there seems to be some correlation with a distinction between inherent vs. occasional possession. There are, however, inconsistencies, although these may be in part due to lack of pertinent cultural information. Some examples are discussed below.

In Huave most nouns that refer to parts of the body, as well as the noun that means 'home', have an inflectional paradigm for person of possessor in which first, second and third person are distinguished, as in (dialect of San Francisco) *siwis* 'my hand', *iwis* 'your hand', *owis* 'his hand'. However, nouns referring to some parts of the body (knee, shoulder, hip, elbow), like all other nouns (including those referring to kin), have an inflectional paradigm in which second and third person have to be specified by an independent pronoun, e.g. *siakos* 'my knee', *mikos jok* 'your knee', *mikos ɲu* 'his knee'; note that both the noun meaning 'hand' and the one meaning 'knee' are obligatorily possessed.

A double pattern for indicating person of possessor is also found in some Otomanguean languages (Chinantec and Mazatec languages). In Quiotepec Chinantec, for example, most nouns that refer to parts of the body and kin, and to some objects (e.g. money, clothes, tortilla, dough, chicken, dish) are inflected for person of possessor, e.g. *kwoh*[1] 'my hand', *kwo*[3]*-ʔh*[3] 'your hand' (the hyphen stands for predictable vowel). In all other nouns, person of possessor is indicated by a free constituent (a possessive pronoun with or without a personal pronoun), e.g. hi^2 $ṭiah^{232}$ book mine 'my book'. This syntactic construction can also be used with the first class of nouns. As in Huave, this difference is independent of the contrast between obligatorily vs. optionally possessed; the terms for 'mother' and for 'grandmother' are both obligatorily possessed, but in the former inflection is used, while in the latter possessor is indicated by a syntactic construction; thus, sah^1 'my mother', $su^2ʔiah^{232}$ $ṭiah^{232}$ 'my grandmother'. A similar difference for marking possession found in other Otomanguean languages will be discussed at the end of 6.4.1.

As in the case of the verb (cf. 6.1.2), Tlapanec marks third possessor in a different way when the possessor is not represented by a free constituent; thus $go^{ʔ2}o^{.12}$ $a^{ʔ3}go^3$ $ci^1ge^{ʔ3}$ her = house woman this 'the house of this woman', but $go^{ʔ2}o^{.13}$ 'her house'.

Inflection for person of subject in nouns has been mentioned and exemplified in chapter 5; it occurs in Nahuatl, Mixe-Zoque languages, most Mayan languages and in Tequistlatec languages.

6.3.2 *Number, gender, definiteness*

Obligatory marking of number is not widespread. Plural is marked regularly in Coastal Chontal, Tarascan, Nahuatl and some Otopamean languages, but in Classical Nahuatl only nouns that designate animate beings were pluralized; those designating inanimate objects were pluralized only exceptionally.

Most Otomanguean languages, some Mayan languages, Miskito, Cuitlatec and Huave do not mark plural in nouns; at most some nouns that designate human beings have a plural form, and sometimes a suppletive one (probably a former collective) as in Tlapanec a^2da^3 'child', $e^3h\tilde{e}^3$ 'children'. In these languages number in nouns is left undetermined or is optionally indicated by a modifier that means 'many'. In languages like Tlapanec, not only is the number of the subject noun indicated in the verb but also the number of the object, although this is not always the case when the noun designates an inanimate object.

Gender is not overtly marked in any language in Mesoamerica. In languages that classify nouns according to gender this is a selective category marked by compatibility with verbs, adjectives, numerals, pronouns and demonstratives indicating gender; the number of gender distinctions is the same as those that were exemplified in the pronominal systems.

Only a few languages – Cuitlatec, Coastal Chontal, Mazahua, Zoque – have a special definite marker; notice Coastal Chontal $ko'sax$ 'corn', $'el-ko'$ sax 'the corn'. It should also be noted that a class of article is comparatively rare; it is found in some Mayan languages (e.g. Tzotzil), some Otomi languages and in Sierra Popoluca.

6.3.3   Case

Morphological case systems are found in a few languages: Copainalá Zoque, Tarascan, Huichol (only in numerals and some quantifiers) and Yaqui. The latter has the simplest system; although functionally the marked form could be considered an accusative, its value is more general and it could be called an oblique case or a form marked for dependency as against the unmarked form (see examples in 7.3). Copainalá Zoque marks nominative–genitive, comitative, instrumental, dative, and (thirteen) various locative notions. The nominative–genitive marks subject of a transitive verb (*teʔ-piʔn-is tʃihku* the = man = nominative did-it 'the man did it'), and possessor in nominal phrases (*teʔ-piʔn-is ţik* the = man = genitive his house 'the man's house'). Examples of some other cases are: *piŋ-hiʔŋ* 'with a man', *niʔ-***pit** 'with water', *niʔ-***aŋi** 'near the water' (comitative, instrumental, locative respectively).

Tarascan differentiates six cases: nominative (unmarked), accusative, genitive, locative, comitative, instrumental. Accusative case is used for direct and indirect object but its use is not obligatory; genitive, besides possession, may mean 'material made of' or 'time at'. Instrumental is also used in a temporal sense; locative only indicates location in general, and according to context it may be translated as 'in', 'from', 'to', etc.

Some languages, e.g. Tlapanec, have some nouns marked as locative, but these forms are probably better analysed as derivational, rather than inflected for case, because many nouns are used in a locative function without having a special marking.

6.4   Classifiers

It is convenient to consider the expression of classificatory notions jointly even though they appear in different parts of the language structure.

6.4.1   Numeral classifiers

Numeral classifiers are elements that co-occur with numerals in counting nouns and which subclassify the nouns according to characteristics of shape, genus or the way they are measured. They are equivalent to the use of forms such as 'handful of', 'piece of' with mass nouns in English, the difference being that in other languages any counted noun is accompanied by a form with this type of meaning. Note the following examples from (Mayan) Chontal: *un-***ts'it** *tʃɔb* 'one candle', *un-***ʃim** *kɔkɔw* 'one cocoa bean', *un-***kʔe** *pop* 'one sleeping mat', *un-***tu** *ahlo* 'one boy', *un-***tek** *teʔ* 'one tree', *un-***sats**ʔ *sum* 'a stretch of rope', *un-***som** *iʃim* 'a handful of ears of corn'; the classifiers (in bold type) are, respectively, used in counting long slender objects, grain-like objects, flat objects, persons and animals, plants and standing trees, measures of approximately an arm's length, and handfuls of something.

Table 18. *Classifiers in common use*

	Papantla Totonac	Yucatec	Tarascan	Classical Nahuatl
'round'	ka·-	-wo·l	-eʈa	-te-ƚ
'long'	kan-	-ts'i·t	-itʃa	-o·lo·-ƚ
'flat'	mak-	-wa·l	-itʃu	(-ipil-li)
'person'	tʃa·-	-tu·l	-kwiripu	-te·kpan-ƚi

Classifiers of this type are found in Mayan languages, Totonac (the locative prefixes discussed in 6.1.3 can also be considered classifiers), Classical Nahuatl and Tarascan. In some Mayan languages, such as Chontal, as well as in Tarascan, Totonac and Classical Nahuatl, classifiers are affixes attached to numerals, while in other Mayan languages, e.g. Tzeltal, classifiers are free forms. In some Mayan languages, e.g. Jacaltec, classifiers can be used as anaphoric pronouns.

Some classifiers (either affixes or free forms) are found only as such, while others are related to nouns, as in Totonac and Nahuatl, or, as in Mayan languages, to a class of roots (which as stems may be nouns, statives or verbs) called positional, which indicate position or shape. For example, the classifier for round objects is the noun meaning 'rock' in Classical Nahuatl, but in Yucatec it is a positional root (*wo·l*) that, derived as a transitive stem (*wo·l-tik*), means 'to make something round', and as stative (*wo·l-is*) means 'to be round'.

The number of classifiers varies considerably from language to language. Classical Nahuatl has seven (three of them only used in counting by twenties), Tarascan has ten, Totonac around twenty-five, Chontal over a hundred, and in a language like Tzeltal there is a set of basic classifiers, but in addition most positional roots can be used as classifiers. Given these differences it is obvious that the number of characteristics specified by classifiers varies accordingly, although some characteristics seem basic in that they occur in all languages that have classifiers; table 18 exemplifies these characteristics. Even so there are discrepancies. The Yucatec classifier for person is also used for animals, whereas Totonac has a different classifier for animals; the Nahuatl form within parentheses is used, like the Totonac one, in counting tortillas and fabrics, but also in counting blankets, hides and papers, and in this use it would better correspond to a different prefix in Totonac, one that is utilized in counting laminate or leaf-like objects (planks, boards, papers).

In some cases the same noun may be counted with different classifiers having different meaning as in the Chontal noun *wop* 'jahuacte' (a type of tree): *un-tek wop* 'one jahuacte tree', *un-tsʔit wop* 'a stick from the jahuacte tree' (*-tek* 'plant', *-tsʔit*

Table 19. *Some Highland Chontal classificatory verbs*

'put upon'	'lower'
ʃ*pef* (something broad)	*ɣah* (a cup, a dish)
ʃ*apφ'i* (something round and big)	*bul* (something big or round)
gapφ'i (something thin and long)	*tṣuh* (something small)
	ɬ*eh* (something grain-like)

'long slender object'). In some languages – Totonac, Yucatec – there is a general classifier used when the speaker does not want to make specific reference to shape, or when he is in doubt as to how to classify the noun.

A different type of classifier is found in the Otomanguean languages. To some extent its characteristics have to be inferred since in most languages these elements are completely fossilized, although they are certainly detectable under over-analysis, e.g. in Zapotec languages, in which most nouns designating animals begin with the same consonant; the same is also true of those designating plants. In Amuzgo they are more easily identifiable because in some cases the noun also occurs without the classifier, e.g. *tṣua⁴* 'cactus', *ka⁴-tṣua⁴* 'wasp' (*ka⁴-* 'animate classifier'). The system is still operational in some Mixtec and Chinantec languages. The differences between these and the types of classifiers discussed above are that here it is always nouns (not necessarily all nouns) that are used with the classifier, and that the classifiers are few in number and make distinctions largely parallel to those found in pronominal systems; that is to say they resemble a gender system. In Amuzgo the following distinctions are made: 'animate', 'thing', 'person', 'feminine', 'masculine', 'fruit', 'familiar person', 'human', 'house'.

Some Otomanguean languages – Amuzgo, Copala Trique, some Mixtec languages, Chichimec – have classifiers that occur in a type of possessive construction. In Chichimec, for instance, person of possessor is indicated by inflection in some nouns (obligatorily possessed nouns belong to this class) as in *na²nte¹* 'my food', *u¹te²* 'your food', but nouns that designate plants, animals, pieces of clothing, foods, and some other notions, are not so inflected, and person of possessor is indicated in an accompanying classificatory noun, as in *nu¹nthi² ma²tũ¹* my-clothing shirt 'my shirt'.

6.4.2 *Classificatory verbs*
The same distinctions that are made by classifiers are also found as semantic properties in certain verbs; in constructions with these verbs, the class of noun, and its position as subject, object, instrument or locative is determined by the form of the verb that is used.

Table 20. *Some Highland Chontal and Totontepec Mixe classificatory verbs*

Highland Chontal	Totontepec Mixe
'to wash'	'to break'
boṯso (clothes)	*kiʔṯs* (clothes)
lapɸ' (grinding stone)	*ket* (grinding stone)
lakʔo (mouth)	*puʔu* (stone)
lou (hand)	*pət* (cord)
ẉiṯsaj (hair)	*tɨh* (branch)
lahʔme (dishes)	
'to put upon'	'to cut'
kʔommof (the head)	*tuk* (fingers)
depɸʔi (a shelf)	*mɨɨʔṯs* (hand)
beṯsu (the ground)	*ṯsuk* (knife)
winapɸ'i (a cushion)	*puʃ* (machete)
	ke·ʔp (scissors)

As is to be expected in a basically lexical domain, the distinctions are less systematic than with classifiers, in the sense that not all the verbs in the class make the same number or kinds of distinctions. Examples from Highland Chontal are given in table 19. The characteristics that the object of the verb must have are indicated within parentheses.

In some cases the reference may be quite specific as to object, instrument or location. Table 20 exemplifies this point from Highland Chontal and from Totontepec Mixe, indicating moreover that the nouns show the same or similar characteristics in different languages from different linguistic families. For the verbs translated as 'to wash' and 'to break' the characteristics given within parentheses refer to the object of the verb; for the verbs translated as 'to put upon' and 'to cut' the characteristics refer respectively to where the object is placed and to the instrument with which the action is performed.

Besides Tequistlatec languages and Totontepec Mixe, these verb types are reported in Tarascan, Mayan languages and some Otomanguean languages. The reference to location is further elaborated in some Otomanguean languages (Chinantec languages, Mazahua, Tlapanec) and also in Totonac. The common meaning of the verb is 'to be located' or 'to exist' (i.e. 'there is/are'). In the examples in table 21 from Mazahua, Papantla Totonac and Tlapanec, it can be seen that Mazahua makes more distinctions according to the genus of the subject, whereas Totonac stresses the position of the subject, and Tlapanec the configuration of the

Table 21. *Some Mazahua, Papantla Totonac and Tlapanec classificatory verbs*

Mazahua	Papantla Totonac
pitʃʔi (tree)	*'ja* (standing or vertical)
poʔo (liquid in a deep container)	*'ma* (on the ground or lying)
kãrã (many animate things)	*'wakʔa* (on a higher place, perched)
hɛsɛ (many fruits or flowers around)	*'lapʔat* (something that moves)
kasa (people in a forest)	
kjaʔa (bread, tortilla)	
kãʔã (fish in a river)	
hɛrɛ (seeds on the ground)	

Tlapanec	
ga²hnoʔ³ (liquid in a deep container)	*gi²daʔ³* (inside a building)
ga²kha¹ (solids in a deep container; people on a lower level)	*gi²wã³* (in the nest, in a sack or hole, in a plantation or park)
kraʔ²ma¹ (upon a rock or sack; on a higher level)	*giʔ¹ma³* (outside but near or on the edge–a house, road, forest)
kwaʔ³ã³ (in the midst of trees or plants; inside)	*gi·¹* (something with broad base; seated)
ri¹gu³ (upon a horse or table or tree)	*we³he³* (standing, a person or a tree)

location of the subject (there are also differences according to the genus of the subject, but they reflect another system, that of animate vs. inanimate which is pervasive in the language).

It should be clear that classificatory verbs are an instance of lexical selection or collocation and that many languages have some examples (cf. with the Totontepec Mixe examples of verbs meaning 'break' (table 20) English *break*, with *branch* but not *cloth*, and *tear*, with *cloth* but not *branch*). What makes a special class out of these verbs is that the differences expressed are parallel to those expressed by classificatory affixes, and these differences are found in a considerable number of verbs; thus, in Tlapanec, the difference between 'solid' and 'liquid' is also made in verbs that mean 'to fill with' and 'to pour', the contrast 'deep' vs. 'flat' is found in verbs that mean 'to throw into/upon', and the contrast between 'open, uncovered' and 'closed, covered' is found in verbs that mean 'to move within/around'.

SOURCES

Amuzgo: (*Guerrero*) Hart 1957. *Chichimec*: Angulo 1933. *Chinantec*: (*Palantla*) Merrifield 1968; (*Quiotepec*) Robbins 1968. *Chocho*: Mock 1977. *Chontal* (*Mayan*): Keller 1955. *Chontal*:

(*Coastal*) Waterhouse 1962; (*Highland*) Turner 1971. *Cora*: Casad 1977, Preuss 1932. *Cuitlatec*: Escalante 1962. *Huave*: Stairs and Hollenbach 1969, Suárez 1975. *Huichol*: Grimes, J. 1964. *Jacaltec*: Craig 1977, Day 1973a. *Mam*: Canger 1969. *Mazahua*: Amador Hernández 1976, Kiemele Muro 1975. *Mazateco*: (*Chiquihuitlan*) Jamieson, C. 1976; (*Huautla*) Pike, E. 1967. *Miskito*: Heath 1913, Thaeler n.d. *Mixe*: (*El Paraíso*) Van Haitsma and Van Haitsma 1976; (*Totontepec*) Schoenhals and Schoenhals 1965. *Mixtec*: (*Coatzospan*) Small 1974; (*Diuxi*) Kuiper and Pickett 1974; (*Jamiltepec*) Bradley 1970. *Nahuatl*: (*Classical*) Andrews, J. 1975; (*North Puebla*) Brockway 1979; (*Zacapoaxtla*) Robinson 1970. *Otomi*: (*Highland*) Echegoyen Gleason 1979. *Pame*: (*South*) Manrique 1967. *Popoloc*: (*Tlacoyalco*) Stark 1976; (*Western*) Williams and Longacre 1967. *Popoluca*: (*Sierra*) Elson 1967. *Tarascan*: Foster 1969, Friedrich 1969. *Tlapanec*: Suárez n.d. *Totonac*: (*Northern*) McQuown 1940; (*Papantla*) Aschmann 1973. *Trique*: (*Chicahuaxtla*) Goode 1978; (*Copala*) Hollenbach and Hollenbach 1975. *Tzeltal*: Kaufman 1971b. *Tzotzil*: McLaughlin 1975. *Varohio*: Miller 1977. *Yaqui*: Lindenfeld 1973. *Yucatec*: Romero Castillo 1961. *Zapotec*: (*Choapan*) Lyman 1964; (*Isthmus*) Pickett 1967, Pickett et al. 1965. *Zoque*: (*Copainalá*) Wonderly 1951–2.

FURTHER READING

The categories of tense, aspect and mode have been rather sketchily handled in descriptions of Mesoamerican languages; Canger 1969 gives a detailed treatment of Mam tenses including constructions with adverbs; Bartholomew and Brockway 1974 deal *in extenso* with the meaning of tenses in a modern Nahuatl language within the frame of discourse; the options as to mode, tense and aspect offered by Southern Tepehuán are treated in Willet 1978; see also the discussion of their respective systems in the sources given for Tarascan (Foster), Jacaltec (Craig), and Northern Totonac (McQuown). For the peculiarities found in connection with negative in a Mayan language see Jacobs and Longacre 1967, in Copala Trique, Hollenbach 1976. Ergative systems have attracted much attention recently; for a full treatment with some references to Mayan systems, see Dixon 1979. A feature that is sometimes connected with ergativity is the hierarchy of grammatical persons, and this is attributed to Mixe languages in some analyses, e.g. Van Haitsma and Van Haitsma 1976; Lyon, D. 1967; Lyon, S. 1967; but the data are not clear.

Casad 1977 covers directionals in Cora as expressed by affixes, particles and adverbs; see also Foster on Tarascan. The Tarascan locative suffixes are treated in detail in Friedrich 1971c. Many examples of locative prefixes in Papantla Totonac can be found going through Aschmann 1973. For directionals in Mam, see Canger 1969; England 1976. Some Otomanguean languages have different verbs of motion which come in pairs and which make distinctions similar to some directionals; see Foris, C. 1978, Kuiper and Merrifield 1975, Pickett 1976, Speck and Pickett 1976.

Formal representations of some pronominal systems are given in Buchler and Freeze 1962, Ros Romero 1979; on Jacaltec see also Day 1973b. On the actual use of a system with honorifics (Nahuatl), Hill and Hill 1978.

An extensive treatment of classifiers in a Mayan language is Berlin 1968; see also the source for Chontal. Classifiers and classificatory verbs are discussed from a general point of view, using Tarascan examples, in Friedrich 1970. Further examples of classificatory verbs can be found in the dictionaries of Highland Chontal (Turner 1971), Mazahua (Kiemele Muro 1975), Totontepec Mixe (Schoenhals and Schoenhals 1965), and Tzotzil (McLaughlin 1975).

7

Syntax I

The distribution of topics in chapters 5–8 has been largely a matter of convenience of presentation since there is of course a good deal of overlap between syntax and morphology. In the present and the following chapters the discussion will refer to and supplement the morphological information given in chapters 5 and 6.

Differences in the order of constituents in a clause are currently used as a way of typologizing languages; as they are easily handled across whole language families, they will be treated early, in 7.1. Section 8.5 will be devoted to a brief discussion of the impact of Spanish on the syntactic structure of Mesoamerican Indian languages. The remainder of chapters 7 and 8 will be devoted to a consideration of various syntactic patterns, organized by language family. Those that will be considered are as follows:

Types of clauses according to number of participants, emphasis and voice.
Ways of expressing existential, identificational, locative, and possessive meanings at clause level.
Forms of interrogative clauses.
Marking of clause constituents according to function.
Forms of verbal phrases containing auxiliaries.
Major features of coordination.
Formation of relative clauses.
Ways of expressing comparison.

Some explanations about the terminology to be used are given in the following paragraphs.

Constructions containing a predicate will be referred to as 'clauses' without distinguishing them from 'sentences'.

'Participant' refers to any clause constituent that is cross-referred to within the verb and/or whose occurrence depends on the choice of the verb; constituents with these characteristics will also be called 'nuclear', and other constituents which are more loosely dependent on the verb will be called 'peripheral'. Participants refer most commonly to animate entities, but some refer to inanimate ones, e.g. 'instrument' or 'location'. Participants are identified by semantic labels deriving from the meanings that may be considered typical (in numerical terms) for constituents which are also formally identifiable, although these labels are extended to cases of these constituents even if in the actual situation referred to differences may be found. Thus, in English, *he* would be considered 'actor' not only in *he threw a stone*, but also in *he saw a horse* or in *he felt pain*; *stone*, *a horse* and *pain* would be considered patients. In single clause constructions with causative meaning the participant that indirectly causes another one (the 'actor') to perform an action or to be in a certain state will be called the 'agent' (the restriction to indirect causation is to distinguish these from those of direct causation as in *John drowned the cat* where *John* is considered 'actor'). The following example illustrates the most commonly encountered participants:

> *ni-mits-kapua-lti-li-s*   *tewal*   *in*   *patʃulimes*
> I = you = pluck = causative = indirective = future   you   the   plants
> *in   lakal*
> the   man
> 'I will make you pull up the plants for the man' [Pómaro Nahuatl]

In this clause the agent is not represented by a clause level constituent (as it could be) but is only cross-referred to in the verb by *ni-* 'I'; the actor is *tewal* 'you'; the patient is *in patʃulimes* 'the plants', and the beneficiary is *in lakal* 'the man'.

'Emphasis' will be used as a cover term for equivalent constructions which in some languages may have different meanings, such as English **John**, *he didn't come*, **It was John** *who didn't come*, **John** *didn't come*, **The one who did not come** *was John*. In fact most of the constructions that will be discussed are like the first English example.

Under 'identificational' clauses those included express identity (*Peter is my son*) and class membership (*Peter is a teacher*).

Auxiliary verbs are considered to be those forms that express modal, temporal, aspectual or other meanings (e.g. negation) which may carry partial or full verbal inflection, which co-occur with verbs that carry lexical meaning and differ from main verbs in peculiarities of inflection.

'Subordinate clause' is used in a broad sense; it may be marked in different ways: introductory particles, special modes, non-finite forms of the verb, or it can even be unmarked. More attention will be paid to these formal mechanisms than to the different types of subordinate clauses according to meaning and function, but specific mention will be made of relative clauses.

Some syntactic characteristics are so widespread in this area that to avoid repetition they are listed below:

Table 22. *Order of constituents within main clauses*

Jacaltec (Mayan)	VSO Pr	NG NA/(AN)	DN NIN AMSt
Isthmus Zapotec (Otomanguean)	VSO Pr	NG NA	ND NIN AMSt*
Tzotzil (Mayan)	VOS Pr	NG AN	DN NIN AMSt
Highland Otomi (Otomanguean)	VOS Pr	NG AN	DN NIN AMSt
Coastal Chontal (Tequistlatec- Jicaque)	SVO Pr	NG AN	DN NIN AMSt
Tarascan (Tarascan)	SVO Pr	NG NA/AN	DN NIN AMSt
Huave (Huave)	SVO Pr	NG NA/AN	DN NIN AMSt
Tetelcingo Nahuatl (Uto-Aztecan)	SVO Po/Pr	NG NA/(AN)	DN NIN AMSt*
Totonac (Totonac-Tepehua)	~ Pr	NG AN/NA	DN NIN AMSt
Tlahuitoltepec Mixe (Mixe-Zoque)	~ Po	GN AN	DN NIN StMA
Chimalapa Zoque (Mixe-Zoque)	~ Po	GN AN	DN NIN AMSt*
Chichimec (Otomanguean)	SOV Po	GN NA	DN NIN AMSt*
Yaqui (Uto-Aztecan)	SOV Po	GN AN	DN NIN StMA
Miskito (Misumalpan)	SOV Po	GN NA/(AN)	DN NIN StMA

A: adjective. D: determiner. G: genitive. M: marker of comparison. N: noun. Nl: numeral. O: object. Po: postpositional. Pr: Prepositional. S: subject. St: standard of comparison. V: verb. /: both orders. ( ): in restricted cases. *: pattern borrowed from Spanish. ~: variable order.

1. There are emphatic clauses which differ from the neutral ones only in that the emphasized constituent occurs first in the clause.
2. Relative clauses can occur without a nominal antecedent ('headless relatives') filling nominal functions; relatives occur after the antecedent when there is one.
3. Questions that bear on some specific constituent of the clause ('constituent questions') are introduced by an interrogative word (exceptions occur in Yaqui and in Miskito, cf. 7.3, 8.4) and these constructions occur as subjects or objects without further changes.
4. Questions that bear on the whole clause ('yes/no questions') when occurring as subject or object are introduced by the same particle that introduces conditional clauses.
5. Subordinate clauses show restrictions as to tense or aspect depending on the tense or aspect in the main clause. Therefore when it is stated that subordinate clauses in a given language have the same structure as main clauses these restrictions are left out of account.

No specific mention of these characteristics will henceforth be made unless they are accompanied by other particular characteristics.

The information is uneven for different languages and language families so that lack of explicit mention of a given characteristic in a language or language family should not be taken as necessarily implying that it is absent.

7.1 **Order of constituents**

Table 22 contains information on the order of constituents within main clauses in fourteen languages representing nine families. The labels attached to constituents have to be understood in a broad sense, that is, 'adjective' refers to a word that indicates quality and is attributive to a noun (formally it may be an adjective or a noun or a verb or a stative); 'genitive' is used for any free constituent that indicates the possessor in a nominal construction; 'preposition' and 'postposition' cover word-types that are (roughly) semantic equivalents to English prepositions (formally they are nouns in many languages in this area); 'marker of comparison' and 'standard of comparison' refer to words or affixes that are equivalent to 'than' and 'John' respectively in 'better *than John*'.

The interest of constituent order for language typology is that some positive correlations have been established between certain features of the basic word order of normal simple assertive clauses and other aspects of linguistic structure. Those for which the table gives information are the following (see table for abbreviations): (i) order SOV is correlated with presence of postpositions, these in turn being correlated with orders GN and StMA; (ii) order VSO is correlated with orders NG and AMSt; (iii) order AN is correlated with orders DN, N1N. Orders SVO and· VOS are less strongly correlated with order of other elements than VSO and SOV, but as it would seem that the most basic is for the verb to be initial or final and to be preceded or followed by O, orders VOS and SVO are closer as to correlations to order VSO than to order SOV.

It should be apparent that the data given in the table fit well with the generalizations above. This is true not only of this sample but also of different and larger samples that have been examined. A good example of the strength of the correlations in table 22 is offered by the contrast between Isthmus Zapotec, representing the type most widespread in Otomanguean, and Chichimec, so far the only language in the family with SOV order.

The following examples from Jacaltec (Jc) and from Yaqui (Yq) exemplify some of the differences between the two types, which we can consider as opposites:

(1)   V   S   O
sk'abnitoχ   *no' oχ*   *sti'*
opened   the coyote his-mouth
'the coyote opened his mouth'   [Jc]

(2)   S   O   V
itom usim   *huka tʃu'uta* *nu'uk*
our   children   this   dog   brought
'our children brought this dog'   [Yq]

(3)   Pr
         yul te⁷ ŋah
         in   the   house   [Jc]

(4)   *kari-po*
         house = in
         'in the house'   [Yq]

(5)   D   N   A
         hune⁷ no⁷   tʃeh saχ⁷iŋ
         a   classifier horse white
         'a white horse'   [Jc]

(6)   *ime⁷e bʷere haamutʃim*
         these big   women   [Yq]

(7)   N   G
         ʃtʃeh   hinman
         his-horse my-father
         'my father's horse'   [Jc]

(8)   G   N
         peota   atʃai
         Peter-'s father
         'Peter's father'   [Yq]

(9)   A   M   St
         qa⁷   itʃam hin sataχ   naχ   pel
         more old   in-front-of classifier Peter
         'I am older than Peter'   [Jc]

(10)   St   M   A
       in   hamut em   maarata   beppa tutu⁷uli
       this woman your daughter over pretty
       'this woman is prettier than your daughter'   [Yq]

From the point of view of linguistic families, most variation is found in the order of subject, verb and object. There are Mayan languages, Chortí for instance, that have SVO order (although this may be due to Spanish influence); within Uto-Aztecan, Huasteca Nahuatl has VSO order. Some languages have more than one basic order, e.g. Chiquihuitlan Mazatec, which has VSO and SVO. In other cases the difference in order may depend on certain features of the clause, as in Tlapanec, where if the subject is animate (as is always the case with Tlapanec transitive verbs) and the object is inanimate the order is VOS, but when both are animate the order is VSO or SVO.

Mesoamerican languages also fit other correlations that have been established for the order of elements, e.g. inflected auxiliaries precede main verbs in prepositional languages but follow them in postpositional ones. On the other hand, deviations that have been found are exceptional, e.g. the fact that in some Otomanguean languages yes/no questions are marked by a final particle, when it is the case that in prepositional languages the expected correlation would be with interrogative clauses marked at the beginning.

7.2 **Totonac-Tepehua**

Totonac will be the only language dealt with in this section because no syntactic information is available for languages of the Tepehuan branch.

An example of a Totonac verb in which five participants were marked was given in 5.1.3; the markers cross-refer to constituents that can potentially occur within the clause. The multiplicity of constituents which have to be marked in the verb, and are therefore nuclear constituents, is one of the most characteristic aspects of the language.

Clauses with actor (intransitive) or actor and patient (transitive) or actor, patient and beneficiary (bitransitive) may be considered basic in the sense that there are verbs that require the presence of these participants. There are, however, other participants that may be marked within the verb, i.e.

Association (or accompaniment).

Location.

Instrument (with verbs that refer to speaking or thinking it is 'theme', i.e. 'speak about').

Interest (the person to whose advantage or disadvantage the action is carried on).

Source (the person from whom something is acquired).

Destination (the person toward whom there is some movement performed).

There are restrictions as to which of these participants may co-occur. Thus, for example, when three of them are marked on a verb, two are selected necessarily from association, location and instrument. Also, not all of these participants may occur with a verb of any type of basic transitivity; source, for example, only occurs with transitive verbs that have meanings like 'buy', 'rent', 'steal'. Up to two of these participants may occur in a bitransitive verb, and up to three in an intransitive or in a transitive verb, so that if the additional participants are added to the participants that occur in clauses of the basic types of transitivity, there are eleven different types of clauses by number of participants. Example (11) illustrates an intransitive clause with location and interest as participants in addition to actor.

(11) *huiʔʃ   ki-lakɬ-to·ˈla-niˈʔ-jaʔ*   *kintʃahu*
you me=on=sit-on=against=you my=corn-cake
'you do me the bad turn of sitting on my corn cake'

This example shows an important aspect in the marking of participants, namely that only for two of them (and this is the upper limit) is the specific grammatical person indicated, the actor (*-ja*) and the damaged participant (*ki-*). However, if the verb were transitive, the prefix *ki-* would be ambiguous because it could represent the patient or the damaged participant, the suffix *-ni·* indicating only that there is a participant to whose detriment the action is carried out; it does not by itself indicate the grammatical person of the participant.

To the combinations of participants mentioned an agent can be added. In (12) there is agent (*ʃata·ta*), actor (*xwan*), patient (*iʔʃtiʔjaʔt*) and source (*wan riko*).

(12) *wan   ʃata·ta   ma·-mak-tama·wa-ni·-ɬ*
the   father   causative=from=he-buy-it=causative=preterite
xwan   iʔʃtiʔjaʔt   wan   riko
John   his-land   the   rich-one
'the father made John buy the land from the rich person'

Further clause varieties are derived by marking the actor, example (13), or the agent as indefinite, in which case the respective participant cannot be represented by a constituent at the clause level.

(13) *wan   tʃiʔʃkuˈ   ki-ma·-te·-ni·-niʔn*
the   man   me=causative=he-bring-it=causative=indefinite-
actor
'the man has me brought' (or: 'the man makes
someone bring me')

This type of clause is one of the equivalents of a passive clause (without actor or agent expressed) in Totonac, there being no distinct passive class in the language. In reflexive clauses, the verb is marked both for a definite actor and for indefinite actor; since the marking of definite actor is the same as that of patient, these clauses are ambiguous; in (14), if the additional constituent that means 'he alone' were not present, the clause could also mean 'they killed him'.

(14) *makni·-ka*   *iʔʃaʔkstu*
he-killed-him=indefinite-actor   he-alone
'he killed himself'

In table 22 variable order is indicated for Totonac, and as the nouns for subject and object are not morphologically marked in many cases ambiguity results as to which constituent is actor and which patient. This ambiguity is often eliminated by the use of two coordinate clauses with the same verb (or synonymous ones) in both clauses, but with one of them marked for indefinite actor, as in (15).

(15) *aˀkli·sta·n   wani   wan   ʃatsi·ˀt,*
      later   she(he)-said-it-him(her)   the   mother,
      wani-kan   wan   rej . . .
      said-it = indefinite-actor   one   king . . .
      'later the mother said to him, it was said to the king . . .' (i.e. 'later the mother said to the king . . .')

In (15) the roles of the participants are ambiguous in the first clause even if *rej* 'king' is added, but in the second clause the marker of indefinite actor indicates unambiguously that *rej* is patient, and consequently *wan ʃatsi·ˀt* 'the mother' has to be interpreted as actor in the first clause.

Identification, location and quality are expressed through a copulative clause (possession by a transitive clause), although when tense is present no copula occurs; these are the only instances of verbless clauses in Totonac.

Yes/no questions are marked by an initial particle.

Clause constituents other than the verb have almost no marking. There are some prepositions (only one of native origin, others being borrowings from Spanish), but most constituents of manner, location, time and instrument are manifested by nominal or adverbial elements without any special marking.

Markers of coordination occur on the level of clause constituents as well as between clauses; in fact most coordinate clauses are linked by a particle, of which several have been borrowed from Spanish.

Subordinate clauses, including relative clauses, are introduced by particles without further changes with respect to a main clause, but in some relative clauses there are changes of order that separate constituents; compare *iˀʃta·ˀtin maria* her-brother Mary 'Mary's brother' with the position of the relative pronoun *aˀnti·* and the noun *iˀʃtakwi·ni* in (16).

(16) *ʃlaˀ   qaɬatin   oˀpʃaˀ   aˀnti· tu·ˀ   iˀkpa·staka   iˀʃtakwi·ni*
      he   one   young-man   who   not   I - remember-it his-name
      'he is a young man whose name I don't remember'

Comparisons are constructed using clauses in which the verb has a special marking and the term of comparison is linked by a particle. In (17), a comparison of superiority, the prefix *ɬaq-* 'more' is obligatory as is *-ʃa·-*, a morpheme that in nominal constructions indicates inherent possession or definiteness.

(17)   *pi·tilu*   *ɬaq-ʃa·-kstuka·*   *la·*   *pa·pilu*
           Peter   more = X = intelligent   than   Paul
           'Peter is more intelligent than Paul'

7.3 Uto-Aztecan

It can be inferred from the morphological characterization of the Classical Nahuatl verb in 5.1.2 that clauses in Nahuatl languages are similar to those in Totonac with regard to nuclear participants, although in Classical Nahuatl these are restricted to agent, actor, patient and beneficiary. In addition, an example was given showing the marking for indefinite actor and patient in a causative transitive clause (in a simple transitive clause, patient and beneficiary can be marked as indefinite). This marking of an indefinite participant is not found in Yaqui, although this language is similar to Nahuatl, but with differences deriving from two types of morphological structure. In Nahuatl the marking is concentrated in the verb, which includes cross-references to participants and can constitute a formally complete clause by itself; in Yaqui the verb can be marked as indirective (i.e. cross-referred to a beneficiary) or as causative, but it has no person inflection, so that even if constituents that represent participants may be omitted when specified in a wider context, they are nonetheless obligatory to constitute a formally complete clause. These constituents themselves are marked in many functions, cf. (18) and (19):

(18)   *ni-mit̲s-mamaki-lti-li-s*   *tewal*   *in*   *kali*
           I = you = sell = causative = indirective = future   you   the   house
           prahedes
           Praxedes
           'I will make you sell the house for Praxedes' [Pómaro Nahuatl]

(19)   *inepo*   *hu-ka*   *hamu-ta*   *batʃi-ta*
           I   this = dependent   woman = dependent   corn = dependent
           bʷaʔa-tua-k
           eat = causative = realized
           'I made the woman eat corn'   [Yaqui]

Classical Nahuatl has passive clauses but without an actor. When the active clause has two objects (patient and beneficiary), it is always the one representing the

beneficiary that is the subject of the passive clause; furthermore, the patient can be
incorporated into the verb; cf. (20) and (21):

(20)   *ni-mak-o·*   *in*   *a·mat͜l*
         I = give = passive   the   paper
         'I am given the paper'

(21)   *ni-ʃotʃi-mak-o·*
         I = flower = give = passive
         'I am given flowers'

In addition a suffix *-lo* marks the indefinite actor (in either transitive or intransitive
clauses); this suffix is also found in some modern languages such as Texcoco
Nahuatl, but the usual way to express indefinite actor in modern Nahuatl languages
is to use a reflexive marker on the verb or by use of the third person plural inflection,
e.g.

(22)   *mjentras*   *mo-aorkaruhtataja*   *in*   *kujol*
         meanwhile   (he) = reflexive = was-strangling   the   coyote
         'meanwhile the coyote was being strangled' [Pómaro Nahuatl]

In Yaqui, on the other hand, the actor can be expressed in a passive clause. The
clause in (23) is active, with the corresponding passive given in (24). Note that the
noun referring to the actor is marked by two suffixes in the passive clause, one that
indicates dependency and the other instrument. ('Realized' is a tense that indicates
action in the past, or result of past action that persists in the present.)

(23)   *wepul*   *oʔoo*   *hu-ka*   *maso-ta*   *meʔa-k*
         one   man   this = dependent   deer = dependent   killed = realized
         'one man killed the deer'

(24)   *hu*   *maaso*   *wepul*   *oʔoo-ta-e*   *meʔe-wa-k*
         this deer   one   man = dependent = with   kill = passive = realized
         'this deer was killed by a man'

Clauses with a noun or an adjective as predicate correspond to the expression of
identification or quality in both Nahuatl and Yaqui. Again, they differ in that nouns
and adjectives are inflected for person in Nahuatl but not in Yaqui. In Nahuatl
these meanings can be also expressed using a copula verb, in which case the noun or
adjective is not inflected; the same copula is used in existential and locative clauses.

Nahuatl languages and Yaqui both have transitive clauses indicating possession.
In addition, Yaqui has a type of clause, (25), in which the possessed item occurs as a

predicate with a tense – aspect inflection, and whenever there is an attributive adjective this is marked for dependency as if it were in agreement with an object noun.

(25)   *inepo   tu⁹i-k   kare-k*
           they   good = dependent   house = realized
           'they have a good house'

In Nahuatl and Yaqui yes/no questions are marked by intonation; an initial particle may occur too but it is not obligatory.

Constituent questions in Yaqui are marked optionally by the same introductory particle that occurs in yes/no questions, and usually by a suffix attached to an indefinite phrase, e.g.

(26)   *haisa*   *hita*   *kari-sa*   *wetʃek*
           interrogative   some   house = interrogative   fell
           'which house fell down?'

In Nahuatl languages, when the questioned constituent depends on a postposition or on a preposition, the interrogative word usually occurs in second position, preceded by the preposition or postposition; in some languages, however, they may also occur in reverse order, e.g. Tetelcingo Nahuatl: *i-ka ƫi* its = with what 'with what', *ki i-ka* who his = with 'with whom?' (in other constructions *ika* is a postposition).

We have already seen that nuclear constituents other than the verb are not marked in Nahuatl languages, but that in Yaqui the object in a transitive clause, (23), as well as the two objects in a causative clause, (19), and the attribute in a possessive clause, (25), are marked with the suffix of dependency; furthermore, this marking extends in many cases to the attributes of the nuclei of these constituents. Number is an obligatory category in Yaqui, and number agreement both on constituent and clause level is a further way in which constituency is marked. Example (24) demonstrates that with certain suffixes nouns are also marked for dependency, so they are always marked when in construction with postpositions. In Nahuatl languages peripheral constituents may be marked by inflected prepositions or by suffixes, and some elements (nouns) occur in both constructions as in these examples from Huasteca Nahuatl: *i-teno nopa altepeƫ* its = edge that town 'at the edge of that town', *no-kal-teno* my = house = edge 'outside my house'.

Clauses and clause constituents can be conjoined in modern Nahuatl languages and Yaqui through coordinating particles some of which are borrowed from Spanish. The second member of a coordination may appear in reduced form, e.g.

(27) *maria kaa jepsak ta peo ala*
   Mary not arrived but Peter X
   'Mary did not arrive but Peter did'   [Yaqui]

The final word in this example is a particle which only occurs in this type of adversative coordination. In Classical Nahuatl coordination was generally unmarked, there being only one true coordinating particle which, according to context, could have additive, alternative or adversative meaning; constructions with reduced clauses, as in (27), do not seem to have been possible.

In modern Nahuatl languages subordinate clauses which are subjects or objects have, in general, no subordinating particle, and if one is used it is *ke*, borrowed from Spanish. Adverbial subordinate clauses are introduced by particles and undergo no internal changes, and the semantic distinctions made by different particles closely parallel those found in Spanish from which some of these particles have been borrowed. Relative clauses are introduced by relative words; there are changes in the order of elements when the noun that is relativized depends on a preposition-like noun; this occurs either preceding or following the relative word, cf.

(28)
ni matʃete i-ka tḷen kimikti nopa kowatḷ ...
the machete its = with which he-killed-it that snake ...
'the machete with which he killed that snake ...'   [Huasteca Nahuatl]

(29) *nopa tsikatḷ tlen i-pan tiatḷiseh* ...
   that jug which its = place we-will-drink ...
   'that jug from which we will drink ...'   [Huasteca Nahuatl]

Classical Nahuatl differs considerably from modern Nahuatl languages. Most subordinate clauses are not marked by subordinating particles, but are simply juxtaposed; adverbs may render the meaning of the subordinate clause more precise although a good deal of ambiguity frequently remains. In fact in many cases the equivalents to subordinate clauses are coordinate ones. On the other hand, Classical Nahuatl (cf. 5.1.2) has a much more productive mechanism for building verbal nouns which can be used in constructions equivalent to subordinate clauses.

Yaqui subordinate clauses may be marked by a suffix in the verb or by an introductory particle, or by both simultaneously; in some of the clauses marked by a suffix, the subject noun or the verb is marked for dependency, e.g.

(30) *empo lottila-ta-kai   kaa jiʔi-ne*
   you tired = dependent = subordinator not dance-expected
   'being tired you will not dance'

Relative clauses in Yaqui are not introduced by relative words but are marked in the verb by a relative suffix which is different depending on whether the relativized noun is subject, (31), or has another function, (32), in the relative clause.

(31)   *itepo   tʃu'u-ta   hipwe kaa hihiibʷa-m-ta*
         we   dog=dependent have   not   eat=relative=dependent
        'we have a dog that does not eat'

(32)   *gwaʔa kari   βem   ama   hoʔak-aʔu   niweela*
        that   house their there live=relative old
        'the house over there in which they live is old'

Note that in (31) the verb of the relative clause is marked for dependency, and that in (32) the subject of the relative clause is in possessive form (*βem* 'their') – had it been a noun instead of a pronoun it would have been marked as dependent; these differences depend on the function of the noun in both clauses. The marking for dependency in the verb, as well as the use of possessive forms as subjects, make these clauses of a participial type. Finally, in (32), although the relativized constituent is locative, no locative suffix occurs, as it would in a main clause (cf. (4)).

Classical Nahuatl does not have a special construction for expressing comparison, a meaning that is given using coordinated clauses, e.g.

(33)   *ok   atʃi   nitʃika·wak   in   aʔmo   natʃiwki   teʔwa·tɬ*
        still very I-am-strong X   not   not-are-strong you
        'I am stronger than you'

In modern Nahuatl languages comparative constructions are calques from Spanish, as in (34): *mas* is a loanword and *tɬen* (a relative particle) is a calque based on the homonymy of Spanish *que* 'that, who' and 'than'; compared with the constructions of Classical Nahuatl, the rule that the verb cannot occur in the term of comparison is a calque from the Spanish pattern.

(34)   *jahaja tekiti   mas   tɬen   wan*
        he   works more than John
        'he works more than John'   [Huasteca Nahuatl]

An example of a Yaqui comparative construction was given in (10); it is a single clause and the term of comparison is a postpositional constituent (in a comparison of equality the postposition would be *benasi* 'like').

No reference has so far been made to Huichol because at each point it has been similar to Nahuatl or Yaqui, but it does show some unusual contrasts in subordinate temporal clauses. They are marked by suffixes in the verb, and the suffix varies according to whether or not the subject of the subordinate clause and the subject of the main clause refer to the same individual, whether the event in the subordinate clause is simultaneous or previous or resultant in relation to the event referred to in the main clause, and whether the event in the subordinate clause is factual or potential.

7.4 Mixe-Zoque

Zoquean languages again show the possibility of four nuclear participants in a clause: agent, actor, patient and beneficiary. The beneficiary may be semantically equivalent to the beneficiary in English, but in constructions with third person subject and an object inflected for third person possessor, (35), the indirective suffix *-aʔj* indicates that the possessor of the object (*ihatuŋ* 'his father') is not the person referred to by the subject (*ʃiwan* 'John') but the one referred to by the beneficiary (*pablo* 'Paul') which could not have been expressed in the clause.

(35)   *heʔm   ʃiwan   ijoʃpadaʔjpa   pablo   ihatuŋ*
         the   John   he-helps-him   Paul   his-father
         'John helps Paul's father'   [Sierra Popoluca]

In some Mixean languages, instead of beneficiary as nuclear participant, instrument is found; the clause in (36) contains an agent, an actor, a patient and an instrument.

(36)
əht̲s̲   paat   matsjet   n-tuk-t̲s̲-pooypj   *ha   hɔɔʔj*
I   Peter   machete   I-him = causative = instrument = cut   the   person
'I made Peter cut the person with the machete'   [Tlahuitoltepec Mixe]

Like Nahuatl and Totonac, Mixe-Zoque languages have clauses with indefinite actor (if transitive or intransitive) or agent (if transitive causative) marked differently according to whether the verb is transitive or intransitive. As in the other languages these clauses are the equivalents of passive ones. As in Totonac, clauses with indefinite actor are found frequently in Sierra Popoluca so as to avoid the ambiguity that can arise owing to the variable order of subject and object, and of their lack of morphological marking. In (37) the first clause has an intransitive verb and specifies the actor, while the second has the same verb as transitive, but with indefinite actor inflection, and it specifies the patient.

(37)   *koʔt̲s̲-o·j*   *'peto·h,   koʔt̲s̲-'ta·*   *iwan*
         (he) = hit = intransitive   Peter,   hit = indefinite-actor   John
         'Peter did hitting, John was hit' (i.e. 'Peter hit John')

Reflexive clauses are marked as such in the verb, but in Sierra Popoluca as in Totonac (cf. (14)) the verb is also inflected for indefinite actor.

Emphasis on an adverbial constituent can be marked not only by its initial position but also by the use of a verb inflected for secondary mode (also called conjunct mode). This construction is found in Mixean languages; (38) and (39) give a neutral clause and the corresponding emphatic one.

(38) *mim-p*   *tu·*   *'migik*
      (it) = come = continuative-primary   rain   hard
      'it's raining hard'   [Sayula Popoluca]

(39) *'migik   i-mi⁹n*   *tu·*
      hard   it = come = (continuative-secondary)   rain
      'it's raining *hard*'   [Sayula Popoluca]

It can be seen in these examples that primary and secondary modes differ in the prefixes that indicate person and in the suffixes that indicate tense. Furthermore, secondary mode also occurs in interrogative clauses and in certain subordinate ones.

Locative clauses may be verbal, with an intransitive verb, as in Copainalá Zoque, or verbless, as in (40), in which the predicate is an adverb.

(40) *tʃa   i·t   kiʃitj*
      here   I   above
      'here I am above'   [Coatlan Mixe]

In Copainalá Zoque there is a single verb used in both locational and existential clauses. With a prefix that indicates association (cf. 6.1.4) it is also used in possessive clauses, e.g.

(41) *nə-ʔiht-u-ma-ha*   *teʔtumin*
      (you-it) = associative = exist = perfective = still   the-money
      [the prefix that indicates subject and associate is a nasal consonant
      that is lost before a following nasal]
      'do you still have the money?'

Other languages have different ways of expressing possession. In Sierra Popoluca, (42), the predicate is a noun inflected for person in the same way as an intransitive verb, and it also has a suffix meaning possession; this type of construction is also found in Chimalapa Zoque, but here possession may also be expressed by a verbless clause, (43), or by a clause containing the verb meaning existence, (44).

(42) *ma·tik   a-hawaŋ-iˀj*
      yesterday I = fever = possessive
      'yesterday I had fever'

(43) *tumista   te·ˀn   nuˀu*
      one-only this-my   dog
      'I have a dog'

(44) *teˀp   tehi   tumi kaˀj   nuˀu*
      this there-is one of-that dog
      'he has a dog'

For identification and attribution of quality, Mixe-Zoque languages have a predicate filled by a noun or an adjective with person inflection; in Sierra Popoluca personal pronouns may have person inflection too, as in dạa-'*he* not I = he 'I am not he' (the inflected pronoun is -'*he*).

Yes/no questions are marked by intonational contour in Sayula Popoluca, by a verb suffix in Copainalá Zoque, and by an optional initial particle and a final particle in Mixe from El Paraíso. In Mixe languages constituent questions have the verb in secondary mode when the questioned element is adverbial (time, location, manner); in Sayula Popoluca when the questioned element is subject or object the verb is in primary mode, but in Tlahuitoltepec Mixe it may be in primary or secondary mode, the difference probably being one of emphasis.

Among nuclear constituents in Zoquean languages, the subject noun in transitive and causative clauses has nominative–genitive inflection (cf. 6.3.3). Peripheral constituents in a language like Copainalá Zoque are in general marked by case inflection in nouns (cf. 6.3.3), but in other Zoquean languages only locative constituents are marked by suffixes, otherwise they either have no marking at all or are prepositional phrases with prepositions borrowed from Spanish.

Mixe-Zoque languages have verbal phrases with auxiliary verbs. The details change from language to language, but a common pattern is to have an auxiliary with tense–aspect inflection followed by a main verb with person inflection; this order is found in Chimalapa Zoque when the auxiliary is modal or aspectual, but in other cases the order is main verb plus auxiliary. In languages that have primary and secondary modes, such as Sayula Popoluca, the auxiliary is in primary mode and the main verb in secondary mode, (45):

(45)
it-p   *i-niʃ-'waˀn*
have-to = continuative-primary   he-secondary = go = future-secondary
'he has to go'

Auxiliary verbs in Mixe-Zoque languages have such meanings as 'be able', 'have to', 'finish', 'come', 'go', 'let's', 'future aspect', 'negative'.

In most of these languages coordinating particles have been borrowed from Spanish, but in spite of that, coordination through mere juxtaposition (with different meanings according to context) is still very common. Nevertheless, Mixe from El Paraíso has two coordinating particles; one links like members grammatically and semantically, (46), the other links unlike members, (47):

(46)   fwan   ʔets   pedro
         John   and   Peter

(47)   tuʔug   jeʔedịhk   ʔe·   tuʔug   toʔoʃhạʔaj
         a   man   and   a   woman

In this language, as in Sayula Popoluca, the second member of a coordination may appear in reduced form through the ellipsis of the elements duplicating those in the first member; this type of construction is rarely found in Mesoamerican languages. Example (48) is from Sayula Popoluca.

(48)   tʃiʔt   inmaʹtʃi·ti   mit   i·   tinʹheʔ
         you-take-out   your-machete   and   I   mine
         'you take out your machete and I'll take out mine'

Subordinate clauses may be marked by verbal affixes and/or subordinating initial particles or by verbal mode. Only in Mixean languages are particles found in this function; in Zoquean languages, temporal and locative clauses mark the verb with a suffix, sometimes accompanied by a subordinating particle borrowed from Spanish; other subordinate clauses are marked by an initial particle. Example (49) contains a temporal clause with a subordinating affix.

(49)   ʔi   ŋ-gen-u-ʔk-amis,
         and   you-it = perfective = temporal-subordinator = already,
         mimbamis   ntsahku   ʔis   ndịhkaŋi
         you-will-come   you-to-leave-it   my   house-at
         'and when you have seen it, you are to come and leave it at my
         house'   [Copainalá Zoque]

In (50) the verb of the subordinate clause is inflected for secondary mode.

(50)
i·ts   tiniʃp   kamʹniʔk   ti-ʃpakwo-p
I   am-going   to-the-field   I-secondary = weed = future-secondary
mo·ʹkwahat
corn

'I am going to the field to weed the corn'   [Sayula Popoluca]

In Sayula Popoluca, location, time and manner clauses also have the verb inflected for secondary mode, and those of location and manner have in addition an obligatory subordinating particle, e.g.

(51)   *a'je   kojw   man   i-'tsi·na   higante*
        that   arrived   where   he-secondary   giant
        'that one arrived where the giant lives'

Conditional, causal and objective clauses are also introduced by a particle, but the mode of the verb depends on the internal structure of the clause, in the same way as if it were acting as the main clause.

In Zoquean languages, relative clauses are participial. In (52) the verb is marked as subordinate by -*aj*, a suffix which is also used to turn some non-verbal forms into noun attributes.

(52)   *a'je   'hajaw   heme   nuʃ-amp-aj*
        that   man   who   go = future = subordinator
        'that man who will go'   [Sayula Popoluca]

This type of construction is found in Copainalá Zoque; in addition, when the relative lacks an antecedent it is marked by the article, and if the relative clause is the subject of a transitive verb, the verb of the relative clause is marked with the nominative–genitive case as though it were a noun. In Mixean languages the verb of a relative clause has no marking; relative clauses as subjects or objects are introduced by relative words, other relative clauses being simply juxtaposed.

In Chimalapa Zoque, comparison is expressed by constructions which are calques from Spanish patterns. In Tlahuitoltepec Mixe, comparison of superiority is rendered by two clauses, one asserting the quality for the item compared, the other negating it for the term of comparison, e.g.

(53)   *jonj   ji⁷   ka⁷ap   its   hatini⁷in   njonj*
        tall   is   not   I   as-much   I-tall
        'he is taller than I am'

7.5 Tarascan

Tarascan is similar to languages already discussed with regard to the number of participants that can occur within the clause nuclei. In (54) the verb is inherently transitive so that it has an implied patient; the suffix -*tʃə* (first or second person object) indicates that the first person referred to by the suffix *-reni* (first person object, second person subject) is a beneficiary, and the suffix *-ku* indicates that there is a second beneficiary.

(54)   '*xwa-ku-tʃə-reni*
         'bring it to me for her!'

As in Mixe-Zoque languages, the beneficiary may refer to a possessor of the object which is not the person referred to by the subject.

Location is in many cases a nuclear constituent. In (55) the suffix *-kʰu* (relative to the arm or hand) is a locative suffix which cross-refers to the noun inflected for locative.

(55)   '*xi   a'paʈkʰu   kʰani   kwin'kwisɨ-ʈu*
         I   burned-   myself elbow = locative
         'I burned myself on the elbow'

In passive clauses no actor can be expressed; moreover, as in Classical Nahuatl, when the active clause has patient and beneficiary, it is the latter that becomes the subject of the passive.

Nouns, adjectives, pronouns and adverbs can be verbalized in Tarascan, and therefore clauses with meaning of identification, quality, location or possession are verbal. In (56) the demonstrative *i'ma*–'that, he, she, it' which appears under the shape *i'me* – is verbalized by the suffix *-e-* and inflected for third person singular (*-thi*).

(56)   *i'me-e-thi*   '*waʈi*
         that = verbalizer = she   woman
         'that is the woman'

Yes/no questions and constituent questions have the verb inflected for clarificational mode (see examples in 6.1.1); yes/no questions are also marked by a suffix.

Most nuclear and peripheral constituents may have a noun or adjective with case inflection (cf. (55)). In some cases, the constituent may include a preposition (borrowed from Spanish) or one of two adverbs that are equivalent to postpositions.

There are two types of verbal phrases with auxiliaries. One is like the English construction with the verb *be* plus a past participle, and also has passive meaning. The other type of verbal phrase consists of an infinitive followed by the verb 'be' or by the auxiliary *ʃa-* 'be' with full inflection; as can be seen in (57), these constructions have progressive meaning.

(57)   '*xi*   *tʰiʼre-ni*   *ʃa-p-kʰa-ni*
              I   eat = infinitive   be = perfect = indicative
              'I have been eating'

The chief mechanism of subordination is through participial and infinitival constructions. There are two active and two passive participles; the construction with the active participle or with the infinitive may take a direct object as in (58) (note that the first infinitive is used as a main verb with value of narrative tense; cf. 6.1.1).

(58)   '*ka*   *siʼeeratsa*   '*xura-ni*   *intsʼpʰekwaɽe-ni*
              and   people-from-the-Sierra   come = infinitive   sell = infinitive
              sununta
              blanket
              'and people from the Sierra come to sell blankets'

The participles and the infinitive can be used as attributes of nouns (being equivalent to relative clauses) or as head nouns inflected for case, or as modal or temporal modifiers. In (59) the passive participle is attributive to a noun and has accusative inflection.

(59)
xi   *paʃkani*   *tsikaku-kata-ni*   *xakʰi-ni*
I   carried   fold = passive-participle = accusative   hand = accusative
'I carried my hand folded'

There are relative clauses introduced by a relative pronoun or a relative adverb and with the verbs inflected for subjunctive mode. 'Relative adverb' refers to the morphological formation since these forms are adverbs with the same relative marker that occurs in relative pronouns, although as to function, the clauses introduced by these adverbs may be objects or have temporal, locative, causal or consecutive value.

Comparison is expressed by simple clauses in which the verb expressing the dimension of comparison has a comparative suffix; in (60) the term of comparison is a pronominal constituent inflected for accusative case (the comparative suffix is -*ku*-).

(60)   *xi*   *aʃpekuʃkani*   *ima-ni*
              I   I-am-better-than   he = accusative
              'I am better than him'

7.6 Tequistlatec-Jicaque

As there is no grammatical information on Jicaque and the two Tequistlatecan languages are syntactically rather similar, the discussion here will focus on Coastal Chontal.

Verbal clauses may have up to three participants: actor, patient and beneficiary, of which only one is marked in the verb (Highland Chontal marks actor and patient or beneficiary). As in Tarascan and Zoquean languages, in many cases beneficiary represents the possessor of the patient, and in clauses with a certain class of verbs there is a beneficiary but no patient (in (61) the beneficiary is *-nga* 'us').

(61)   *'kuʃ'ki-nga   laɬpitʃʼaleʔ*
         got-sour = us   our clothes
         'our clothes got sour on us'

Reflexive clauses are marked in the verb which lacks person inflection; the stem of the reflexive verb may be both transitive and intransitive, e.g.

(62)   *'wʔap-osi   iṭu'waʔ*
         walked = reflexive   himself
         'he walked all by himself'

There are suffixes that mark a verb as passive, but in the clauses in which these occur no actor can be expressed.

A construction which is similar to those Zoquean and Totonac constructions that avoid ambiguity as to the function of the constituents is also found in Coastal Chontal, but here it is·the beneficiary and patient functions that are differentiated. In (63), the first clause has a verb meaning 'give' which takes a single object (patient), while in the second clause the verb meaning 'give' takes two objects, a beneficiary (in this case marked by zero in the verb, although other persons would be overtly marked) and a patient which is implied by the verb, although not marked, and potentially occurring as constituent.

(63)
'ku-pa   el'meḽu,   paj-pa   li'wʔa
give = punctual = (it)   the-money,   give = punctual = (him)   his-son
'he gave the money, he gave it to his son' (i.e. 'he gave the money to his son')

There are four types of verbless clauses: locative, identificational, possessive and qualitative. Locative clauses obligatorily have two constituents, a nominal expression and a locative particle or a noun with locative inflection, e.g.

(64)   *'ma-jɲega*   *lakuɬwe*
               locative = cornfield   the-man
               'the men are in the cornfield'

Identificational clauses obligatorily consist of two nouns or noun phrases, and optionally of a third nominal constituent which specifies the owner of the item identified, e.g.

(65)   *la'kanʔo*   *'ɬʔe* *l-i-'xuṭi*
               the-woman   it   the = her = waterjug
               'that is the woman's waterjug'

Possessive clauses, which indicate possession in a very broad sense, have an obligatory constituent represented by a noun inflected for possession (but without locative or definite inflection; cf. *l-i-'xuṭi* in (65)) and an optional nominal constituent, e.g.

(66)   *i-puʃki*   *'lubia*
               her = health   Lubia
               'Lubia has health' (i.e. 'Lubia is well')

Quality clauses also have two nominal constituents, although one belongs to a subclass of nouns which, uninflected, are used to indicate quality. As can be seen in (67), the normal English translation has a very different structure; in other cases the English translation of the predicative noun would be, for example, 'is made of palm' or 'has fever'. A more literal translation, taking into account that Coastal Chontal has no separate class of adjectives, would be 'is palmish', 'is feverish', 'is crowish'.

(67)   *'kope* *'kope* *liw'xax*
               crow   crow   his-head
               'his hair is very black'

Note here that the predicate noun is reduplicated to indicate intensity.

Yes/no questions are marked by intonation and optionally by a particle, the same particle that is used in constituent questions for subject, object or indirect object; these clauses are negated by the same particle that is used in imperative and in subordinate clauses.

A noun as subject or object has to be marked as definite. Among peripheral constituents only those with locative meaning may be marked with locative inflection, although this is not always so; other constituents have no marking, e.g.

(68)   *'mana'pola* *'puro* *e'paɬma*
               they = died   just   fever
               'they died just from fever'

With the exception of those built by the verb that means 'make' plus a Spanish infinitive (a mechanism for incorporating Spanish verbs in the language), there are no verbal phrases.

Constituents of the clause and clauses may be linked by coordinating particles; in Coastal Chontal some of these particles are native, but in Highland Chontal all particles with this function are borrowings from Spanish.

In Coastal Chontal, subordinate clauses, including relative clauses, are introduced by particles and have a different negation from main clauses. In Highland Chontal, objective clauses, purpose and manner have no subordinating particle, other subordinate clauses being marked with particles borrowed from Spanish. Relative clauses are marked only in the verb, one of the markers being the definite prefix which is also prefixed to nouns, e.g.

(69)   *kal* *ʃans* *ł-ipamma*   *isna*
         the man   the = he-went-out   drunk
         'the man who went out was drunk'   [Highland Chontal]

There are special comparative patterns which appear to be calques from Spanish.

SOURCES

MIXE-ZOQUE. *Mixe*: (*Coatlan*) Hoogshagen 1974; (*El Paraíso*) Van Haitsma and Van Haitsma 1976; (*Tlahuitoltepec*) Lyon, D. 1967, 1980, Lyon, S. 1967. *Popoluca*: (*Sayula*) Clark 1962; (*Sierra*) Lind 1964, Elson 1960, 1967. *Zoque*: (*Chimalapa*) Knudson 1980; (*Copainalá*) Wonderly 1951c, 1952b; (*Ostuacan*) Engel and Longacre 1963. TARASCAN: Foster 1969, Wares 1974. TEQUISTLATEC-JICAQUE: (*Coastal Chontal*) Waterhouse 1962, 1967; (*Highland Chontal*) Turner 1967b, 1968a, b, Waterhouse 1980. TOTONAC-TEPEHUA: (*Northern Totonac*) McQuown 1940, Reid et al. 1968. UTO-AZTECAN. *Huichol*: Grimes, J. 1964. *Nahuatl*: (*Classical*) Andrews, J. 1975; (*Huasteca*) Beller 1979; (*Pómaro*) Robinson and Sischo 1969; (*Tetelcingo*) Tuggy 1979; (*Texcoco*) Lastra de Suárez 1980a. *Yaqui*: Lindenfeld 1973.

FURTHER READING

Any one of the sources quoted above inevitably gives more information than has been possible in this chapter, but in general the descriptions are rather sketchy. Below only some general works and those of a reasonable breadth are indicated.

Typological surveys of the area are Escalante 1975, Kaufman 1974a, Pickett 1978. The volumes of the *Archivo de Lenguas Indigenas de México* (the first two volumes issued as *Archivo de Lenguas Indigenas del Estado de Oaxaca*) exemplify basic syntactic patterns through c. 900 sentences (the same sentences for all languages) with morpheme-by-morpheme as well as with free translation; ten volumes have been published, see Daly 1977, Hollenbach and Hollenbach 1975, Jamieson, A. and Tejeda 1978, Knudson 1980, Lastra de Suárez 1980b, Lyon, D. 1980, Mock 1977, Pickett 1974, Rupp 1980, Waterhouse 1980. Langacker 1977 surveys the entire Uto-Aztecan family typologically and serves as background for the more detailed descriptions of Nahuatl languages included in Langacker 1979. For different descriptive approaches to these languages see Law 1966, Pittman 1954. For Classical Nahuatl Andrews, J. 1975 deals systematically with syntax. Lindenfeld 1973 is a detailed and clear presentation of the basic structures of Yaqui. Reid et al. 1968 offer a description of Totonac that pays much attention to number of participants in main clauses and to coordinate and subordinate clauses. Waterhouse 1962 on Coastal Chontal deals in considerable detail with main clauses, but subordinate clauses are exemplified rather than described.

The reader should consult some of the sources given for Mixe languages where the analyses make a distinction between subject oriented and object oriented clauses, a contrast that does not seem to belong to the level of clause but rather to person marking in the verb; these languages show traces of ergativity but the patterns appear rather blurred. The presentation in this chapter is based on a reinterpretation of these analyses that drastically reduces the types of clauses.

8

Syntax II

8.1 Mayan

This section will focus mainly on two languages – Jacaltec and Tzotzil – with occasional references to other languages.

Nuclear participants, namely actor, patient and beneficiary, are the usual forms. The latter may occur in a language like Chamula Tzotzil, but only in clauses that also have a patient, and, as in Zoquean languages or Coastal Chontal, it may refer to the possessor of the patient.

An agent can occur in Jacaltec clauses, although the causative construction includes the verb that means 'make', with agent as subject and actor as object, and a second verb without either person or tense inflection, marked by a special suffix. When this verb is transitive, as in (70), the actor occurs as an indirect object (the form that manifests it is a preposition inflected for possessor). It should be noted that in spite of the fact that there are two verbs, these constructions are analysed as containing a single clause (compare the Huave causative construction in 8.3).

(70)   ṣ-*a*ʔ   *iχa*ʔ   *i*ṣ   *ja*ʔ   *taw-et*
          (she) = past = make   carry   she   her-water   your = to
          'she made you carry her water'

Passive clauses may have a constituent indicating the actor; this constituent contains a preposition (or prepositional phrase) inflected for person, and is formally identical to the constituent that indicates cause. In (71) the form indicates the actor in a passive clause, but in (72) the cause in an intransitive active clause.

(71)   *i-ʔak*ʔ-*ba-t*   *j-u*ʔ*un*   *ti*   *antse*
          he = give = indirective = passive   her = by   the   woman
          'it was given to him by the woman'   [Chamula Tzotzil]

(72)   *tej*   *it∫am*   *o∫vo*   *k-u*ʔ*un*
          there   they-died   three-people   my = by
          'there three people died because of me'   [Chamula Tzotzil]

117

As can be deduced from the translation of (71), the beneficiary is the subject in a clause that also has a patient.

Jacaltec has more than one suffix marking a verb as passive; with some of these suffixes the construction of the clause is like that of (71), but with one of them no actor is expressed or implied so it can be considered as an impersonal construction; with another suffix, an actor may or may not be expressed, although it is always implied, and the construction is equivalent to one with indefinite actor.

Reflexive clauses are marked by a reflexive pronoun as object.

As in other languages, emphasis in Jacaltec is expressed with the emphasized constituent in initial position, although in one type of clause the emphatic element is also represented in the neutral position by a pronoun; in another type of emphatic clause the constituent is preceded by a particle (obligatorily if the constituent is a pronoun), and if the constituent is the subject of a transitive clause the verb is marked with the suffix *-ni* (a marker that will be found in several constructions in what follows). Furthermore, if the subject is third person the verb will not be inflected for person, as in (73). This type of construction (like the one in (77)), in which, rather than the transitive features that the English translation would lead us to expect, we have intransitive features (most typically the actor not being expressed as a subject (as in (77)) is characteristic of ergative languages and is called the 'antipassive' construction. Like the passive construction it serves to put emphasis on a constituent that is not the actor.

(73)   *ha⁹   naχ   ṣ-maq'-ni   iṣ*
          emphasis he   past = hit = X   she
          'it is he who hit her'

With this example, it should be recalled that Jacaltec has VSO as neutral order.

Clauses that indicate identification or attribution of quality have a noun or an adjective (or stative verb) inflected for person of subject as predicate, but in Jacaltec, with some adjectives, an invariable copula is obligatory; with other adjectives the quality is permanent when the copula is present, but transitory when no copula is present. In spite of Jacaltec being a verb-initial language the copula occurs in second position within a clause.

There is another type of clause in Jacaltec in which a verb fills the second position. It consists of an adjective, (74), or a noun, the verb that means 'do' inflected for tense, and a clause in which the verb is inflected for person but not for tense; this type of clause is used as the normal way for expressing manner.

(74)   *b⁹eh   ṣ-u   hin-to   watut*
          direct   past = do   I = go   my-house
          'I went home straightaway'

Another class of copulative clause has an invariable copula in first position both in Tzotzil and Jacaltec; depending on the other constituents present, it may express existence, location or possession:

(75) *aj*   *w-autut*   *bʔetuʔ*
      there-is   my = house   there
      'my house is there'   [Jacaltec]

(76) *aj*   *hin-tʃeh*
      there-is   my = house
      'I have a house'   [Jacaltec]

(the difference in the shape of the person prefix in (75) and (76) is not significant, depending simply on whether the noun stem begins with a vowel or with a consonant).

Yes/no questions are marked by intonation in Jacaltec, by an interrogative initial particle in Quiché, and in Huixtan Tzotzil by the same particle that marks conditional clauses. In constituent questions, when the questioned constituent in Jacaltec is the subject of a transitive clause the verb is marked by the suffix -*ni* and lacks inflection for person of actor. Although the mechanism is very different, this type of marking in the verb when the subject of a transitive verb is questioned or emphasized (cf. (73)) may be considered to fulfil the same disambiguating function as to which constituent is subject or object as the use of two clauses in Totonac, Mixe-Zoque and Coastal Chontal (cf. (15), (37), (63)). The same marking is found in Jacaltec when the questioned constituent is instrument, but in addition the preposition marking instrument in a declarative clause is absent, and the actor of the declarative clause appears represented by the construction that indicates actor or cause in passive clauses, (77). In the interrogative clause the instrument can be considered as subject, although it is interesting to note that one reason that militates against such an analysis is that an otherwise inanimate noun in Jacaltec (as in other Mesoamerican languages as Achí and Tlapanec) cannot be the subject of a transitive verb.

(77) *tset*   *ʃ-maqʔ-ni*   *metʃ*   *tʃ'iʔ*   *haw-u*
      what   past = hit = X   classifier   dog   your = because-of
      'what did you hit the dog with?'

In Huixtan Tzotzil some question words inflect, like nouns, for person of subject so that they constitute the nucleus of a stative clause; compare the noun *'kaʃnil-ot* 'you are my wife' and the question word *'mutʃʔu-ot* 'who are you?' In cases such as *'mut'ʃu i'tʃam* 'who died?' the verb *i'tʃam* may therefore be analysed as the subject of a stative clause whose predicate is the word meaning 'who'.

It can be seen in the examples above that nominal nuclear constituents are not marked except by order. Peripheral constituents are frequently marked by prepositions, these being inflected for person; in Tzotzil the article may also mark peripheral constituents.

Verbal phrases have an auxiliary verb inflected for aspect or tense and, in Chamula Tzotzil, a main verb inflected for person. Auxiliaries have meanings such as 'go', 'come', 'pass', 'finish', 'begin'. Details vary in different languages. In Mam, for example, the auxiliary is inflected for person and tense; the main verb occurs in participial form, although when transitive it is inflected for person of actor and the auxiliary inflects for person of patient. There are also verbal phrases in Mam in which the main verb is followed by the auxiliary and then by the verb that means 'be'.

An aspect of verbal phrases that is in general quite complex in Mayan languages is the marking of person. Note in (78) and (79) from Chamula Tzotzil that the affixes which indicate 'second person plural object' are different.

(78)   *muk*   *ta*   *x-kolta-oʃuk*   *bal*
       not   incompletive   I = help = you-pl.   going
       'I will not help you go'

(79)   *muk*   *bu*   *tʃ-a-x-max-ik*
       not   restrictive   incompletive = you = I = hit = 2nd-pl.
       'I will not hit you'

In these examples the choice of a given person marking is determined by the presence of a particular aspect marker (*ta* and *t-*); in other cases it is determined by the presence of an auxiliary or by subjunctive inflection. With some aspectual or modal elements (variously analysed as modifying particles, auxiliaries or main predicates, the difference being chiefly one of analysis), the verb has the same person inflection as it has in subordinate clauses, and the difference in person marking between transitive and intransitive verbs (cf. 6.1.2) is obliterated. These contrasts in verb inflection are to some extent parallel to those found in the use of primary and secondary modes in Mixean languages (cf. 7.4) and in Huave (cf. 8.3).

Coordination is made largely through juxtaposition in Huixtan Tzotzil. In Tojolabal, the same mechanism is found, although there are coordinating particles borrowed from Spanish; in addition, coordinate clauses may be marked in the verb in a similar way to that discussed above for person inflection, i.e. transitive verbs lose the transitive marker they have in main clauses. Jacaltec has a more elaborate system of coordination. When the clauses are juxtaposed the verb in a transitive clause is marked by the suffix *-ni* when it is the second member of the coordination. There is a particle within the tense system (cf. 6.1.1) that means 'and then', and this only occurs in a clause preceded by another clause. Also there are coordinating particles meaning 'and' (linking clause constituents but not clauses), 'or' (there are two, one used in declarative clauses, another in interrogative ones), 'but', 'but on the other hand'. With one of these particles the second clause in a coordination lacks a verb, (80), a type of construction that is also found in Tojolabal, a construction which, as stated in 7.4 in reference to Mixean languages, is uncommon in this area as an indigenous characteristic (cf. 8.5).

(80)   *slotoχ*   *iṣ*   *manku⁷*   *wal*   *naχ*   *hune⁷*
         eats   she   mango   but   he   orange
         'she eats a mango but he an orange'

Subordinate clauses may be unmarked, like some objective clauses in Tzotzil and Jacaltec. There are also subordinating particles, although their number and function vary in different languages. Jacaltec has two particles which mark objective clauses (with no internal changes); Huixtan Tzotzil has a particle with locative or temporal meaning ('as far as', 'as long as', 'when'), a particle that means 'until' which has been borrowed from Spanish, another particle for condition, and finally, some objective and subjective clauses, (81), marked by the article.

(81)   *ivuunaʃ*   *ti*   *ʃka⁷*   *ti*   *te⁷*
         it-appeared   the   is-rotting   the   wood
         'it appeared that the wood is rotting'

Some subordinate clauses in Jacaltec have a verb without tense inflection and marked by the suffix -*ni* when transitive, but with transitive person inflection when intransitive. The contrast between transitive and intransitive person inflection can be exemplified with *tʃ-in* **haw-***ila* incompletive = me-you = see 'you see me', and *tʃ-* **atʃ** *waji* incompletive = you-sleep 'you sleep'; in (82) the verb of the subordinate clause is intransitive but inflects as though it were transitive.

(82)   *ʃtsala*   *naχ*   *haw-ul*   *jatut*
         he-happy   he   you = come   his-house
         'he is happy that you came to his house'

Other subordinate transitive clauses have the verb inflected for person and for future tense; this construction is found in cases in which the (semantic) actor of the subordinate clause is identical to either the subject of the main clause or the object, e.g.

(83)
tʃ-oŋ   *s-tʃeχ*   *naχ*   **ko-***ts⁷is-a⁷*   *kalem*
non-past = us   he = order   he   (it) = we = sweep = future   garbage
'he orders us to sweep the floor'

Relative clauses in general are not introduced by a relative word, although in Huixtan Tzotzil those lacking an antecedent do contain a relative word; in other cases the relative clause is often marked only by the article.

In Jacaltec, there is a locative word only when the relativized constituent is locative; when the relativized constituent is the subject of a transitive clause, the verb is not inflected for person and has a suffix *-ni*. When the relativized constituent depends on a preposition, either this remains in its main clause position with a classifier filling the position of the relativized word, (84), or the preposition occurs after the antecedent noun and introduces the relative clause.

(84) *ʃtsʼah*   **teʔ**   **kaʃa**   *tʃinkʼuba hintsetet*   **j-ul**   **teʔ**
     it-burned   the   chest   I-keep-it   my-thing   its = in   classifier
     'the chest I keep my things in burned'

Comparative constructions can be either simple or complex in Jacaltec. In both cases the term of comparison is introduced by the preposition meaning 'in front of' (9), and in the complex clause the preposition is followed by the word meaning 'the way', (85); the subordinate clause is marked as in other cases, that is, suffix *-ni* with transitive verb, transitive person inflection with intransitive verb; furthermore the subordinate clause lacks elements common to the main clause.

(85)
kaʔ   *tʃawotʃe*   *hawilni*   *saxatʃ*   **sataχ haka ʔ**   *wotʃe*-**ni**
more   you-like-it   you-see-game   in-front-of   the-way   I-like-it = X
'you like to watch the game more than I like it'

8.2   Otomanguean

Although some grammatical characteristics are widespread in Otomanguean languages, there is still considerable diversity among them. Moreover, since not many languages have been described within each subgroup, statements about particular characteristics appearing in such and such a subgroup are to be understood as meaning that the characteristic is found in more than one language within the pertinent group, not necessarily that it is general within it. As a result, reference will be more to individual languages than to subgroups.

In Otomanguean languages, the number and combinations of nuclear participants which can occur in a clause is smaller than it is in Nahuatl or Mixe-Zoque languages. Clauses with an agent occur in Mixtec, Zapotec and Popoloc languages, but an agent in combination with a beneficiary would seem to be unusual, and even when in combination with a patient it is uncommon; furthermore, the agent is formally not clearly distinguished from actor, since causative and transitive verbs are made up in the same way (i.e. with a prefix that is still recognizable as a reduced form of the verb that means 'make'). A participant with the meaning of instrument is found in several languages (cf. 6.1.4) but in at least some of them (e.g. Tlapanec) it is not usually found in combination with patient, i.e. it occurs predominantly in intransitive clauses. Beneficiary is common in Popolocan and Otomian languages, but again, in Eastern Otomi it occurs only in transitive clauses.

In other branches of Otomanguean, beneficiary is a nuclear participant only when the predicate is a verb belonging to a small class that inherently takes a patient and a beneficiary, with meanings such as 'tell', 'give', 'ask'; otherwise beneficiary is expressed by a peripheral locative constituent containing the locative noun meaning 'surface, face' or 'hand' and the noun referring to the beneficiary; this construction is found, for example, in Ayutla Mixtec, (86), in Trique and Tlapanec.

(86)　　$ni^2sa^2ta^{\eta2}$　　be^1tu^1　　$\text{\textltailn}u^3nu^{\eta2}$　　$nu^3u^{\eta2}$　　pe^1lu^1
　　　　bought　Bob　bag　face　Peter
　　　　'Bob bought Peter a bag'

Even so, in Tlapanec it is more common to indicate beneficiary – when it is expressed at all – by a possessive modifier, so that the clause in (86) would turn out in literal translation as 'Bob bought Peter's bag' or, as in (87), through an additional clause that refers to the use the beneficiary will make of the patient.

(87)　　ne^3tse^3　　$\text{\textesh}u^1ba^3$　　$ma^3hmu\cdot^3$　　$a^{\eta3}go^3$　　$\underline{tsi^1ge}^{\eta3}$
　　　　I-bought-it　plate　she-will-use-it　woman　this
　　　　'I bought a plate in order that this woman will use it'
　　　　(i.e. 'I bought this woman a plate')

An agent participant can also be expressed in both Trique languages, in Ayutla Mixtec and Tlapanec, but it appears as subject of an additional clause with the verb that means 'make' as predicate, as in (88) from Copala Trique.

(88)　　$u\cdot n\tilde{a}\cdot h^{21}$　　$gwa\cdot jo^{32}$　　$\text{\textglotstop}ja\cdot h^3$　　$gwa\cdot^{32}$　　$\hat{a}\cdot h$
　　　　is-running　horse　makes　John　affirmative
　　　　'John makes the horse run'

This construction is not an instance of a main clause with a clause as object, for in that case the clauses would be in reverse order; besides, in Tlapanec the semantically subordinate clause cannot be marked by the particle which in other cases marks objective clauses. A construction more similar to the English one with the verbs *make* or *cause* is found in Rincón Zapotec, (89), although the subordinate clause is locative, not objective.

(89)   *beeba⁷   ga   gwijɛ⁷*
        I-did   where   he-went
        'I made him go away'

Marking of indefinite actor does not seem common, but in Tlapanec it can be marked both in active (*na³-ti³-ngo³-ho³* present = indefinite-actor = sell 'they sell it') and passive verbs (*na³-wa³-ta³-ngo³-ho³* present = passive = indefinite-actor = sell 'it is sold by somebody').

A nuclear constituent formally different from those already mentioned occurs in Yatzachi Zapotec and Tlapanec with verbs meaning 'forgive', 'remember' and 'forget'. In Tlapanec, for example, it is filled by a word inflected for two persons and which occurs only in this construction (90). By its inflection this word historically seems to be a transitive stative verb like the one meaning 'have', i.e. it has subject – object inflection but no tense inflection.

(90)   *ni²mbo²ma·²   ʃta³j-o⁷²   (ʃta³j-a·⁷²³)*
        you-forgot   X = you-I   (X = you-him)
        'you forgot me (him)'

Reflexive clauses can have a transitive verb and a reflexive pronoun as actor–patient, although in Mazahua the verb is marked as reflexive, and in Diuxi Mixtec, (91), they may take the form of an ordinary transitive clause.

(91)   *te²ɲu⁷²u¹   -te¹   me²te¹*
        is-burning   = he   him
        'he is burning him' or 'he is burning himself'

Passive verbs are found in languages of different subgroups: Eastern Popoloc, Texmelucan Zapotec, Highland Otomi, Tlapanec. As in other linguistic families, in passive clauses with a patient and beneficiary the latter is the subject, and there is no actor constituent. The actor can be expressed in Tlapanec by the same construction that was discussed in connection with agent: a passive clause indicates the patient, a following one containing the verb meaning 'make' indicates the actor, e.g.

(92)   *na²wi²t̪si¹   a⁷³da³   e⁷²ne²   ʃu³wã¹*
        he-is-being-bitten   child   he-makes-it   dog
        'the child is being bitten by the dog'

Emphasized constituents occur in initial position and may be marked in various ways. In Quiotepec Chinantec, verbs, adjectives, nouns and pronouns have a special inflection for emphasis, for example *hna⁷h¹³* 'we (exclusive)', *hna⁷¹o⁷h²³* 'we (exclusive), emphatic'. A different marking is found in Palantla Chinantec; here the emphasized constituent is followed by a copula-like particle. In Tlapanec, there is a special marking in emphatic clauses, but only when tense is present; in this case a prefix *iʔ-*, *eʔ-* is used instead of the present prefix *na-*, *ne-*. Although Tlapanec is a verb-initial language, verbs with that prefix cannot occur as an initial constituent, and they only occur in clauses with an emphasized constituent, which can be anything except the verb. Included in the set of constituents that can be emphasized are the questioned and the negative elements; the verb can also be marked in this way in clauses referring to the agent in causative constructions or to the actor in passive constructions (cf. (92)).

The commonest marker of yes/no questions is an initial particle, a variant of which is found in Chocho where an initial and a final particle are used simultaneously. In Copala Trique, the particle is final, and furthermore, it contrasts with the obligatory markers of affirmative and negative clauses which are also final particles (cf. 88). When the questioned element depends on a preposition it remains in the same position it occupies in a declarative clause (becoming separated from its term) in Tlapanec and in Copala Trique, or it occurs after the questioned element in Palantla Chinantec and in Chiquihuitlan Mazatec.

Most languages have clauses in which an adjectival predicate attributes a quality to a nominal subject, and in Copala Trique clauses with that meaning have a copula in addition. Identificational clauses are nominal in most languages, but again in Copala Trique there is a copula in this construction; in some languages nominal and copulative clauses are alternative ways of indicating identification, and in Tlapanec and South-Eastern Popoloc the negative counterpart of an affirmative nominal clause is obligatorily copulative.

There are some characteristics of copulative clauses that are found in more than one language. Morphologically the copula may be a demonstrative, (93); it occurs in second position or in last position, (94), even though these languages are verb-initial.

(93) *laʔabe   nga   majstru*
      he   that teacher
      'he is a teacher'   [Isthmus Zapotec]

(94) *pe¹dro³   ʒa²kũ²   ja²hũ·²*
      Peter   priest   is
      'Peter is a priest'   [Tlapanec]

In addition, when copulative clauses are negated, the negative particle is not in direct construction with the copula but with the nominal complement in Tlapanec or with the subject, as in (95). It is likely that in both languages the negation could be analysed (in copulative constructions) as standing in construction with the rest of the clause.

(95)   *kadi   xwan   di   nga   maistru*
        not   John   emphatic   that teacher
        'John is not a teacher'   [Isthmus Zapotec]

Copulative clauses are more common in Otomanguean languages than in languages of other families; Huautla Mazatec has four copulas: one for identification, two indicating appearance (one for things or people, another for places or the weather), and a fourth is used with quantitative complements.

Locative and existential clauses may have an intransitive verb as predicate; in Tlapanec, a stative verb is used. In some languages, like Isthmus Zapotec, there is a locative verb that may be used practically for any type of location, while languages like Mazahua, Tlapanec or Lealao Chinantec have a large class of verbs with locative meaning (cf. 6.4.2).

The expression of possession varies considerably, and one or another of the types of clauses already discussed occurs in different languages. In Isthmus Zapotec, they are transitive clauses; in Tlapanec, they are also transitive but the verb is stative and does not have a passive form. In Chiquihuitlan Mazatec, (96), the clause contains the existential verb inflected for beneficiary.

(96)   *thĩ²-na²   nku²   na²ɲa²*
        there-is = me   one   dog
        'I have a dog'

Chocho has a nominal clause for expressing possession, although a copula can be added.

Nuclear nominal constituents are usually unmarked. Peripheral constituents are marked depending on the existence of prepositions, which in general are few in Otomanguean languages, some languages lacking them entirely. As in many Mesoamerican languages, locative constructions contain a locative noun that refers to parts of the body (cf. 86), but frequently any function is filled simply by a noun, adjective or adverb.

Verbal phrases with auxiliaries are uncommon. Some Zapotec languages and Quiotepec Chinantec have a verbal phrase consisting of the verb that means 'make' and a Spanish infinitive; as in the case of Tequistlatecan languages (cf. 7.6) it is simply the way Spanish verbs are incorporated into the language. In a few languages – Choapan Zapotec, Chichimec, Tlapanec – a verbal phrase consists of a verb of motion plus a verb which instead of a tense prefix has a special one that is only used in this construction and indicates simultaneous event; in Tlapanec, it is inflected for person, in the other two languages it has no person inflection.

Another type of verbal phrase consists of an auxiliary with tense inflection and a main verb with tense and person inflection; this type of verbal phrase is found in Copala Trique and Tlapanec; the auxiliaries mean 'finish', 'be able', 'begin'.

Coordination of clauses or of constituents of clauses may be marked by particles, but the most common mechanism is simple juxtaposition; some languages like Tlapanec lack coordinating particles altogether. Coordination of clauses is more common than that of clause constituents, as in examples (97a, 97b) from Tlapanec.

(97a) $na^2d\!\!\!\!\!/a^2\tilde{u}^{.2}$ $mi^{?3}pha^{.3}$ $na^2d\!\!\!\!\!/a^2\tilde{u}^{.2}$ $\int ti^1lo^3$
      I-hear   Tlapanec I-hear   Spanish
      'I understand Tlapanec and Spanish'

(97b) $a^{.1}$ $\int ku^2ni^{.2}$ $wa^1ja^{.\prime3}$ $a^{.1}$ $mi^{?2}\int a^{.1}$
      interrogative black-he your-horse interrogative white-he
      'is your horse black or white?'

Note in (97b) that the particle $a^{.1}$ is the marker of yes/no questions and that it marks a whole clause as interrogative. It is even uncommon for some languages to have a noun modified by two attributes with the same internal structure, e.g. two adjectives; if two quality modifiers occur one is an adjective and the other a relative clause ((98), from Tlapanec), and a construction with as many as three modifiers, corresponding to English *old small white dog*, hardly occurs.

(98) $\int u^3w\tilde{a}^1$ $mi^{?2}\int a^{.1}$ $\underline{t}si^1$ $la^1hw\tilde{\imath}^{.1}$
     dog   white   who small-he
     'small white dog'

Coordinate clauses in which common elements are suppressed in the second clause do not seem to occur, except for constituents like subject or object in those languages which mark them within the verb, a type of suppression that also occurs in simple clauses. Note (99) in which the subject and object are omitted but in which the verb is obligatory in spite of the fact that the word 'also' is inflected for person in cross-reference with the subject, a feature that would make of it a perfect pro-form.

(99) pe^1dro^3 ma^3do^2 $d\tilde{u}^{.2}$ $\int u^{?1}kho^3$ $ma^2ng\text{-}\tilde{u}^{.1}$ ma^3do^2
     Peter   will-sow-he-it chile this-way also = I   will-sow-I-it
     'Peter will sow chile and I will too'   [Tlapanec]

Some subordinate clauses are marked by subordinating particles and have the internal structure of a main clause. The number of subordinating particles varies from language to language, but a widespread characteristic is the presence of a particle which only marks subordination, its particular meaning varying according to context; the particle is clearly deictic in some languages, at least historically.

Thus, in Coatzospan Mixtec there is a particle that marks objective, causal, relative and purpose clauses, and furthermore it functions as a nominalizer, marks the term of comparison and is used in nominal constituents with temporal meaning. On the other hand, there are subordinate clauses that are simply juxtaposed; this occurs particularly frequently in subjective, objective and purpose clauses.

Relative clauses without a relative introducer are found in Copala Trique, for example; in other languages these clauses have an introductory word, but it rarely seems to be specifically relative, being in many cases a generic subordinating particle as in Coatzospan Mixtec. In Chocho relative words are classifiers and may be preceded by the article, e.g.

(100)

$ba^{\eta 1}\S e^2$	sa^1	$\dot{3}u^3$	$ndoa^3$	sa^1	$\dot{3}u^3$	$ku^{\eta 3}nia^1$	u^2	nie^{13}
went-out	the	classifier	man	the	classifier	killed	I	dog-of

'the man whose dog I killed went out'

Since coordinate clauses as well as subordinate ones can be simply juxtaposed without internal marking, the difference between the two types becomes somewhat indeterminate in Otomanguean languages, and many clauses which are translated in English by a subordinate clause are better considered as coordinate in the original. Consider examples (101) and (102) from Yaitepec Chatino.

(101)

$nguhwi^1$	$j^{\eta}\tilde{o}^{12}$	$nguhwi^1$	$st\tilde{i}^1$
died	mother-my	died	father-my

'my mother and my father died'

(102)

ha^4	$kwi^{\eta}ja^{32}$	$n\tilde{o}^2$	$t\tilde{i}^{\eta}\tilde{i}^2$	$lju^{\eta 1}$	a^2
not	will-carry-you	thing	heavy	lesser-you	very

'you are not to carry heavy things as you are so little'

While there may be little doubt as to the semantic relation between the two clauses in each case, it derives from the meaning of the clauses and not from their form. The second example could be translated preserving basically the same meaning as 'you are not to carry heavy things; you are so little'. In other cases the tenses (or aspects) in each clause give a clue as to the meaning relation, but this is also the case in independent clauses that follow each other in connected discourse; even so in (103), (104) and (105), from Tlapanec, the contrasts made in the two translations given for the last two examples cannot be differentiated formally in that language.

(103)

$ni^{\eta 3}kha^3$	$\int a^3bo^3$	$\mathbf{ni}^2ra^1me^3$
came-he	man	whistled-he

'the man came and whistled'

(104)   *niꞋ³kha³   ʃa³bo³   **na²ra¹me³***
          came-he man   whistles-he
          'the man came whistling' or 'the man came and he was whistling'

(105)   *niꞋ³kha³   ʃa³bo³   **ma³ra¹me³***
          came-he man   will-whistle-he
          'the man came in order to whistle' or 'the man came and he will whistle'

This type of coordinate clause occurs frequently in many languages as the equivalent of a manner clause.

There are various constructions that express comparison. Besides cases like that of Isthmus Zapotec in which comparative constructions are calques of Spanish patterns, comparative constructions in some languages consist of two full clauses with correlative elements, e.g.

(106)   *l̪a³ʃi³   kʷé·⁴a⁴   diꞋ¹   kʷé̥·j⁴*
          as   am-tall-I as-much is-tall-he
          'he is as tall as I am'   [Lealao Chinantec]

In Chiquihuitlan Mazatec, (107), and in Copala Trique, (108), comparison is made in simple clauses using a complement of association in the former, and with the same type of constituent that is used for beneficiary in the latter.

(107)   *ta⁴nkŭ⁴   Ꞌnka²   tʃa²   ko³-na²*
          same   tall   he   with=me
          'he is as tall as I am'

(108)   *ʒakã̃⁵   zoꞋ³   doh³   riã³⁴   Ꞌũh⁵   âh*
          tall   he   more face-of I   affirmative
          'he is taller than I am'

Comparison of equality in Copala Trique is expressed by a two-clause construction like the one of Lealao Chinantec (cf. (106)); in turn comparison of inequality in Chiquihuitlan Mazatec is also a two-clause construction but with the verb that means 'can' in the subordinate clause, (109).

(109)   *iꞋ⁴t̪s³-sa³   Ꞌnka³   tʃa²   ʃi²   ku²⁴mã-na²   nkã³⁴*
          a-bit-more tall   he   that is-possible=me   I
          'he is taller than I can be' (i.e. 'he is taller than I am')

8.3 Huave

Huave is a language with four mutually intelligible dialects differing syntactically in details only; the exemplification in this section will be from the dialect of San Mateo del Mar unless otherwise stated. (The transcription used keeps phonemic contrasts distinct but it is also partially a practical one because the data allow a wide margin for divergent phonological interpretations.)

There are few nuclear participants. Beneficiary occurs only when the verb belongs to a small class (meanings are roughly the same as in some Otomanguean languages, e.g. 'tell', 'give') and there is also a patient. On the other hand, an agent (as the term is used in this book) does not occur: the construction with causative meaning, (110), involves a main verb meaning 'give' to which an objective clause is subordinated; both the subject of the main verb and the subject of the subordinate verb are actors (cf. the comments on the Jacaltec causative construction in 8.1).

(110) maria   ti·t̠s̠   mamiaj   a   nine
       Mary   she-gave she-subordinate-sleep   the   child
       'Mary made the child sleep'

Indefinite actor can be marked in both intransitive (111) and transitive (112) clauses, and in these cases the verb is marked by a suffix that indicates indefinite actor, and is inflected for plural subject.

(111) ahiə^ŋg-ar-an   na^ŋgos   nɨt
       dance = indefinite-actor = plural   sacred   day
       'they danced at the fiesta' ('there was dancing at the fiesta')

(112) ^ŋgow   it-er-an   kiət
       when   eat = indefinite-actor = plural   fish
       'when is fish eaten?'

Note that the clauses in these examples lack a subject constituent; as was the case in other languages already discussed, the construction in (112) is equivalent to a passive clause without the actor being expressed.

Reflexive clauses are marked in the verb; compare the verb in the transitive clause (113) with the verb reflexive clause (114).

(113)
ta-ʃot   mi-saral   mi-ci·g   neh
past-he = hide   possessed = trousers   possessed = young-brother   he
'he hid his younger brother's trousers'

(114) kiah   neh   te-ʃot-ɨj   til-iəm
       that   she   past-he = hide = reflexive   in = house
       'she hid herself in the house'

Only those clauses that mean identification and have two nominal expressions as constituents are verbless.

Other types of clauses are verbal. Possessive clauses are transitive, and quality clauses are stative, having a verb marked as stative or an adjective (both differ from active verbs in lacking tense inflection); locative and existential clauses both have the same intransitive verb as predicate, but some locative clauses show a different construction. In (115) we find the ordinary verb used for location – existence, and a proclitic form of the verb *aɦn* 'remain' that adds durative meaning; in (116), however, the same proclitic is added to an adverb which is the nucleus of the predicate.

(115) *ⁿgiane al= ma-hɦj xwan*
      where durative he-subordinate = be John
      'where is John?'

(116) *neh al= naⁿgij*
      he durative = here
      'he is here'

Yes/no questions are marked by intonation and optionally by a final particle which is also optional in constituent questions. In the latter type, when the questioned element depends on a preposition, this may occur in the same position as it does in an affirmative clause, becoming separate from its term, or it may occur immediately after its term (i.e. the question word).

Nuclear nominal constituents have no marking, except that the subject, when it occurs after the verb and is not possessed or determined by a demonstrative, must be accompanied by the article. Some peripheral constituents such as locative or instrument may be prepositional constructions, although this is not always the case; in (111) above the locative complement is an unmarked nominal phrase. As in other families, a locative constituent may be a nominal phrase with a possessed noun that refers to part of the body.

There is a verbal phrase that, as in Tequistlatec and in some Otomanguean languages, is used for incorporating Spanish verbs, but, while in those languages the auxiliary means 'make', in Huave the auxiliary means 'begin'. Other verbal phrases contain an auxiliary verb (some inflected for tense) and a main verb that in some cases is inflected for independent mode and in others for subordinate mode, e.g. *tiⁿgi=ahɦj* past-continuative/he-walks-independent-mode 'he was walking'. These proclitic auxiliary verbs are on the verge of becoming inflectional prefixes. It is worth noting that the future tense construction is historically a verbal phrase in which the auxiliary is the verb meaning 'go' and the main verb is inflected for subordinate mode.

The use of subordinate mode is in fact more complex than the discussion in this section shows; in connected discourse, main verbs may occur in subordinate mode. In this mode no tense distinctions are made.

Another type of verbal phrase consists of a modal auxiliary with tense inflection and a verb inflected for subordinate mode. The auxiliaries mean 'be possible', 'be allowed', 'be necessary', 'finish'. The negation could be considered as an auxiliary since the accompanying verb is inflected for secondary mode, although the negation is not inflected for tense.

In most cases coordination is marked with particles borrowed from Spanish, and the constructions with a reduced second clause match the Spanish patterns so closely that these have probably been imitated too. The verbs may be juxtaposed, the second being equivalent to a manner modifier (117).

(117)   *taw*   *imiən*   *tiⁿden*   *ma-tepiaj*   *sik*
        he-went-out he-comes the house he-subordinate = greet I
        'he went out of the house to greet me' (more literally:
        'he went out of the house coming to greet me')

This example also contains a purpose clause which is found with verbs of movement; to this type of subordinate clause, but without being dependent on a movement verb, belong those that indicate 'in the company of', e.g.

(118)   *neh* *i·t*   *ma-ki·əp*   *sik*
        he   he-eats he-secondary = accompany I
        'he eats with me'

Subordinate clauses with temporal, conditional, causal or purpose meaning are marked by particles; in temporal, conditional and causal clauses the verb is inflected for independent mode, (119), in adversative and purpose clauses the verb is inflected for subordinate mode, (120).

(119)   *tahawas* *wiʃ*   *sa-kʷiər*
        I-saw   when I-independent-run
        'I saw him when I was running'

(120)   *saran*   *nahiət* *pa*   *na-hiər*   *sejaj* *tomiən*
        I-make work   in-order-to I-subordinate = have much   money
        'I work in order to have much money'

Objective clauses have no subordinate particle and have the verb inflected for independent mode except when the main verb is one whose meaning falls within the range of 'desire'; note (121) and (122).

(121)   *sahaw   osep   i-riə^mb   latiək*
        I-know   tomorrow   you-independent = go   Tehuantepec
        'I know that you go tomorrow to Tehuantepec'

(122)   *sandiəm   osep   me-riə^mb   latiək*
        I-want   tomorrow   you-subordinate = go   Tehuantepec
        'I want you to go tomorrow to Tehuantepec'

Relative clauses are not introduced by a relative word except, as in Jacaltec, when the relativized constituent is locative; the verb is inflected for independent mode. Note in (123) that as the language has SVO order the sentence could be interpreted as one with two coordinate predicates.

(123)   *aɣa   pet   ta^ntsor   tatsa^mb   sik*
        this   dog   he-barked   he-bit   I
        'this dog that barked bit me'

Comparative constructions of inequality are calques from Spanish (with borrowing of comparative particles). For comparison of equality there is a construction (124) semantically parallel to that exemplified for Chiquihuitlan Mazatec (cf. (107)), although in Huave the term of comparison is a subordinate clause.

(124)   *atotow   ahal   oliahiw   ma-ki·əp   mik^wal*
        same   it-is-long   his-leg   he-subordinate = accompany   your-son
        'he is as tall as your son'

8.4 Misumalpan

The only language that will be examined in this section is Miskito because no information is available on the other languages of the family concerning syntax. The transcription used may not be phonemic.

There are clauses with actor, and with actor and patient participants, but it seems that there are no clauses with a beneficiary as nuclear constituent.

Verbless clauses are found in emphatic constructions, e.g.

(125)   *jang   sika   jamni*
        I   emphasis   good
        'it is I who am well'

There are also another two particles which are used in emphatic clauses with different meanings ('as for x's part, x ...', 'x is the one who ...').

A whole clause can also be emphasized by having the copula inflected for third person and occurring at the end of the clause, e.g.

(126) *witin   balbia   sa*
       he   he-will-come   is
       'it is a fact that he will come'

There are constituent questions that are emphasized too; in this case the interrogative word occurs at the end of the clause, e.g.

(127) *man   wamtla   ha   ani*
       your   house   the   which
       'which is your house?'

In some non-emphatic interrogative clauses, as in (128), the interrogative word does not occur at the beginning of the clause (in languages with SOV order such as Miskito a rule requiring that this type of interrogative word necessarily occurs at the beginning of the clause – as is the case with VSO languages – is never found).

(128) *aras   an   brisa*
       horse   how-many   he-has
       'how many horses does he have?'

Yes/no questions are marked by intonation and optionally by a final particle.

Only personal pronouns have different forms when they are subjects or objects; other forms are not marked, but the subject may be marked with a postposed particle in cases of potential ambiguity because the basic SOV order can be changed into OSV. Peripheral constituents are usually marked by suffixes or by postpositions.

There are at least three types of verbal phrases with auxiliaries. One consists of the verb that means 'commit' plus an infinitive and has intentive meaning; another contains a gerund followed by the copula and has progressive meaning; a third contains an infinitive and the copula, and has the meaning of duty or intention.

Miskito has a considerable number of coordinating and subordinating particles. Particles that coordinate clauses go in between the clauses, with a few exceptions like the particle *sin* 'and' which occurs after the second member of the coordination; the particle *sin* may link clauses or clause constituents (there is another particle meaning 'and' but that only coordinates clauses). Subordinating particles follow the subordinate clause and have temporal (129), conditional or adversative meaning.

(129) *witin   nani   balbia   bara,   jawin   plun   pibia*
       he   plural   will-come   when   we   food   will-eat
       'when they come, we will eat food'

Relative clauses are marked at the end by a demonstrative or by the article, (130); they can be marked at the beginning by an optional demonstrative (a marking used chiefly when the relative clause is long).

(130)　　*baha　waikna　naiwa　balan　ba　baku　win*
　　　　　that　　man　　came　　today　the　said　so
　　　　　'the man that came today said so'

There are also participial constructions in Misumalpan. The participle may precede a noun with which it is in construction, the nouns taking the same form they have when preceded by an adjective (differing from the form of the noun when followed by the adjective). When attributive to a noun, temporal clause, (131), or coordinate clause in construction with a verb the participle may be equivalent in meaning to a relative clause.

(131)　　*aisi-si*　　　　　　　*balamni*
　　　　　speak = past-participle　I-will-come
　　　　　'when I have spoken, I will come'

In this example the implied actor of the participle has the same referent as the subject of the main verb, and this is a necessary condition in this construction; if the implied actor of the participle were different from the subject of the main verb, the subordinate verbal form would be different. Compare (132) with (131).

(132)　　*aisa-ka*　　　　　　*balamni*
　　　　　speak = subordinator　I-will-come
　　　　　'when he has spoken, I will come'

For comparison of superiority the construction is similar to that of Chiquihuitlan Mazatec (cf. (107)), that is, the marker of comparison means 'with'; comparison of inferiority is made also with a postpositional constituent as in (133) (compare this with the Yaqui construction in (10)).

(133)　　*witin　jang　ninara　tukta*
　　　　　he　　I　　behind　child
　　　　　'he is younger than I'

8.5　The influence of Spanish

We have referred repeatedly in chapter 7 and in the present chapter to borrowing from Spanish. The most obvious manifestation of the impact of Spanish is in the grammatical patterns of indigenous languages, and the extent of this type of borrowing runs counter to the traditional view that grammatical words are seldom borrowed. Table 23 registers the occurrence of fourteen Spanish grammatical words in ten languages. This is only a sample of the languages in which those words

Table 23. *Spanish function words borrowed into Indian languages*

	N.T.	O.Z.	H.C.	H.	M.O.	I.Z.	T.N.	P.	Hv.	T.
como 'as, like'	x	x	x	x		x		x		
con 'with'	x		x	x						
cuando 'when'		x						x		
de 'of, from'	x		x		x	x			x	
hasta 'till, until, even'	x	x	x	x	x	x	x		x	
(*lo*) (*de*) *que* 'that, which'		x			x	x	x		x	x
mas que 'although'	x						x			
o 'or'	x					x	x	x	x	
para 'for, in order to'	x	x	x		x	x	x		x	x
pero 'but'	x	x				x	x	x	x	
por 'because of'	x		x		x	x	x			
porque 'because'	x	x	x			x	x	x		
pues 'then'	x	x					x	x	x	
y 'and'	x	x		x				x	x	

H.: Huichol. H.C.: Highland Chontal. Hv.: Huave. I.Z.: Isthmus Zapotec. M.O.: Mezquital Otomi. N.T.: Northern Totonac. O.Z.: Ostuacan Zoque. P.: Pokomán. T.: Tarascan. T.N.: Tetelcingo Nahuatl.

have been incorporated, selected so as to exemplify the extent of the phenomenon in languages of different families or in different subgroups within a family. Nor are these Spanish words the only grammatical ones that have been incorporated, although they are the ones attested in the greatest number of languages; in a smaller number of languages other words are found, e.g. *sino* 'but', *casi* 'almost', *mientras* 'while', *entonces* 'then, therefore', *desde* 'since, from', *también* 'also', *todo* 'all', *cada* 'each'.

These borrowed words have rarely replaced a native element with the same function, so one of the effects of these borrowings has been that more syntactic constructions are overtly marked; in addition, coordinate and subordinate constructions are more neatly differentiated. For example, the word *para* 'for, in order to' has been one of the most widely borrowed (see table 23) and marks purpose clauses which in many languages are only marked by future tense or incompletive aspect, and which could be interpreted as coordinate clauses (cf. (105)). In other cases, in which the borrowed Spanish word is semantically equivalent to an indigenous element, there may not only be syntactic but also morphological changes. Thus, the incorporation of *con* 'with' into Totonac and Mezquital Otomi is eliminating the use of the instrumental affixes in the verb; therefore, at the level of the clause the constituent with meaning of instrument changes its status from nuclear to peripheral. Also the incorporation of *de* 'from, of' into Nahuatl languages has certainly contributed to the decrease of the frequency of nominal composition.

A different way in which Spanish has influenced the grammars of aboriginal languages is through calques of syntactic patterns, sometimes with concomitant borrowing of grammatical words. In some cases the change may be a rather minor one, as for example in Tlapanec, in which Spanish *tener que* 'have to' (and *tener* 'have, own') has been imitated with $gu^{?1}do^2$ 'have to' (formerly used only for indicating possession), and Spanish *deber* 'owe, have to' with $gi^{?1}ma^{.2}$ which natively only means 'owe'; both Tlapanec verbs have changed their syntactic subclass since they can now have a clause as object (with the meaning 'have to') whereas formerly they took only a nominal phrase as object. More radical changes, including the introduction of a new syntactic pattern, have been produced by the calque of comparative constructions as can be seen by comparing the construction imitated from Spanish in Huasteca Nahuatl (cf. (34)) with semantically equivalent constructions in other Uto-Aztecan languages (cf. (1), (33)). Another example of calque of a syntactic pattern is found in Tlapanec. The language lacked a native particle with the meaning 'and'; in certain cases the nearest equivalent was a construction with the word meaning 'with' (a word that inflects for two grammatical persons), i.e. 'John came with Peter' = 'John and Peter came'. This word occurred only as a constituent of the predicate in native patterns, but in imitation of the Spanish pattern it is also used now to link two nouns or nominal phrases, without person inflection (i.e. 'John with Peter came'). Even if this construction can still be interpreted as meaning 'X with Y' instead of 'X and Y', a construction using a noun modified with a prepositional constituent is new for the language.

It may be suspected that this process, or a similar one, has occurred in other languages, and indeed, there are several instances of a language in which the particle meaning 'with' also coordinates clauses with the meaning 'and'. Moreover, patterns of coordinate clauses in which common elements between the two clauses are not repeated in the second clause are probably calques from Spanish patterns, at least in those cases in which closely related languages lack these patterns; additionally, a construction like *When and where did you see me?* (instead of *When did you see me, where did you see me?*) seems to occur only in the few languages in which the coordinating particle is /i/, a borrowing from Spanish.

There have as yet been no systematic comparisons of old grammars and texts with modern languages in order to determine the extent of this type of borrowing, but we can guess that calque from Spanish patterns is behind several uses of coordinating and subordinating native particles in Mesoamerican languages.

SOURCES

HUAVE: Stairs and Hollenbach 1969, Stairs n.d. MISKITO: Thaeler n.d. MAYAN. *Jacaltec*: Craig 1977, Day 1973a. *Mam*: Canger 1969. *Quiché*: Burgess and Fox 1966. *Tojolabal*: Furbee-

Losee 1976. *Tzotzil*: (*Chamula*) Jacobs and Longacre 1967. (*Huixtan*) Cowan, M. 1969.
OTOMANGUEAN. *Chatino*: (*Yaitepec*) Pride, K. 1965. *Chichimec*: Angulo 1933. *Chinantec*:
(*Lalana*) Rensch 1963; (*Lealao*) Rupp 1980; (*Palantla*) Merrifield 1968; (*Quiotepec*) Robbins
1968. *Chocho*: Mock 1977. *Mazatec*: (*Chiquihuitlan*) Jamieson and Tejeda 1978; (*Huautla*)
Gudschinsky 1959, Pike, E. 1967. *Mixtec*: (*Ayutla*) Hills and Merrifield 1974; (*Coatzospan*)
Small 1974; (*Diuxi*) Kuiper and Pickett 1974; (*Peñoles*) Daly 1973, 1977. *Otomi*: (*Highland*)
Echegoyen Gleason 1979; (*Mezquital*) Hess 1968. *Popoloc*: (*Eastern*) Austin and Pickett 1974;
(*South-Eastern*) Williams and Longacre 1967. *Tlapanec*: Suárez n.d. *Trique*: (*Chicahuaxtla*)
Longacre 1966; (*Copala*) Hollenbach and Hollenbach 1975. *Zapotec*: (*Choapan*) Lyman 1964;
(*Isthmus*) Pickett 1960, 1967, 1974; (*Rincon*) Earl 1968; (*Texmelucan*) Speck 1978; (*Yatzachi*)
Butler 1980.

FURTHER READING

Craig 1977 is not only recommended for Mayan languages, it is also one of the best syntactic
descriptions of a Mesoamerican language. For Otomanguean languages the most detailed
descriptions are those indicated in the sources for Mezquital Otomi, Isthmus Zapotec and
Yaitepec Chatino. The source for Yaitepec Chatino deals at considerable length (under the
label 'colon types') with the type of syntactic relation intermediate between coordination and
subordination typical of Otomanguean languages; for the same point see also Longacre 1966,
and Austin and Pickett 1974.

   The influence of Spanish on the syntax of an Indian language (Nahuatl) is discussed in
Karttunen and Lockhart 1976, Suárez 1977b; on the influence of Spanish loanwords in
Nahuatl morphology, Hill and Hill 1977.

9

Preconquest literary traditions

It is not the purpose of this chapter to deal with the present-day oral literatures of Mesoamerican languages. They naturally exist, and a considerable body of texts has been published to which reference will be made in the suggested readings. In many groups, especially Mayan ones, these oral traditions have preserved, although in a transformed way, many elements of pre-Hispanic origin; in other groups, these elements are few and have been replaced by traditions in which postconquest or directly Hispanic elements predominate. Studies of these works from a linguistic point of view are, however, almost entirely lacking.

We will be concerned, instead, with literary manifestations of preconquest origin. Again there is almost a total absence of such studies from a linguistic point of view, and even from a literary viewpoint the pertinent studies are meagre. But these old literary works are extremely important as a characteristic which otherwise does not recur or at least was insufficiently recorded in other Amerindian groups. As will be discussed in the next chapter, Mesoamerica reached the stage of cultural complexity known as civilization, and, as is to be expected, this was reflected in the development of more elaborate literary works than may be found in simpler societies. Consequently the present chapter aims to give only an idea of the extent and variety of materials available as a potential field of study.

9.1 The aboriginal literary tradition

An important characteristic of some Mesoamerican Indian groups is that, after the conquest, they developed a written form which was to serve not only as a vehicle for teaching the Catholic religion but also as a means of recording preconquest culture.

The writing system in Central Mexico was at a very rudimentary stage; that of the Mayan area (whatever its characteristics) is still undeciphered. Nevertheless, part of the production gathered in the Latin alphabet represents a highly fixed form of oral tradition that harks back to events of past centuries. In the native centres where culture was highly developed there were pictorial books which registered historical traditions, genealogies, rituals, astronomical knowledge and songs for which an oral version was memorized; some of this oral tradition, that connected with the calendar, for example, might have been as old as the Classic period (see table 24). Naturally, the fact that friars taught Indian students to write their own language was conducive to the preservation of these traditions; most important was the information gathered systematically from his students by Bernardino de Sahagún, a Franciscan friar who was active in New Spain from 1529 to 1590. His work, in which part of the old pictorial books was also reproduced (most of them having been destroyed by the Spaniards), is an encyclopedia of Aztec ethnography covering such topics as religion, astronomy, astrology, economics, daily life, medicine, rhetoric, mineralogy, native history and the history of the Spanish conquest.

Languages for which this type of written material, although in variable quantity, is extant are Nahuatl, Yucatec, Quiché and Cakchiquel. The most important works, naturally, are those set down in writing during the sixteenth century (the extant copies do not always belong to that century), although during the course of the seventeenth century authors of native origin wrote historical works into which material of preconquest times found its way.

9.2 Writings in the Nahuatl language

The richest corpus of this type of material exists for Nahuatl, and it is not only the richest in the large number of works that survive in it but also in its variety. Different genres such as historical annals, poetry, formal talks and proverbs can be clearly distinguished, although some of the materials, at least from a modern point of view, seem to belong to other genres or subgenres.

There are some five or six historical works of the annal type. While Spanish influence may be detected, they nevertheless largely consisted of comments about pictorial books organized by years (against which some of them can be checked). The oldest, according to the time in which we know they were written, are the *Annals of Tlatelolco*, one of whose parts is dated 1528 (seven years after the conquest). It consists of five documents, four of them containing lists of rulers and genealogies, the fifth being a history of the city of Tlatelolco – a city in the Valley of Mexico – from 1250 to 1525; this means that it also covers the narration of the conquest viewed from the Indian side. In general, it has to be remembered that the keeping of time records was one of the achievements of Mesoamerican cultures.

These types of annals are chiefly concerned with migrations into the Valley of Mexico and wars between the cities which were founded there, and they reflect, in the main, the narrow viewpoint of the successful Aztecs. The time span covered by some of these chronicles is considerable, the *Annals of Quauhtitlan* dealing with the period from A.D. 635 to 1519, and the *Toltec – Chichimec History* from 1116 to 1544. The telling of events is sometimes quite dry, as in the case when, for some year, it is stated that 'nothing happened', but the narration is sometimes expanded and then it incorporates songs, myths and even what may be considered (from a modern viewpoint) short stories. To these kinds of writings must be added those written at the turn of the sixteenth century by acculturated Indians like Domingo Chimalpahin and Fernando Alvarado Tezozomoc, writings which largely preserved many characteristics of the native style of historical works, and which were based on native traditions.

Poetry represents an important aspect of ancient Nahuatl literature. There is a small corpus of sacred hymns (preserved by Sahagún) which were sung in honour of the gods, and among which some of the presumably oldest specimens of Nahuatl language can be found. Another collection – the so-called *Mexican songs* – was written down during the sixteenth century, and while there are instances of Catholic influence most of the content belongs to preconquest times. The topics of these songs are varied; there are lyrical poetry, war songs, mourning songs, and some that express philosophical viewpoints; others have a burlesque content. The content of some of these songs suggests that they were sung by a choir and soloists, and others represent a rudimentary form of drama. That the Aztecs had such performances is stated explicitly in more than one Spanish testimony, although to what extent texts of this type can be identified in the corpus of poetry is not clear. On the other hand, two interesting features of Nahuatl poetry were that some songs were attributed to definite individuals and that others were identified as being in the style of a city or region, a fact that points to a developed sense of literary form.

These poems were not only sung but also accompanied by music. The manuscript contains what can be interpreted as rhythmical instructions for drums, but nothing is actually known about the musical accompaniment, nor about the formal arrangement of the text; the writings show no formal structure. Nahuatl songs – and even what is unquestionably straight prose – are usually presented both in the original texts and in translations with stanza organization. This practice is founded on a hypothesis about the rhythm of the songs, and it should be noted that the hypothesis is based neither on the way in which songs are written in the manuscripts, nor in statements by contemporaries, nor in what is known about Classical Nahuatl phonology, nor on the study of the prosodic characteristics of modern Nahuatl languages. On the other hand, some features of style are obvious: the use of multiple compound words (a feature already pointed out by old grammarians), the use of parallel expressions (a widespread characteristic of the ancient and modern texts from this area), and a rather repetitive imagery referring to precious stones, bird feathers and flowers. Metaphorical expressions were frequent in Nahuatl, and Sahagún transmitted a selection of them with explanation, as well as a series of proverbs and riddles.

A different type of genre was that of formal speeches. These were delivered by elders on different occasions: the coming of age of a daughter or son, births, or the election of a chief. They are didactic in nature and highly stylized in expression.

While these are among the more readily identifiable genres the topics listed above and contained in Sahagún's work may give an idea of the variety of subjects for which, in one way or another, there is a written account reflecting the native viewpoint, even though they may be more or less influenced by the friars' teaching.

To these writings representing the aboriginal traditions has to be added the extensive corpus of Catholic religious writing composed in Nahuatl, as well as religious and literary works translated from Spanish. Among these works an important place should be given to the catechistic plays written and performed during the sixteenth century. There were also some commemorating victories of the Spanish army against the Arabs. In a much transformed and decayed form, plays with similar plots are still performed nowadays in native Nahuatl villages.

Finally, Nahuatl continued to have written manifestations during the Colonial period (sixteenth–eighteenth centuries), but the content of the documents is of a different sort: they are wills or legal documents concerning, for the most part, land disputes.

9.3 Writings in Mayan languages

Works written in Mayan languages were probably first translated into the Latin alphabet in the middle of the sixteenth century. As in the case of Nahuatl writings, they were composed partly from oral traditions, partly from the example of pictorial books, and presumably also from inscriptions and books written in the still undeciphered Mayan script. The earliest extant documents, however, are from the eighteenth century and some belong to the nineteenth century, which means much more exposure to Spanish influences.

The most important texts in Yucatec are contained in the collection called the *Books of Chilam Balam*. The name comes from a member of the priestly class who lived in the city of Maní before the coming of the Spaniards and who prophesied the advent of a new religion, Chilam being the name given to the priestly class and Balam being a family name. It is assumed that copies of the original book written in Maní went to other places and that local native priests made additions to it, so that there are a series of manuscripts, identified by the place where they were found, which coincide partially in content. The subject matter is highly heterogeneous and even includes Spanish religious and literary texts translated into Yucatec. Among the materials of native origin are religious texts, explanations of the native calendar, historical accounts, prophecies, rituals and treatises in astrology and medicine. As in Nahuatl texts, chronicles are concerned with relating the migrations of groups into the Yucatan Peninsula, and there are also accounts of the arrival of the Spaniards and the conquest. Prophecies connected with the calendar are particularly abundant; another genre contained in these books is that of riddles.

Poetry in Yucatec is chiefly preserved in *The book of the songs of Dzitbalché*, a collection of fifteen songs in a manuscript probably belonging to the eighteenth century. These were songs which, like the Nahuatl ones, were accompanied by music and dance. Some of them are purely lyrical, others are prayers, and two describe the sacrifice of a captive, a ceremony also known through Spanish chronicles.

Writings of native origin in Quiché are rare, but those which exist are among the most significant of those preserved for Mesoamerican peoples. The most important are the *Popol Vuh* and the *Rabinal Achí*.

The *Popol Vuh*, also called *The book of counsel*, was originally written in the middle of the sixteenth century on the basis of a previous hieroglyphic code, and although since lost, it was copied in the seventeenth century. Some Western influences are detectable in the book, but they appear to be minor ones. It is the most organic work we have of old Mesoamerican literature, and it tells the mythical and historical story of the Quiché people. It begins with the origin of the world and the successive creations of different kinds of men, the adventures of two heroes in a war of gods, and the origin of the various Quichean groups, their migrations and their wars until the Quiché obtained supremacy. It contains a wealth of mythical, historical and ethnographic information. The use of parallel expressions as the major stylistic procedure is as prominent as it is in Nahuatl writings.

The *Rabinal Achí* is the only preserved example of pre-Hispanic drama, although it was not recorded until the nineteenth century. The piece little resembles a Western drama, being composed of long duologues. It is highly repetitious in content and very simple in its plot which concerns a victor and a war captive who will be eventually sacrificed. Rudimentary as it may seem viewed by modern Western standards, it exemplifies the type of theatrical work that we know also existed among the Aztecs and the Yucatecs.

From the Cakchiquel group there are several chronicles, some telling of the wars between Quichés and Cakchiquels, but more significant is the *Annals of the Cakchiquels*, in various respects a parallel of the *Popol Vuh* in its mythological and historical content; it also covers the Spanish conquest.

The foregoing exposition has been restricted to those native works for which the text in the Indian language is preserved, but there are also some for which the original text has been lost and which are known only through a Spanish translation. Furthermore, the extant writings may represent only a fraction of a much larger semi-oral literary tradition, a supposition not only suggested by the references in old Spanish chronicles but also by the known fact that a large quantity of native books were destroyed by the conquerors.

FURTHER READING

An overall view of ancient Mesoamerican native literature, with extensive quotations from the texts and a full bibliography, is León-Portilla, M. 1969. On the problems of Mesoamerican indigenous scripts see Dibble 1971, Kelley 1976. An appraisal of the work done on native Classical languages is to be found in Suárez 1968; see also Carmack 1973 on Quiché studies.

For the religious drama written in Nahuatl see Horcasitas 1974; for the legal documents of the Colonial period see Anderson, Berdan and Lockhart 1976.

The reader who is willing to go to the original texts will get an idea of the difficulties by comparing different editions and translations of the same work; Garibay, K. 1965–8 and Schultze-Jena 1957 are two editions of the *Mexican songs*, with Spanish and German translation respectively; Schultze-Jena 1944 and Edmonson 1970 are important editions of the *Popol Vuh*, with German and English translation respectively, and which have the advantage that the former can be checked by using the appended analytical vocabulary, and the second by using the dictionary and grammatical description by the same author (Edmonson 1965, 1967a).

Book vi of Sahagún 1950–63 is the most important from a linguistic point of view as it reproduces formal speeches, proverbs, riddles and metaphors. The importance of Sahagún's work is such that it is convenient to consult some papers on it, e.g. Cline 1973, Nicolau d'Olwer and Cline 1973, Nicholson 1973.

The problems concerning the *Rabinal Achí* and its structure are discussed at length in Acuña 1975.

For a bibliographical guide to modern Mesoamerican oral literature see Edmonson 1967b. Analyses on the level of discourse of these languages are Jones and Longacre 1979, Reid et al. 1968, and Van Haitsma and Van Haitsma 1976. The complex native classification of types of verbal traditions in two Mayan languages is discussed in Gossen 1971, and Furbee-Losee 1976. Gossen 1973 analyses Tzotzil proverbs.

10

The prehistory of Mesoamerican Indian languages

The title of this chapter refers not to the information that can be obtained through reconstruction of protolanguages but to the types of correlations that can be established between linguistic groups on the one hand and documentary and archaeological data on the other. Nevertheless linguistic reconstruction will be of importance in the discussion below.

These types of correlations would ideally involve determining when and whence the languages reached their historically known locations, problems which are easier to deal with on the shallow time depth typical of dialect studies or little differentiated languages. However, our perspective is more properly the treatment of individual languages or linguistic families, so the focus of this chapter will be the broad correlations with Mesoamerican cultural history. From this perspective not much is known with reasonable certainty; neither is what is known very startling when one compares it to what can be assumed through an examination of language distribution and of linguistic genetic relationships. As some of the hypotheses advanced by scholars are important but questionable they must be approached critically.

10.1   Correlations with documentary and archaeological data

Identifications of linguistic and historical-cultural data are important for any linguistic group, but in Mesoamerica this aspect has a special significance because the area is delimited on the basis of cultural characteristics and is one of the regions in the Americas in which native cultures reached the level of complexity called civilization.

Some of the features which characterized Mesoamerica were dependence on intensive agriculture (with several basic crops such as maize, beans and squash and in some places with irrigation systems or other types of water control); heavy emphasis on religion, with an elaborate pantheon manifested materially in ceremonial centres with monumental architecture; developed art styles; urban centres; expansionist political units; a stratified society with full- or part-time specialists; a

Table 24. *Mesoamerican archaeological periods*

I	Early hunter-gatherers	before 7000 B.C.
II	Archaic	7000 B.C.–2000 B.C.
III	Formative	Early 2000 B.C.–1000 B.C.
	(or Preclassic)	Middle 1000 B.C.–300 B.C.
		Late 300 B.C.–A.D. 300
IV	Classic	Early A.D. 300–A.D. 600
		Late A.D. 600–A.D. 900
V	Postclassic	Early A.D. 900–A.D. 1200
		Late A.D. 1200–A.D. 1520

market system and extensive trade; elaborate calendars and hieroglyphic writing.

The features listed – as well as others – were found throughout the area, although not everywhere and not with the same degree of elaboration. The whole area, however, was under the influence of centres which had reached the most complex levels of development. The northern limit was not static, and the one marked on the map indicates the northernmost limit of the area; at the time of first contact it had already receded southward. The southern limit seems to have been more stable, but the southern area represented a merging of Mesoamerican and Central American (also South American) features.

Since the cultural stage characterized above was the result of a long development it is necessary to refer, however sketchily, to some important phases in this development. As a temporal and spatial guide for the discussion that follows the reader is referred to table 24 which lists the main archaeological periods, and to map 2 in which a few archaeological sites are plotted.

The evidence for plant cultivation is found in the Archaic between 5200 B.C. and 3400 B.C., in the sites of Tamaulipas and Tehuacan. During the Early Formative (*c.* 1500 B.C.), fully agricultural cultures are already attested. The size of human groups found during the first phases of the archaeological record has been estimated at between 12 and 24 persons, which implies a family organization. By 3400 B.C. the groups had increased to approximately 240 persons, that is to the type of social organization called bands. From *c.* 3400 B.C. onwards there is evidence of semi-permanent settlements, and by the Early Formative period permanent settlements are established.

What can be considered as the typical culture pattern of Mesoamerica appears during the Middle Formative. One of its most important manifestations is the existence of ceremonial centres. To this period belong the sites of La Venta, on the southern Gulf Coast, Monte Albán in the Valley of Oaxaca, and Kaminaljuyú in the Guatemalan highlands. The culture of La Venta – and of neighbouring sites not indicated in the map – is called Olmec culture; it flourished at La Venta between 800 B.C. and 400 B.C., but at certain places it can be traced back to 1300 B.C., and according to some specialists it already had the basic characteristics of the later archaeological phases. Olmec culture is particularly important because the influence of its art, with its religious associations, was far reaching, although the actual extent of the influences and the way they were exerted – mere trade contacts or intrusion by Olmec groups – are highly controversial. There are also different interpretations as to the type of social organization this culture reflects, in such questions as the size of the population, the potential urban character of the settlements and the complexity of its political organization. These points can naturally be of importance in estimating the linguistic influences which a group may exert. Another point that has a bearing on the type of cultural and linguistic contacts is that while Olmec influences are found in Monte Albán, the cultural tradition here appears to have evolved in unbroken form since *c.* 1200 B.C.

Of the sites indicated on the map, not only Monte Albán and Kaminaljuyú belong to the Classic period, but also Tikal in the lowland Mayan area, Dzibilchaltún in Yucatan (i.e. the northern Mayan area) and Teotihuacan in the Valley of Mexico. The latter already represented a full urban centre, covering a built-up area of 7 square miles with a minimum population of 50,000 inhabitants. Its influences were far-flung, and in a place like Kaminaljuyú they were of such quantity and quality that the actual presence of Teotihuacan groups is suspected. Although there is not as yet enough evidence to determine the type of control that Teotihuacan may have exerted, there is the possibility that it already represented an expansionist state, and that its ruling hierarchy may have already contained military elements, as against the predominant priest-rulers assumed for earlier periods.

Teotihuacan was destroyed in A.D. 600 and the Classic centres in the lowland Mayan area were abandoned by A.D. 900. At about this time Monte Albán ceased to be a ceremonial centre and was converted into a necropolis.

In the Postclassic period, groups originating in the northern region, some probably closely related to hunter-gatherer peoples, entered the Valley of Mexico. The first to gain dominion were the Toltecs with a centre in Tula. They represent a rather drastic cultural change, with emphasis on war, prisoners and human sacrifices; during this period the cities became walled and fortress-like. To the Toltec period corresponds the maximum extension of the Mesoamerican area. Toltecs were certainly an expansionist group, conquering the region of the Guatemalan highlands. The site of Chichen Itzá in northern Yucatan – built in Late Classic times – was also conquered by groups under strong Toltec influence or even led by Toltec elements. Toltec power collapsed *c.* A.D. 1160, overrun by invaders from the north.

In the suceeding period several centres in the Valley of Mexico became increasingly hegemonic, destroying each other's power, until the Aztecs, who had founded Tenochtitlan in 1325, allied with the cities of Tlacopan and Azcapozalco dominated the Valley of Mexico after 1430 and started their expansion. At the time of the conquest their territory had reached the limits marked on map 3. As can be seen, there remained some independent states (or chiefdoms) within the Aztec dominated territory. Of these, the Tarascan state naturally spoke Tarascan, and the groups in Guatemala and Yucatan spoke respectively Quiché, Tzutuhil, Cakchiquel and Yucatec. Tlaxcala was ruled by people speaking Nahuatl, but there were also elements of Otomi speech. Teotitlan del Camino was probably also ruled by Nahuatl speakers but included Mixtec and Popolocan speakers as well. Yopitzingo spoke Tlapanec and Tataltepec was a Mixtec Kingdom. The Valley of Oaxaca and the Isthmus of Tehuantepec on the Pacific coast were Zapotec domains with Mixtec intrusions, and also under heavy pressure from the Aztecs. As can be seen by comparison with the map of present-day distribution of languages, the regions under Aztec control included groups that were Huastec, Totonac, Otomian, Popolocan, Mixtecan and Mayan speakers, as well as other small groups whose languages have not been preserved.

Within the time span covered in the above outline the Toltec period is a breakthrough as far as historical information is concerned. Whatever their actual historical value, most of the traditions gathered in postconquest times go back to that period, so that from there onwards we are, relatively speaking, in historical times. It is therefore convenient to start from conquest times to see to what date and place language groups can be traced back.

The Aztec group of Nahuatl speakers, according to historical information, was in the Valley of Mexico after A.D. 1256, and they had a tradition of having come from a place located to the north-west, which is not surprising since the rest of the Uto-Aztecan languages are located to the north of that area. Because of a differentiating phonemic trait Nahuatl, Nahuat and Nahual varieties are distinguished; 'Nahua' refers to any of the groups. Nahuatl groups occupy approximately a central position; Nahual groups are found from the central part toward the west; Nahuat groups occupy part of the northern area, the Gulf Coast and regions further south. However, the Aztecs were not the first people in the area belonging to their linguistic subgroup; several of the groups located in the Valley of Mexico were of Nahua speech, and so too, according to tradition, were the Toltecs, at least partially. It is possible that in some cases the known Nahuatl groups were formerly speakers of a different language; this, for instance, has been assumed for the group of Xolotl, who were still hunters when they appeared in the Valley of Mexico after the fall of Tula, and who became absorbed into Mesoamerican culture.

There are also traditions that a Nahuat speech group called Pipil, which was located later in Guatemala and further south, had migrated – via the southern Gulf Coast – from the Valley of Mexico c. A.D. 800. As that migration is reported to have been the consequence of the struggle for supremacy among different groups after the destruction of Teotihuacan, it can be assumed that Nahua speech groups were in the Valley of Mexico at least since the fall of that place, i.e. A.D. 600. Furthermore, as the historically attested Nahua language group and its closest relative Pochutec share the vocabulary for typical Mesoamerican culture characteristics, it can be assumed that speakers of the Aztec subgroup of Uto-Aztecan were already within Mesoamerica well before the fall of Teotihuacan (the glottochronological date for the split of Pochutec is A.D. 400), although the time or place cannot, with present knowledge, be rendered more precise. Since most Uto-Aztecan groups are spread in keeping with the closest linguistic affiliation, Aztecs may have been near the Corachol group (assuming this is its closest relative), but the disappearance in north-west Mexico of groups which were probably of the Uto-Aztecan family, and which might have been closer to the Aztec subgroup than Corachol – from which it is considerably differentiated – renders any attempt at more precision in determining the prehistoric location of the Aztecan group very hypothetical.

Within the Otomanguean family the Mixtec group can be traced back through documentary evidence to northwest Oaxaca (site of Tilantongo (no. 7 in map 2)) during the seventh century A.D.; also, on the somewhat more indirect historical information, Mixtec groups may have extended in the thirteenth century to the Valley of Mexico. Using criteria of cultural identity Zapotecs can be located with certainty in Monte Albán after A.D. 400. There is also sufficient evidence that Otomian groups were in the area where they were encountered historically since at least the period of Tula's dominance, since Otomi speech groups were certainly part of Toltec groups. On the other hand, the identification of the northern invaders of hunting culture in post-Toltec times (e.g. the so-called Chichimec of Xolotl) with groups close to the historically known Pamean speech groups is doubtful on purely linguistic grounds, since Pamean languages have a vocabulary for agricultural items that is proto-Otomanguean. Finally, although it depends on a more hypothetical interpretation of indirect historical data, it is likely that groups of Mazatec and Popolocan speakers were to be found among the Toltecs.

According to some historical traditions the Chiapanec-Mangue group migrated from a region south of the Valley of Mexico some time before A.D. 900, and then split at the place where the Chiapanec were first found historically, the Mangue migrating further south. However, there is a conflicting tradition according to which the Chiapanec split from the Mangue in Nicaragua and migrated to the north; although the first tradition is the one generally accepted the second cannot be discarded entirely.

Subtiaba and Tlapanec are rather closely related, a fact that gives credibility to the glottochronological date of A.D. 1100 for the time of split. But the Tlapanecs have a tradition of having migrated from a place near the Malinche mountain in the Mexican State of Puebla, so that the place where the Subtiaba group started its migration may not have been in the State of Guerrero, the historical location of the Tlapanecs.

As for the Mayan family, groups of Mayan speech can be identified with certainty – through the presence of inscriptions – in the lowland Mayan region from the third century A.D., but no direct evidence exists as to which Mayan language was spoken there. On the basis of the presence of loanwords from Cholan languages (implying a cultural superiority) into other Mayan languages, some experts assume that the people of classical lowland culture spoke Cholan; the validity of the argument depends on the possibility of determining the chronology of these loanwords, since the borrowing may have occurred in later times. The grouping of Chicomuceltec with Huastec seems certain, and the degree of differentiation is such that it makes plausible the glottochronological date of A.D. 1100 for the time of separation, presumably the Chicomuceltec migrating to the south. As in the case of Subtiaba and Tlapanec, the glottochronological date is reasonable because of the fact that it falls in a period of known unrest and migrations in Central Mexico.

For other groups data are either lacking or refer more or less to conquest times. The Tarascans are reported to have taken hold of their area in relatively recent times, displacing and subjugating previous groups, but there is no information from where they might have come; linguistic data are of no help in this case because Tarascan cannot be linked linguistically with any other group. Totonacs had their centre at Cempoala at the time of the conquest, and they may have been the carriers of the important Tajín culture (from Late Classic to the Postclassic period); the identification is, however, hypothetical. The Huastecs must have split from the main Mayan group before Classic times since they share no cultural elements corresponding to that period, although identification by archaeological data may place them in their historical location no further back than A.D. 1000. Other historical information only points to movements within a restricted area, as is the case for example with the Tequistlatec group which extended more to the west and was confined to its historical territory by Mixtec and Zapotec expansion; and the Huaves, who occupied a larger territory toward the north neighbouring Mixe-Zoque groups but who were pushed into the coast by Zapotec expansion just on the eve of the Spanish conquest.

In the previous paragraphs mention was made of plausible data which indicated either the presence of a given group at a previous time in the historically known location or a marked displacement of the group. Further linguistic identifications have been proposed for different groups to which historical documents refer, but they rest upon much more indirect evidence involving, chiefly, movements of groups around the Valley of Mexico in Toltec or post-Toltec times. As it seems certain that these groups were of diverse ethnic composition, the identification becomes more difficult. In these cases, however, it is a question of interpreting documentary evidence; as we go back from Toltec times identification is based on linguistic and archaeological data and is therefore extremely hypothetical.

On the basis of unbroken cultural development the archaeological tradition that leads from 1200 B.C. to Monte Albán culture could be attributed to Zapotec speakers. On the same grounds we could assume the presence of Mayan groups in the lowland area from approximately 800 B.C., although it is not clear how long groups of Mayan speakers may have been present in Kaminaljuyú or in the northern Yucatan area. Elaborate schemes for correlating Mayan groups with archaeological data have been proposed, but while the relations between the groups imply different times of divergence and can be backed by linguistic reconstruction, the assignment of each stage of differentiation to particular archaeological cultures does not in general seem to correlate with data that suggest a change of population. In addition, it relies too heavily on glottochronological dating and operates with a model of 'least moves', a model which is of doubtful validity as it assumes that simplicity has something to do with historical development and interpretation.

A linguistic identification for the carriers of Teotihuacan and Olmec cultures is difficult. Totonacs had a tradition of having been the builders of the pyramids in Teotihuacan, and there is some ethnographic evidence that would strengthen the hypothesis. However, it can in fact be assumed that the pattern known from later times (that political units included diverse ethnic groups) already existed in Teotihuacan, so that the right question to ask (and much more difficult to answer) would be: to what speech group did the rulers that had built Teotihuacan belong? For the rest, the presence of Mazatecan, Mixtecan, Nahuatl, Otomian and Popolocan speakers have been proposed on the basis of rather impressionistic hypotheses.

On archaeological grounds there has been a tendency to assume a Mayan linguistic affiliation for Olmec culture. Another hypothesis has been advanced, chiefly based on linguistic data, that Olmec culture is to be identified, at least partially, with Mixe-Zoque speakers, more precisely with speakers of proto-Mixe-Zoque. The suggestion based on geographical contiguity of the historic location of Mixe-Zoque groups – and absence of evidence for their migration in recent times – is known, but linguistic arguments have been added. These are: (1) the coincidence between the archaeological dating of the beginnings of Olmec tradition and glot-tochronological dating for proto-Mixe-Zoque; (2) the reconstruction for Mixe-Zoque of a vocabulary referring to the typical Mesoamerican pattern of cultivated plants, maize complex and religion; and (3) the borrowing of lexical items of cultural significance into several Mesoamerican languages. The argument based on glottochronology depends on the reliability that one is willing to ascribe to the method, but in addition the date is within a time range for which, even accepting the method in general, results become difficult to check. The argument for borrowings, which seem less extensive than assumed (cf. 10.2), encounters problems; the direction of the borrowing is not clear in every case, and the possibility of a genetic connection of Mixe-Zoque with Totonac and Mayan – two of the language families involved in the borrowings – includes the possibility that some of these items are actual cognates; borrowings into languages like Paya and Lenca may have hardly been direct, so that they become irrelevant to the issue; finally, the possibility exists that some loanwords may be later acquisitions, especially those attested only in neighbouring Mayan languages and/or in Huave and Tequistlatec.

Furthermore, the interpretation of the occurrence of these loanwords as reflect-ing the influence of the first known Mesoamerican culture would be valid for the borrowings that belong to the religious domain (although it depends in turn on the controversial view of Olmec culture as the Mesoamerican 'mother' culture) but certainly not for those within the agricultural domain, because for this aspect there is no evidence for assuming a single centre of diffusion. Summing up, the arguments that make Mixe-Zoque a candidate for the language associated with Olmec culture are based on geographical location and on the character of the reconstructed vocabulary.

The possibility of linking Olmec culture with the Mixe-Zoque group would also solve the problem of identifying the most recent homeland of this linguistic group. The restriction as to 'most recent' homeland is due to the obvious fact that the group had migrated from somewhere north into the Mesoamerican area, although the aforementioned possibility of connection with Totonac-Tepehua and with Mayan would probably pose the problem of determining a homeland for the enlarged group still within Mesoamerica. However, except for Uto-Aztecan lan-guages and for Paya, the problem of when and from where the other groups entered the Mesoamerican area does not seem susceptible to a purely non-hypothetical solution, at least for the time being. This is so because these groups have been not proven to be related on a level of reconstruction with groups outside Mesoamerica, and therefore no evidence for original place of migration is available. Besides, everything points to the presence of the Mayan and Otomanguean groups in Mesoamerica at least as far back as the period when the area began to develop its distinctive characteristics; for both families it is possible to reconstruct a vocabulary which refers to these basic cultural characteristics.

Concerning the Uto-Aztecan languages, it would be premature to identify homelands for subgroups such as Corachol plus Aztecan before they are well established as such. As for the whole family, it certainly did not begin to differentiate in the Mesoamerican area and it represents a migration from the north. In addition, Paya seems to represent an intrusion into Mesoamerica; historical and archaeological data point to a marginal cultural position, and there is no evidence for a retreat of other Chibchan languages toward the south – on the contrary they may be a reflux from South America into Central America.

For the Mayan group the highlands of Guatemala have been repeatedly proposed, but the arguments for it seem to be rather weak. There is no association with a definite archaeological culture, the reconstructed vocabulary does not clearly point to a definite geographical region, and other arguments are rather speculative, e.g. that it is more likely that migrations were downriver than upriver.

The Valley of Tehuacan has been proposed as the homeland of the Otomanguean group. The hypothesis relies on the coincidence of glottochronological dating for the protolanguage with the dating of an archaeological phase, and on the matching between plants and animals associated with that archaeological phase and the reconstructed vocabulary, in which there are items naming those elements. That some Otomanguean groups may have been associated for a long time with the culture of Tehuacan is very likely because of the historical location of some of these groups and the unbroken cultural development there, but as a homeland for the whole family it presents problems. The main one is that it fails to account for the historical position of the Otopamean subgroup that would represent marked displacement toward the north; in the absence of archaeological evidence for the migration it could be assumed to have been in the opposite direction, and a site like Tamaulipas (see map 2) could serve equally well for the correlation with the reconstructed vocabulary. Again, even accepting the data from glottochronology as valid, as it was stated in 2.5, there is no reliable estimation of the percentage of cognates for the whole family, the one used – giving 4500 B.C. as time of differentiation – having been made on a rather impressionistic basis without the control of systematic reconstruction. Additionally, the fact that there is no conclusive evidence for establishing more inclusive subgroups within Otomanguean (cf. 2.3) is a severe limitation on the inferences that could be made from the purely linguistic viewpoint.

The recently established relationship between Tequistlatecan and Jicaque automatically poses the problem of determining for the family both the homeland and the direction of migration, given the distance at which they are located. But comparative work is still too recent even for an estimation of the degree of differentiation, a point which would imply a considerable difference as to the possibility of migration in one or another direction. The fact that among the reconstructed items of vocabulary are some that refer to agriculture is a hint that the time of separation may not be too remote.

The identification of linguistic groups with archaeological cultures is in general very difficult. Moreover, for the specific case of Mesoamerica one has to take into account the many gaps still existing in the archaeological knowledge of the area, and also the fact that the historical study of the linguistic families has not reached the degree of refinement necessary for tackling these problems on a firm basis.

10.2 Language contacts

Several of the cultural characteristics of Mesoamerica imply intense and widespread cultural contacts, and therefore the presence of linguistic borrowings is to be expected. In spite of this, what seems striking is that in general examples of borrowings among Indian languages are comparatively few, with the exception of the southern periphery, and even there the number of loanwords is not great. As will be discussed in 10.2.2, there is only one certain case of another type of borrowing.

10.2.1 *Loanwords*

The case in which the greatest number of loanwords is attested is that of Quichean languages. These loanwords are of Nahuatl origin – probably from a variety similar to that spoken in the southern Gulf coast – and were incorporated into Quichean languages as a consequence of Toltec influence. Most of the borrowed words belong to the religious and military domains, e.g. 'altar', 'incense', 'demon', 'axe', 'cotton cuirasse' and 'palace', although there are a few within the domain of everyday life, such as words for 'cradle' or 'net for catching fish'. Including doubtful cases, around eighty loanwords are found in these languages. This fact indicates a widespread influence but it is not significant for any particular language since not all those loanwords are actually attested in a single one. Those languages with the highest number have about thirty loanwords, which is a rather modest number when contrasted with other cases of lexical borrowing. By way of comparison – and without taking an example of truly mass borrowing – in a collection of modern Chol texts which refer to traditional aspects of the culture about 100 loanwords from Spanish are found.

Mayan languages, in turn, have been a source of loanwords for Xinca, Lenca, Jicaque and Paya. Those borrowed into Xinca – only about twenty-five – show a clear pattern, but in different domains from those of Nahuatl into Quichean languages. Several loanwords are names for cultivated plants, a fact which has been interpreted as pointing to a former status of the Xincas as non-agriculturalists. What is rather puzzling (taking into account that the language may have been in the area for a long time) is the presence of names for animals among the loanwords, although other instances within the same domain are found among other languages in the area.

Other common items of vocabulary in the domains of cultivated plants, flora and fauna are found in Jicaque, Xinca, Miskito and Matagalpa, but the direction of borrowing cannot as yet be determined. In any case, it is likely that the amount of borrowing in this area has been somewhat exaggerated. Some of the assumed loanwords can hardly be true loanwords as they have meanings like 'wind', 'stone', 'white' or 'good' which, even in cases of mass borrowing, are unusual as loanwords. It should be taken into account that as in the case of cognates mere resemblance is not sufficient proof of common origin, and there are at least two problems which render the determination of loanwords still more difficult in these cases: (1) there is not enough historical knowledge about some of the languages (which for practical purposes are isolated); (2) in the absence of many instances of loanwords which could serve to establish patterns of adaptation it is difficult to ascertain whether differences in shape are the result of erratic adaptation or whether the resemblance is simply casual. The assumed loanword for 'snake' (in undetermined direction), Xinca *ampuk(i)*, Lenca from El Salvador *amap*, Subtiaba *apu*, may serve as an example. The Subtiaba form is sufficiently similar to the Xinca one to suggest a borrowing, but it happens that it is a cognate of Tlapanec $a^3bõ^{?3}$ and of other words in Otomanguean languages that reconstruct as *$(n)k^wa n$ (the Subtiaba word does not require the initial nasal). This excludes the possibility of a borrowing from Xinca or Lenca, and as a borrowing in inverse direction – in itself highly unlikely since Subtiaba is a newcomer in the area – it would be difficult to explain why the other languages should have added a nasal. Therefore the resemblance of the Subtiaba form appears fortuitous.

A further difficulty is that for some of these languages the material was recorded very recently when some of these were practically dying languages, and one may wonder whether their receptivity to loanwords may not reflect a state of dissolution of the language; otherwise it is quite anomalous (given the total number of loanwords) to find the unmistakably Pipil word *nakat* 'meat' borrowed into Matagalpa.

The possibility that a loanword may be recently acquired is strong for borrowings from Nahuatl languages; that is why borrowings from Pipil into other languages in the southern area were not mentioned above. Some of the loanwords are obviously postconquest because of their meanings, e.g. Pipil *tiupan* (*tiu-* 'God', *-pan* 'place of'), Honduras Lenca *teiban*, Matagalpa *teopan*, all meaning 'church'. Even some of the Nahuatl loanwords found in Quichean languages may be of the postconquest period.

A case in point may be the word *masa* 'deer' from Nahuatl *masa-tl* which seems to have been borrowed because the native word meaning 'deer' had shifted to the meaning 'horse', obviously a postconquest phenomenon; the hypothesis is strengthened by the fact that exactly the same process of shifting the meaning of the native word and borrowing of the Nahuatl word occurred in North Pame. It would seem as though Spanish acted as a catalyst through the preference given by Spaniards to the Nahuatl language and by the presence of Nahuatl speakers allied to the Spaniards. Thus there is no reason to expect Nahuatl loanwords in Malinaltepec Tlapanec as the region had been subjugated by the Aztecs at the time the Spanish conquest started. Nevertheless, there is an attested Nahuatl loanword *la¹ʃa³* 'orange', from Nahuatl *laʃa*, which in turn is borrowed from Old Spanish/*na'ranʃa*/. Again, languages with few if any preconquest borrowings, such as Ixcatec, Mixe, Tzotzil and Huave, have borrowed the word meaning 'goat': Nahuatl *tentsu*, Totontepec Mixe *tɛɛnts*, Tzotzil *tentsun*, Huave *tiants*; this is again clearly a postconquest process.

For the rest of Mesoamerica the case that could demonstrate a number of borrowings is the previously mentioned case of the Mixe-Zoque loanwords. These would be important, not through sheer number (there are about fifty in total, and single languages do not have more than a dozen), but because of the time of borrowing (Olmec times), the domains they refer to (cultivated plants, maize complex, religion), and the number of languages involved: Mayan, Otomanguean, Chontal-Jicaque, Lencan and Xinca languages plus Nahuatl, Huave, Tarascan and Paya. However, on close inspection many of the assumed loanwords can be rejected. It was mentioned in the preceding section of this chapter that most borrowings into Jicaque and Paya are probably through Mayan languages, so they are not instances of borrowing from Mixe-Zoque but of ultimate Mixe-Zoque origin. Among those borrowed into Otomanguean languages only the word meaning 'paper' in Mixtec can be considered a certain borrowing; most of the remaining words reconstruct well as cognates within Otomanguean, but in some cases with quite different shape.

This may serve as a further example of the cases of casual resemblances discussed above: Mazahua *ʃihmo* has been considered to be a loan from proto-Mixe-Zoque **tsima* 'gourd', but the Mazahua form is a cognate of the Chichimec form *nimo* 'gourd', and, as a rule, in the usual Otomanguean pattern the final syllable is the root; furthermore, in this case it is the same one that appears in the Ixcatec word *ʃwa³* and in Tlapanec *ʃu²wa²*, and it derives from proto-Otomanguean **(n)wi(h)n*. (The part of the Ixcatec and Tlapanec forms cognate with Mazahua and Chichimec

-*mo* is -*wa*. Correspondences within Otomanguean are too complicated to be explained in detail here.)

Borrowings from Mixe-Zoque into Nahuatl (with the exception of one similar to the word for 'cacao' – most probably not a direct borrowing) are difficult to justify owing to unexplained differences in shape, existence of cognates in northern Uto-Aztecan languages (a reborrowing from Nahuatl into Tarahumara or Varohio is hard to imagine), and geographical and temporal discontinuity. It has to be remembered that while Olmec culture has been identified since 1200 B.C. it flourished between 800 B.C. and 400 B.C., whereas proto-Aztecan may have been present in north-western Mexico at the beginning of the Christian era.

If one takes into account that borrowings into Tequistlatecan languages and into Totonac are few in number, and that those into the former, as well as those into neighbouring Mayan languages and Huave, may be relatively recent loanwords, it has to be concluded that the certain linguistic influences from Mixe-Zoque at Olmec times are reduced to quite modest proportions.

Although of Mixe-Zoque origin too, the loanwords found in Isthmus Nahuatl (located in the southern Gulf coast) have been incorporated at a later time, after the group migrated from Central Mexico (cf. 10.1). Some may be rather early borrowings, but the fact that most of them have a scanty distribution in the Nahuat dialect – a group which probably did not start to differentiate before the arrival of the Spaniards – suggests that their incorporation may have been in many cases relatively recent. There are around forty loanwords identified, but again no single variety has more than fifteen. Most words refer to the fauna (predominantly maritime fauna) and flora of the area. On the other hand, while Nahuat loanwords are not apparent in the Mixe-Zoque languages, some languages of the Zoquean branch have borrowed from Nahuatl the function word *iga* 'that', 'in order that'. It is interesting that some cases of loan translations (calques) have been found, e.g. Nahuat *si·n-go·jama*, Popoluca *mog-itsim* 'boar', both words literally meaning 'ear-of-corn-swine'.

It should be clear from the preceding discussion of loanwords in the Mesoamerican area that we need to explain why they are comparatively uncommon. The situation is not unexpected, however, considering certain characteristics of social and political organization. Mesoamerican 'states', including the Aztec empire, were rather loose political aggregates that switched alliances without concomitant important changes in the internal organization of the groups which participated. Each basic unit centred in a town or city which had a type of internal differentiation that allowed integration at different levels without much affecting lower levels. Even in bigger units different ethnic groups could coexist side by side, but seemingly without a great deal of intermingling. The sphere of influence of the

Aztec empire probably represented the most cohesive kind of integration at the state level in the development of Mesoamerica, but even so power was exerted chiefly through tribute and control by punitive raids whenever the necessity arose, not by real integration into a unified and directly controlled political whole. It is significant that in cases of real conquest, like that of the Quichean territory by Toltecs, the result was not a state dependent on an already existing centre, and it was the ruling class who became linguistically assimilated to the subjugated population. There is another example of this kind of process: according to the native tradition, the founders of the Mixtec kingdom of Tilantongo were intruders who became assimilated linguistically. That this should have been so is supported by the fact that at the time of the Spanish conquest there was still a special vocabulary used by commoners when referring to the members of the upper class, forms which were not of the Mixtec language and which have been partially identified as occurring in other Otomanguean languages (chiefly Cuicatec). This special vocabulary, in spite of having been used by commoners, did not survive the collapse of native political units.

In more general terms a hypothesis advanced from the archaeological side, and which aims to explain the seemingly contradictory facts of outside influences and locally well characterized unbroken development, is pertinent to the problems associated with the loanwords. In simplified terms it assumes that cultural contacts were the results of interest in keeping prestige on the part of the ruling class. This agrees with the fact that the most widespread borrowed words or those that seem to have been easily borrowed independently at different places belong by their meaning to the religious and military domains or to that of luxury items. This is the case of the widespread loanwords from Mixe-Zoque meaning 'incense', 'cacao', or the occurrence everywhere of the vigesimal number system. The otherwise puzzling borrowing of some names that designate animals, e.g. 'rabbit' from Mixe-Zoque into Yucatec, has been plausibly explained as being due to the fact that they were calendrical terms; days were associated with names of animals and plants in the Mesoamerican calendars, and these were the responsibility – and privilege – of the priestly class. A word for 'turkey' is common to some Mayan languages and Mixe-Zoque (which is probably the source of the borrowing), and it is possibly the same one that occurs in Jicaque and Tequistlatec; Huastec Nahuatl and Huastec share the word for 'male turkey' (the direction of the borrowing is undetermined), and in several Otomanguean languages occupying a continuous territory (Trique, some Mixtec languages, Chatino, some Zapotec languages and Tlapanec) there is a common word for 'male turkey' which, because of its phonological shape, could only be the result of normal development in Zapotec languages, from which the form may have been borrowed. The interest of these examples for the point at hand is that, at least in the Mixtec area, the turkey was a luxury item.

The character of the Nahuatl loanwords found in Quichean languages has already been discussed, and as a final example one might mention the frequent cases where groups, on taking hold of new territory, kept previous place names by means of loan translation, a practice that can be assumed not to be in the hands of commoners.

It can be seen, then, that several facts point to a situation in which linguistic contacts were primarily among the upper classes and that their potential effects reached lower groups only sparingly. Consequently it indicates that the very frequent references to bilingualism involving Nahuatl and another language found in the *Relaciones Geográficas* (cf. chapter 1) and other sources should be taken with a qualification as to the generality of the phenomenon. It may have been so in cases like that of Nahuatl and Zoquean languages (cf. above), but for the most part one has to assume that bilingualism was restricted to the ruling class; were it the case, as is accepted by some modern scholars, that bilingualism was general, the scarcity of Nahuatl loanwords in other languages would be anomalous.

The implied conclusion that the lower strata of society developed in a situation of marked linguistic isolation from other groups is reinforced by the present-day linguistic fragmentation which was discussed in chapter 2. It would seem that Mesoamerican political units did not produce linguistic unification even at close range; the fragmentation may have been favoured by the Spanish policy of isolating cultural groups, but it was not its result. As the following quotation (Córdova 1886 [1578]: 119) makes clear, it already existed: 'It has to be noticed that among all the towns that speak this language – I mean those that are pure Zapotecans – there is no town that does not differ from another little or much.'

Some patterns appear persistent in Mesoamerica, and although little information is available on present-day linguistic contacts among native groups, some instances exist in which the casual traveller may see what appears to be a single town but which in reality contains two linguistically and ethnically different groups coexisting but with little intermingling between them.

10.2.2 *Linguistic area traits*

Within a given geographical and cultural area languages, whatever their genetic affiliations, may share structural characteristics which are not inherited but which are the result of diffusion; this phenomenon is called 'area traits' or 'language association' (or by the original German term *Sprachbund*). Area traits are of special historical interest insofar as they are in fact due to diffusion, for otherwise, if due to common origin, they are part of the historical study of the language families, or, if casual, they belong to the typological characterization of the area.

As against some approaches for which this type of diffusion would constitute a phenomenon different from ordinary borrowing, a process in which some not directly attested mechanism is involved, here it is understood that area traits cannot but be an instance of borrowing. Therefore, on the basis of what is known of influences among languages – that the part of a language that is most easily influenced is vocabulary – it would be quite unusual if borrowing of phonological and grammatical traits could occur in the absence of straight borrowing of lexical items.

In fact no definite proposals as to the diffusion of phonological or grammatical traits have been advanced for Mesoamerica, but it has been proposed that this area shows a coincidence of features characteristic of a linguistic area. Even in this preliminary form the proposal does not seem to be supported by the facts.

In relation to phonology the data presented in chapters 2 and 3 hardly suggest a recurrence of traits characteristic of a linguistic area. Actually the hypothesis referred to the phonological systems of the protolanguages, but then it becomes self-defeating because in a linguistic area progressive convergence would be ex-pected, not the opposite. Furthermore, at the time of the protolanguage some of the groups would have had the social organization of a band or a small tribe, which is not the type of social organization that would favour this kind of linguistic contact. Nevertheless, many of the alleged common features are negative ones, for example the absence of voiced fricatives; negative features have the same value for area traits as retentions have for subgrouping, that is, they are neutral (cf. chapter 2). Other features adduced are too natural to be significant, as for example voicing of obstruents after nasals, chiefly when the language lacks contrast of voice in the obstruent series. Other characteristics occur discontinuously, such as the voiceless laterals that are found in Tequistlatec, Cuicatec and Totonac, or the aspirated stops occurring in Tarascan and Jicaque. Otomanguean languages cannot be adduced for this point because, although having Ch clusters, the aspiration in this position is the result of a process of metathesis hC > Ch that is still going on in some languages like Tlapanec. Only for the glottalized stops could a case be made on the basis of Mayan languages, Xinca and Lenca, but not Jicaque which shares them with its genetically related group Tequistlatec.

The last point mentioned is important; one of the ways through which an area trait can be detected is when it occurs unexpectedly (i.e. not explainable as an inherited characteristic) in a language or languages of a given family, although this is not the case for all the phonological area traits proposed. Thus, for instance, tones occur either within a genetic group, e.g. Otomanguean – and there is no evidence that the particular system of a given subgroup may have been influenced by the system of another subgroup – or in some languages of a family, e.g. Mayan, where they can be explained as regular developments, or as a yet unexplained trait (e.g. in a dialect of Huave and in some Uto-Aztecan languages) in languages which, so far as it can be determined, have not been in contact with tone languages, or, if they have, where the contact is very recent.

In connection with grammar, coincidental traits adduced are common and general, e.g. nouns that designate body parts being obligatorily possessed, marking of pronominal object in the verb, directional elements within the verb phrase, use of nouns referring to body parts in locative phrases, etc. On this level of generality most of the characteristics listed in chapter 6 could be considered particular to given areas, but by the same token the given area could progressively cover a good part of the Americas. For a characteristic to be significant it has to be either specific enough (although attention was called in chapter 6 to the differences that were found under the same general category label), or it has to represent a particularly elaborated notion, as is the case of directionals in Corachol and Tarahumara-Varohio, but these languages are Uto-Aztecan. Again, in other cases, the characteristics are either found discontinuously or constitute isolated common features when it is the case that a certain clustering of common characteristics would be expected in area phenomena.

The same objection can be raised with regard to common semantic traits, with the exception of the already mentioned vigesimal systems of numerals which clearly constitute an area trait which has to be explained by diffusion.

In spite of the rejection of these proposals, Mesoamerica presently constitutes an obvious linguistic area, but its characteristics have probably been overlooked because of the view that separates area traits from instances of ordinary borrowing. Mesoamerican as a linguistic area is the result of the influence of Spanish on the native languages. The extent of the common characteristics can be seen by looking back at chapters 3 and 8. They originate from a definite and identifiable source, are widespread and they involve diffusion of phonemic contrasts and of clusters of phonemes, grammatical elements (function words) and grammatical patterns which sometimes disrupt inherited ones (e.g. prepositions in postpositional languages, marking with particles instead of marking affixes, subordination by particles instead of subordination by juxtaposition, etc.); they represent direct borrowings as well as calques. To these structural characteristics a considerable number of loanwords must be added, and, as would be expected, there is an almost total absence of borrowing of morphological elements. On the other hand, this case is an example of the care with which hypotheses about the diffusion of particular characteristics should be made; the fact that a given characteristic, say contrast of voice in stops, has diffused from Spanish does not mean that any occurrence of it in Mesoamerica is an instance of the area trait.

It will be important for the discussion of the topics dealt with in the next chapter that Spanish is involved in this type of phenomenon. Spanish intrusion in

Mesoamerica not only ended the native cultural development and thrust it in a new direction, but also brought in a type of cultural influence that was previously seemingly absent in the area.

SOURCES

Most of the data given in this chapter can be found in the bibliographical references under Further Reading, but a few points require a specific reference. The difficulty in assuming Pamean linguistic affiliation for northern tribes of hunters because of their common agricultural vocabulary with Otomian languages was pointed out by Carrasco 1950: 306–7. Thompson 1943: 25 argued for the postconquest character of the borrowing of the Nahuat word for 'deer' into Quichean languages; for the same word as borrowed by Northern Pame, Gibson and Bartholomew 1979: 311. The word 'turkey' in Mixe-Zoque, Mayan and Tequistlatec-Jicaque has been identified by Campbell and Kaufman 1976: 86; for the turkey as a luxury item in Mixtec areas, Spores 1967: 8. Zoquean loanwords into Isthmus Nahuat are identified by García de León 1976: 50–3. The identification of the words of the special Mixtec vocabulary have been made by Arana Osnaya: 1955.

FURTHER READING

Some general presentations of archaeological data and culture development are Wolf 1959; Willey, Ekholm, and Millon 1964; Willey 1966; characterization of Mesoamerican societies in Carrasco 1971a; of the Aztec empire in Gibson, C. 1971. On the important issue of the character and influence of Olmec culture see the different points of view represented by Coe 1965, 1968, and Sanders and Price 1968. The hypothesis on the mechanism of and motivations for cultural influences in Mesoamerica is advanced by Flannery 1968.

The native traditions are summarized in Carrasco 1971b. Basic general treatments of linguistic identifications of groups through documentary evidence in Jiménez Moreno 1942, 1954–5, 1959. For treatments of particular groups: Carrasco 1950; Dahlgren 1954; Brand et al. 1960; some references to linguistic identifications for preconquest times are given in Harvey 1971; Spores 1965; Miles 1965.

Hypotheses about migrations and archaeological identifications of Mayan groups in Diebold 1960; McQuown 1971; Kaufman 1978; see also the cautious views expressed in Willey 1971. For the identification of Mixe-Zoque with Olmec culture on the basis of linguistic evidence see Campbell and Kaufman 1976. On Tehuacan as homeland of the Otomanguean group, Amador Hernández and Casasa García 1979, Hopkins 1977. An attempt at tracing migrations of linguistic groups into Mesoamerica through correlations with archaeological data is Manrique 1975. A careful correlation (Mixtecan and Amuzgo) of reconstructed vocabulary with archaeological data is Longacre and Millon 1961.

On loanwords from Nahuat into Quichean languages, from Mayan languages into the languages of the southern periphery and among the latter see Campbell 1972, 1976b, 1977; for the borrowings from Mixe-Zoque, Campbell and Kaufman 1976. On general problems in the identification of loanwords, Thompson 1943; although restricted to cases in which Spanish is involved, the observations in Bright 1979 are much to the point in dealing with loanwords among Indian languages. For a case of contemporary co-territorial groups with little inter-influence see Albores 1976.

Proposals for considering Mesoamerica as a linguistic area: Kaufman 1973; Campbell 1979.

11

Indian languages after the conquest

11.1 Language policies

As stated in chapter 2, an indeterminable number of Indian languages became extinct as a consequence of the conquest. Looking at a map of language distribution at the time of first contact it can be seen that except for northern languages located beyond Mesoamerica proper, most of those which disappeared were spoken by groups occupying small areas in regions of great linguistic diversity, chiefly along the coast and nearby inland fringes in the present-day Mexican States of Guerrero, Michoacan and Colima. For the most part, languages became extinct rather early during the sixteenth century chiefly because of the sharp decline in population caused by epidemics. In some cases whole groups were probably wiped out; in others a decimated group may have shifted linguistically to Spanish or to other Indian languages.

Replacement of a given language by Nahuatl certainly occurred, although it has not been clearly demonstrated in how many cases the shift actually took place. Nahuatl groups which the Spaniards brought along with them, either by force or as allies, settled in regions where different languages were spoken, and the favouring of Nahuatl by Spaniards may have been conducive to language replacement. On the other hand, that the friars may have taught and enforced the use of the Nahuatl language to certain groups, as it is sometimes stated, could hardly have been possible: there was always a shortage of friars to attend to Indian communities, most towns in a parish being merely *visitas* ('visits'); thus for a region in the Mixe area, it has been estimated that it took a month for the parson to make the tour of the towns in his jurisdiction, so that in these conditions it is difficult to imagine how a parson could have taught a language to a whole population.

The conquest began in 1519 and by the end of the sixteenth century most of Mesoamerica was under Spanish control, although by the end of the seventeenth century there were still some groups which had not yet been completely subjugated, and from the sixteenth century right through to and including the nineteenth numerous Indian uprisings occurred. Outside Mesoamerica proper, some even took place during the first third of the present century. Some of these uprisings were nativistic in character, others were struggles for land rights. The rule of Spain as well as that of its heirs exerted effective control of the native populations, which were not merely tributaries, as under the Aztecs, but became, at least theoretically, free subjects of the Crown and later citizens of the respective Republics.

The fact that almost five hundred years after the first contact there are still over five million people who speak an Indian language shows a remarkable persistence. It is difficult to point out the conditions which either favoured Hispanicization or furthered the maintenance of indigenous languages; there are many variables involved in this type of process which cannot be merely guessed at, and there are no in-depth studies dealing with this problem. Nevertheless, the state of Indian languages may have been conditioned by some general facts which are worth mentioning. These are: the official language policy, the system of control of Indian communities and interethnic relationships.

It is doubtful whether language policy had any important effect on the linguistic situation, but it reflected official attitudes toward native languages, and the policy during the Spanish period has additional interest in that its architects were one of the first legislative bodies to face explicitly the problem of multilingual states.

Up to 1770 the Spanish Crown had a double language policy with different goals and reflecting conflicting interests. As was the case in reference to the study of native languages, mentioned in the first chapter, the relationship with the dominated Arabs in Spain served as background for Spanish attitudes toward Indian languages. In this connection a prominent figure like Cardinal Jiménez de Cisneros – advisor to Queen Isabella, Prime Minister of Castile, and later regent of the Kingdom of Castile – favoured an immediate assimilation of the Moorish population through forced conversion and the learning of the Spanish language, believing that the preservation of the Arab language would make its speakers persist in their religious beliefs. This argument would be used later in relation to the Indian population. In fact, the teaching of Spanish may be considered to have reflected the point of view of the Spanish government.

From 1516 there were written statements favouring the teaching of Spanish, and one of the arguments adduced for the assumed benefits of the system of *encomienda* was that the Indians would acquire the Christian religion and the Spanish language through their close contact with Spaniards. On the other hand, the application of an ordinance in 1550 enforcing the teaching of Spanish was resisted by the friars, and in 1555 the first Mexican Council established that it was necessary to convert people using their own language, requiring parsons to know the language spoken in their parish, a resolution endorsed by the Crown in 1565.

Nonetheless, the friars found the difficulty of coping with so many languages almost insurmountable and looked for a remedy in choosing Nahuatl as the vehicle for conversion; as a consequence, a Crown ordinance of 1570 made Nahuatl a kind of official language. It has to be borne in mind that, for the friars, the conversion of a group at first meant the conversion of its chief who in fact may have already known Nahuatl. Knowledge of Nahuatl by whole populations is, however, very doubtful, as was pointed out in 10.2. As for the ease with which Indians learned Nahuatl, the true situation was probably similar to the one described years later by a friar, reporting on the attempts to teach Nahuatl, who considered the difficulty that the friars had learning Chinantec and stated that 'no benefit derived from it [i.e. teaching Nahuatl], on the contrary, it was realized that it caused more confusion and misery' (Barreda 1960 [1730]: p. 14 of the facsimile).

The lack of sufficient friars who knew the Indian languages, as well as the assumed unfitness of native languages for the teaching of the Catholic religion without distortion, were arguments advanced from the last years of the sixteenth century to press Colonial and Peninsular authorities to further the spread of Spanish, but at that time the Spanish Crown resisted enforcing the outright teaching of Spanish because the Council of Trent (1545–63) had sanctioned the use of native languages as the vehicle of conversion. Nevertheless, the trend favouring the Spanish language became progressively more prominent. It was argued, for example, that if the Indians knew Spanish then, in legal suits, there would be no need for translators who could be bribed to act to the detriment of the Indians; furthermore, after the sixteenth-century missions declined and friars were relegated to peripheral areas, secular priests were never very enthusiastic about the use of Indian languages; also, by the end of the seventeenth century even the ecclesiastical authorities became alarmed at the fact that few Indians knew Spanish and that many resisted learning it; a resolution of 1690 established that preference should be given to persons who knew Spanish in the appointment of native officials.

Furthermore, in the eighteenth century there was an important change in the intellectual climate: Peninsular and Colonial authorities, both civil and ecclesiastic, were men of the Enlightenment and supporters of absolute monarchy for which linguistic uniformity was considered a necessary ingredient. It was in this atmosphere that a Royal Cedula issued in 1770 enforced the teaching of Spanish with the avowed purpose that Indian languages should disappear. While this decree is important as a testimony of official attitudes in the last period of Spanish rule in America, its effects were in all likelihood minor given the educational conditions of the epoch (witness the survival of native languages). Besides, it is a fact – all too commonly forgotten in evaluating this type of linguistic policy – that the only effective way to cause the extinction of a language is to eliminate its speakers, otherwise the 'killing of a language' is only a worn-out metaphor.

Probably more important than language policy was the way in which control of Indian population was exerted. This may be characterized in general as an indirect control. From the middle of the sixteenth century the *encomienda* system in the Mesoamerican area was for tribute only, without personal service and without land granting; it was also the system which provided the labour force for public works and mining, the so called *repartimiento* ('allotment'), working on a rota system, Indians being assigned to it for a fixed period. These systems, moreover, functioned through the intermediacy of native chiefs; Spaniards kept the stratified native social system on the community level, and from the middle of the sixteenth century there were in Indian towns – kept apart from Spanish towns – native councils in charge of collecting tribute, allotting Indians for the required works and which also performed other surveillance functions. Also, although at first Spanish laws favoured the contact of native population with Spaniards as well as intermarrying, later complaints were raised about the bad example that the behaviour of the Spaniards presented to the Indians, and the authorities became alarmed at the rate at which the number of mestizos increased. As a result a number of laws were issued forbidding non-Indians, i.e. whites, mestizos and blacks, to live in Indian towns.

Furthermore, the sharp decrease in the population had the effect that by the end of the sixteenth century native chiefs lost power and importance because they did not have enough people from whom to collect the tribute demanded by Spaniards. At that time a system which was to become well established in the following century began to take shape; this system provided Indian towns with an organization parallel to that of Spanish towns; it embraced civil and religious spheres with an elaborate hierarchy of posts that were filled in prescribed order. This system still persists, and it seems to have been one of the factors that gave cohesion to Indian communities and became one of the chief forces behind their survival as distinct entities. Also, the period from the beginning of the eighteenth century saw a certain weakening of Spanish control that still further increased the isolation of Indian towns, and in some cases seems to have allowed the reemergence of old native characteristics that had been suppressed but not eradicated.

All of these elements may have favoured the relative isolation and autonomy of Indian communities, and consequently were conducive to the preservation of the native language, although there were also opposite forces at work. At the end of the seventeenth century *haciendas* (large landholdings) emerged and with them the system of peonage. Although in theory this was free labour, impoverished Indians who had to pay their tribute were in fact forced to engage themselves as workers in *haciendas*; the owners, in turn, needing a large labour force, tried to ensure that Indians contracted debts, thus tying them to the *hacienda* so that free labour turned into debt-bonded work. In spite of efforts on the part of the Indian communities, they were unable to stem the flow of Indians who went to establish themselves in *haciendas*. Despite the limited amount of Spanish required for that kind of work, the mere fact of people moving out of their communities – even temporarily – should have been one of the main agents of Hispanicization, if not, in some cases, of progressive loss of the native language.

A process in the reverse direction also ran counter to the isolation of Indians and counts as a factor leading to the spread of the Spanish language. In spite of both the legislation against the mixing of ethnic groups and of the development of theoretically more severe 'caste' systems neither law nor prejudice prevented the process of racial and social mixing. The mestizo class grew steadily, and while it tended to come in between and separate the more European groups from the more Indian ones, it also started to encroach into Indian towns and Indian lands.

While the conditions under the Spanish period were not uniform for the entire area, neither was legislation valid in all jurisdictions – much of the legislation was introduced to resolve specific problems which arose among the diverse Indian groups. With the rise of the newly independent countries a new element of diversification appeared: although in general the approaches to the problems posed by Indian communities have been similar, policies have not been implemented at the same time. The following remarks will focus on Mexico since developments there are better known than in the other countries.

At first the approaches to the Indian problem were conflicting and similar to those in the Spanish period, but finally the criterion that prevailed was that the Indians were to be treated as citizens and thus did not warrant any special legislation. Afterwards, in the mid-nineteenth century, laws were issued to eliminate the communal ownership of land. This was a severe blow to the Indian communities which suffered heavy losses of land. As in other cases, the native populations had their already limited possibilities of subsistence further curtailed and had to look for work outside their communities. On the other hand, those communities which could persist relatively undisturbed were those located in the most isolated and unproductive areas that nobody wanted.

The revolutionary uprising begun in 1910 was again unfavourable for the maintenance of native languages. In certain areas the native population was involved, actively or passively, in the Revolution, and people frequently had to move to other towns. This situation naturally furthered the process of Hispanicization. The Revolution restored the communal ownership of land, but Indian groups were not those most affected by that measure. On the other hand, the view was held that these groups should be fully incorporated into national life, which meant among other things that they had to speak Spanish. For several years the use of native languages was forbidden in schools, a measure which acquired special weight after 1921, when an amendment to the Constitution established the Federal Educational System in which no special education was provided for Indian groups. Programmes which were launched to raise the standards of the rural population did not in general prove to be very effective for Indian groups, many of whom did not speak Spanish and whose teachers did not know the native languages. But to a greater or lesser degree the period from 1910 to the 1930s can be considered as a period of expansion for Spanish.

However, since at least the late 1930s it is difficult to determine the extent to which official policies have been actually implemented. This is because they have not been embodied in written legislation which could be enforced. As a consequence, since they are primarily the reflection of opinions of various government officials, it may happen (as occurred in the Spanish period) that different or even the same departments may carry out conflicting policies at the same time.

This official view began to change in the mid-1930s. The chief barrier to the integration of these groups was considered to be of a cultural nature. Indian groups, it was now thought, should be motivated to adapt culturally, preserving their ethnic identity as much as possible. Education should be bilingual, starting with literacy in the native language with a progressive shift to Spanish. This approach is the one that has prevailed, at least in theory, until now, and although no objective evaluation (in fact, no evaluation at all) has been made of its effects, very little seems to have been achieved. No group has become literate in its own language, and the progressive spread of Spanish has probably been independent of those programmes. Properly speaking, there was no methodology employed to teach Spanish except that based on the wrong premise that literacy in the native language made the learning of another language easier.

In recent years a method has been developed and applied for the teaching of Spanish. It relies on the native language as a medium for basic communication but makes the oral teaching of Spanish, and eventually literacy in it, independent of literacy in the native language. Also, in relation to the whole problem of Indian communities, there seems to have been a shift toward considering them as part of the wider problem of 'depressed areas' without distinguishing them from non-Indian communities.

11.2   Indian languages at the present time

Tables 25 and 26 give the number of speakers for single languages and for groups of languages in Mexico and Guatemala, according to the latest official data. Mexican figures correspond to the 1970 census and those for Guatemala to the 1950 census, but figures of the 1940 census are given in brackets because the differences are such as to cast serious doubts on the reliability of the 1950 census. For Guatemala there are total figures from the 1973 census which are given below, but figures for speakers of each language are not yet available.

Table 25. *Number of speakers of single languages*

Yucatec	454675	Cuicatec	10192
Cakchiquel	167363 [328991]	Chontal (Mayan)	9854
Kekchí	153971 [246414]	Aguacatec	8401 [6794]
Mazahua	104729	Huave	7442
Tzeltal	99383	Yaqui	7084
Tzotzil	95383	Huichol	6874f
Chol	73253	Cora	6242
Huastec	66091	Zoque (Oaxaca)	5352
Tarascan	60411	Chontal (Highland)	4309
Kanjobal	41622 [39685]	Tepehuán (Southern)	3607
Pocomchí	37540	Varohio*	3000
Tlapanec	30804	Pima*	3000
Mayo	27848	Chontal (Coastal)	2271
Ixil	25025 [15160]	Amuzgo (Oaxaca)	1973
Zoque (Chiapas)	21036	Matlatzinca	1792
Miskito	20723	Tepehuán (Northern)	1189
Tzutuhil	18761	Black Carib	1116 [3317]
Jacaltec	G.13491 [12107]	Chichimec*	500
	M.*1000	Chocho*	993
Tojolabal	13303	Papago*	700
Uspantec	12089 [4778]	Sumu	700
Chortí	12048	Lacandon	G. 215
Pokomán	11434		M. 200
Amuzgo (Guerrero)	11426	Ocuiltec*	393
Chuj	G.10771	Ixcatec*	119
	M. 700		

[ ] Figures from the 1940 Guatemalan census.
*   Indirect estimate since the census does not register the language.
G: Guatemala. M: Mexico.

Table 26. *Number of speakers for language complexes*

Nahuatl	799394	Mixe	54403
Quiché	339232 [441705]	Chinantec	54145
Zapotecan	283345	Popoloc	27818
Mixtec	283235	Tarahumara	25479
Otomi	221062	Popoluca	18633
Mam	G. 178308 [268512]	Chatino	11773
	M.*10000	Trique	5897
Totonac	124840	Tepehua	5545
Mazatec	101541	North Pame*	2600

[ ] figures from the 1940 Guatemalan census.
*   indirect estimate.

Some differences may be noted in comparing these tables with table 1: some languages which in the classificatory table are entered as single languages appear in table 26 as groups of languages. This is owing to the fact that in some cases the census lumps together different languages that have the same name, and consequently the component languages cannot be identified separately through the census data; also table 1 reflects standard classifications, but as the criteria for differentiating languages from dialects are not uniform only languages for which no indication exists of the inclusion of unintelligible varieties have been set out in table 25.

The disparity in number of speakers for single languages is apparent in table 25. Almost 50% (taking the lowest figures for Cakchiquel and Kekchí) of the total number is made up of three languages. Although the estimates are approximate a similar disparity is found in the groups in table 26. There are probably three or four Nahuatl languages with *c.* 100,000 speakers – Huasteca Nahuatl may have *c.* 200,000 – but Pómaro Nahuatl has only 1,640 speakers. Most of the figures for the Quiché group correspond to what is probably a single language; on the other hand, in the Mixtec and Zapotec groups, a variety with 10,000 speakers may be considered large because many probably have between 2,000 and 4,000 speakers.

The total number of speakers of Indian languages for the area including the whole of Mexico, Guatemala, Belize, Honduras, El Salvador and Nicaragua (figures for the last four countries are old and represent approximate estimates) is *c.* 5,500,000. The majority of these speakers are from Mexico with 3,111,411 and Guatemala with 2,260,023 (1973 census). (It should be noted that the figures of the Guatemalan census are considered too low by scholars working in the area. For considerably higher estimates see Kaufman 1974a, b.) Indian speakers constitute 6·4% of the total population in Mexico and 43·7% in Guatemala. In both countries there has been a significant decrease in comparison with the year 1940 when speakers of Indian languages made up 15% of the population in Mexico and 68·3% in Guatemala. As one goes further back the percentage was still higher, and in the first half of the last century, it is estimated that Indian speakers constituted some 73% of the total population of Mexico. Note that in spite of the decrease in percentage terms, the absolute number of speakers of Indian languages has increased by 775,127 in Guatemala and by 620,502 in Mexico since 1940.

There are sharp differences among languages in terms of monolingualism and bilingualism. It can be seen in table 25 that Mazahua and Tzeltal have approximately the same number of speakers, but in Mazahua monolinguals represent only 11% while in Tzeltal they constitute 76% of the total number. A similar difference is found in languages with a small total number of speakers; in Zenzontepec Chatino with *c.* 3,500 speakers, 62% of them are monolinguals while in Oaxaca Zoque with *c.* 3,700 speakers, 25% are monolinguals.

In historical perspective the general trend in Mexico has been one of decreasing monolingualism in Indian languages: in 1940 the percentage of monolinguals was 50%; in 1970 it was 27·6%, but again there are marked differences between individual languages. In Tarascan the number of monolinguals decreased from 44·3% to 17·5% between 1950 and 1970, a fact that indicates a rapid shift toward bilingualism. In Huichol, on the other hand, there has been a slight increase in the number of monolinguals during the same period from 30% to 34%; taking into account that the total Huichol population was 3,449 in 1950 and 6,874 in 1970, it is clear that the native language has yielded little to Spanish. In other languages like Huastec, Tzeltal, Tlapanec and Tzotzil the decrease in the number of monolinguals has been a moderate one; in Tzotzil, for example, monolinguals constituted 58·9% in 1950 and 52·7% in 1970. In other cases, the most conspicuous being Yucatec, the number of monolinguals has remained static, but they represent a low percentage of the total number of speakers, namely 15%; this indicates a situation of stable bilingualism. Yaqui and Isthmus Zapotec are similar cases.

An interesting fact found in some situations is that the variation in the number of monolinguals and bilinguals is not always correlative. Thus, in the State of Oaxaca (Mexico) the number of monolinguals decreased by 90,996 and the number of bilinguals increased by 84,925 between 1960 and 1970, but within the same time span in the State of Hidalgo monolinguals decreased by 23,883 and bilinguals by 8,088. Part of the decrease of bilinguals may be due to migration to another state – there were 6,821 Otomi speakers outside their home states in 1970, although they are not necessarily from Hidalgo because Otomi speakers are also native to other four states. The decrease in monolinguals without a correlative increase in bilinguals may also be due to the circumstance that younger generations grow up as monolinguals in Spanish. This type of drastic shift is certainly occurring in communities like San Francisco del Mar and Santa María del Mar – both of Huave speech – in which parents purposely speak to their children in Spanish.

Another aspect which influences the status of a language is whether it is spoken in an area with a high density of speakers of Indian languages or in an area with a low density of Indian population surrounded by speakers of Spanish. The first case is the more common, that is, the greatest number of these languages cluster in certain areas, which is obvious looking at the map of their distribution, but there are a considerable number of communities in the second situation. Naturally the latter are more subject to the inroads of Spanish. A case in point is furnished by the Nahuatl language spoken in the State of Morelos: speakers number 14,787 (there are 1,496 monolinguals) and constitute 3·2% of the total population; moreover there is only one *municipio* where they represent a respectable percentage (41·3) of the total population, then there is a sharp drop to 18% (two *municipios*), and then to 5% and lower. But this type of correlation, which may be widened to cover the aspect of relative physical isolation of a community, is far from perfect. There are communities with bad communications, in areas of high density of Indian population which are predominantly bilingual and which may show a clear trend toward monolingualism in Spanish, while other communities that are close to important Spanish-speaking urban centres, although bilingual, may show no trend toward losing their language. It is difficult to determine the causes for the latter type of contrast which depends on what may be called cultural conservatism. Again, the correlation between general cultural retention and retention of the language may be imperfect, as is to be expected, but practically no study in depth has been made of the problem. There are at least a few communities which retain their native language but which may otherwise be indistinguishable from a Spanish-speaking community, and it would seem that there are some cases where although the native language has been lost several characteristics that are peculiar to Indian communities have been retained. Nevertheless, as a rough generalization, most of the Guatemalan area and the adjacent Mexican area, where Mayan languages are spoken, can be considered more 'Indian' than the rest of the area.

In spite of all these differences there are characteristics common to the status of these languages which reflect more general conditions. In chapter 2 the marked dialectal fragmentation was discussed, and in chapter 10 mention was made that this fragmentation may have been furthered by Spanish and later Republican isolating policy, but that, certainly, it antedated them. This situation agrees with a characteristic stressed repeatedly in anthropological studies all over this area, namely that group consciousness and group alliances do not usually extend beyond towns which coherently are markedly endogamous units. That means that from this point of view there are no groups that may be called Zapotec, or Otomi or Quiché, even less an Indian group, so therefore these groups cannot be equated properly with ethnic minorities. It is not surprising, then, that no general dialect has been reported in any area; the nearest equivalent may be those dialects among which a marked asymmetry in interintelligibility was registered; but while this fact indicates that some of them are more prominent, there is no evidence that they are used as vehicles of communication between speakers of other non-mutually intelligible language varieties. On the contrary, at least in certain regions – Zapotecan, Mixtecan – speakers of varieties which could be reasonably interintelligible without much effort resort to Spanish as the vehicle of communication. None of these languages has developed a written form, not even those in which there is stable bilingualism and which have a certain number of speakers who are literate in Spanish. Given this situation, it is unlikely that a standard variety could develop. Besides, the fact that the development of a standard language has usually been accompanied by outright political, economic and cultural supremacy renders it doubtful that a centre with these characteristics could develop within Indian communities, and, from the point of view of practical government policy, whether it would be desirable that such a process should take place. Promoters of the development of standard varieties seem to fail to realize that they might be furthering within native groups the very evils they try to keep these communities away from in relation to the official culture. That this may be so can be deduced from the fact that some groups have seemingly developed what is called 'ethnic identity' and have also adopted some of the traits of the dominant culture, using them against other Indian groups.

All these groups, to a greater or lesser extent, have been and still are under pressures which have little to do with the ideal patterns of development programmes. The encroachment into Indian lands on the part of outsiders, the impoverishment of Indian communities, the need for their members to look for work elsewhere, the increasing dependency on the national economic systems are all continuing processes and they are always reaching more communities. It is not surprising, then, that being in such conditions of inferiority, these groups transfer a negative evaluation to their languages so that efforts directed at creating a conscience of the dignity of the native language seem to attack a chain of causation from the wrong end.

Also, even disregarding the problem of linguistic fragmentation it is doubtful that a written form of these languages would fulfil any function other than as an aid to literacy in Spanish: policies about not only bilingual but even bicultural education fail to specify which contents of the non-official cultures are distinct enough, after four centuries of acculturation, to warrant being included as part of a formal curriculum; the fact that official education is in some aspects utterly inadequate does not appear to derive from its remoteness regarding specifically Indian communities, but from its remoteness regarding most non-urban areas.

There are languages, particularly in Central Mexico, which are certainly declining toward extinction. There are not many possibilities of survival for a language like Ixcatec, for example, a language spoken by only 119 persons. For many or most of them, however, no such fate is foreseeable in the near future. On the other hand, everything points in the direction of their continuing survival in oral form only. The frequent reaction of parents who do not see the point of their children being taught the native language at school on the ground that 'they already know it' may not only reflect a feeling of inferiority impressed upon them through centuries of oppression, but also a deep understanding of the way their language fulfils a function, that is, orally within a restricted environment as a vehicle for cultural aspects which by their very nature require no formal teaching, even less an orthographic tradition.

FURTHER READING

The cultural, economic and political characteristics of the Spanish period in America are authoritatively summarized in Gibson, C. 1966, Konetzke 1965, Parry 1966. A treatment focussed on the Indian population up to the present time is to be found in Wolf 1959, with an excellent annotated bibliography.

Konetzke 1964 is a balanced panorama of Spanish language policy. Heath 1972 gives detailed information on the same subject from the conquest to the present time in Mexico, but it is rather uncritical of the modern period in that it takes at face value official pronouncements and programmes. For additional information on this subject, and with a different approach, see Zavala 1977a, b. For language policy in relation to legislation about ethnic relations see Mörner 1967b; on the wider subject of race mixture, Mörner 1967a, 1974.

On the teaching of Spanish to speakers of Indian languages see Bravo Ahuja 1977. An early (and isolated) view on the function of Indian languages, advocating direct teaching of Spanish independently of literacy in the native language is Pozas and Pozas 1956.

For official attitudes toward and programmes for Indian communities since the rise of the independent countries see Adams 1967, Ewald 1967; for the modern period these surveys summarize the points of view of the official indigenists – not necessarily what has been accomplished – and on these matters appraisals of the role and future of Indian groups are naturally committed politically; for different points of view see Pozas and Pozas 1972, Instituto de Investigaciones Antropológicas 1980.

Data on number of speakers of Indian languages for the entire area in Marino Flores 1967, Mayer and Masferrer 1979 (the figure given for individual groups in the last paper should be taken very cautiously as they do not reproduce census data but estimates by individuals or national agencies on a non-specified basis, and some of the figures seem grossly exaggerated). The data pertinent to speakers of Indian languages from the 1970 Mexican census are given in Horcasitas de Barros and Crespo 1979 which also contains charts with number of bilinguals and monolinguals and their distribution by States, migration of speakers, comparative data with earlier censuses, and two maps with the distribution of monolinguals and bilinguals. Using data from the 1960 census, Nolasco Armas 1972 gives detailed information for the State of Oaxaca in Mexico and has a map where the complex linguistic situation of this State can be appreciated in detail. Maps attempting to give a quantitative typology of monolingualism and bilingualism in Mexico, in Uribe Villegas 1970, Paulín 1971. Whetten 1961 has a map with the density of speakers of Indian languages in Guatemala according to the 1950 census.

Types and trends in bilingualism in Mexico are summarized in Lastra de Suárez 1978; a sociolinguistic characterization of bilinguals in Tzotzil-Spanish and Tzeltal-Spanish in McQuown 1962. On Indians' attitudes toward learning of Spanish see Paulín (de Siade) 1974. On the process of acculturation, Beals 1967, Spicer 1962.

Ethnological sketches of twentieth century Indian groups in Wauchope and Vogt (eds.) 1969; it should be noted that these summaries are based on studies done, when most recently, around thirty years ago, and consequently the situation for some groups may have changed considerably. Ethnological surveys by topics in Wauchope and Nash (eds.) 1967.

Sources for the sentences quoted in chapters 7 and 8

Examples not cited in the Appendix are from the author's unpublished material.

1	Craig 1977: 399	37	Elson 1967: 277
2	Lindenfeld 1973: 70	38	Clark 1962: 192
3	Craig 1977: 9	39	Clark 1962: 192
4	Lindenfeld 1973: 55	40	Hoogshagen 1974: 42
5	Craig 1977: 10	41	Wonderly 1952b: 195
6	Lindenfeld 1973: 50	42	Lind 1964: 349
7	Day 1973a: 67	43	Knudson 1980: no. 60
8	Lindenfeld 1973: 56	44	Knudson 1980: no. 60
9	Craig 1977: 39	45	Clark 1962: 189
10	Lindenfeld 1973: 55	46	Van Haitsma and Van Haitsma 1976: 75
11	Reid et al. 1968: 36		
12	Redi et al. 1968: 40	47	Van Haitsma and Van Haitsma 1976: 75
13	Reid et al. 1968: 41		
14	Reid et al. 1968: 41	48	Clark 1962: 194
15	Reid et al. 1968: 30	49	Wonderly 1952b: 192
16	Reid and Bishop 1974: 234	50	Clark 1962: 194
17	McQuown 1940: 108.3	51	Clark 1962: 194
18	Robinson and Sischo 1969: 65	52	Clark 1962: 188
19	Lindenfeld 1973: 105	53	Lyon, D. 1980: no. 528
20	Carochi 1892: 433	54	Foster 1969: 127
21	Carochi 1892: 433	55	Foster 1969: 183
22	Sischo 1979: 322	56	Foster 1969: 78
23	Lindenfeld 1973: 38	57	Foster 1969: 67
24	Lindenfeld 1973: 38	58	Foster 1969: 189
25	Lindenfeld 1973: 61	59	Foster 1969: 85
26	Lindenfeld 1973: 34	60	Foster 1969: 128
27	Lindenfeld 1973: 129	61	Waterhouse 1967: 360
28	Beller 1979: 293	62	Waterhouse 1962: 29
29	Beller 1979: 293	63	Waterhouse 1962: 25
30	Lindenfeld 1973: 82	64	Waterhouse 1962: 35
31	Lindenfeld 1973: 72	65	Waterhouse 1962: 35
32	Lindenfeld 1973: 70	66	Waterhouse 1962: 33
33	Carochi 1892: 491	67	Waterhouse 1962: 31
34	Beller 1979: 263	68	Waterhouse 1962: 30
35	Lind 1964: 345	69	Waterhouse 1980: no. 484
36	Lyon, S. 1967: 32	70	Craig 1977: 367

71	Jacobs and Longacre 1967: 372
72	Jacobs and Longacre 1967: 372
73	Craig 1977: 11
74	Craig 1977: 335
75	Day 1973a: 79
76	Day 1973a: 79
77	Craig 1977: 17
78	Jacobs and Longacre 1967: 340
79	Jacobs and Longacre 1967: 340
80	Craig 1977: 38
81	Cowan, M. 1969: 45
82	Craig 1977: 237
83	Craig 1977: 239
84	Craig 1977: 199
85	Craig 1977: 40
86	Hills and Merrifield 1974: 286
88	Hollenbach and Hollenbach 1975: 119
89	Earl 1968: 274
91	Austin and Pickett 1974: 57
93	Pickett 1960: 55
95	Pickett 1974: 121
96	Jamieson and Tejeda 1978: 65
100	Mock 1977: 147

101	Pride 1965: 106
102	Pride 1965: 107
106	Rupp 1980: no. 529
107	Jamieson and Tejeda 1978: 123
108	Hollenbach and Hollenbach 1975: 136
109	Jamieson and Tejeda 1978: 123
110	Stairs n.d.: no. 360
113	Stairs Kreger and Scharfe de Stairs 1981: 83
114	Stairs Kreger and Scharfe de Stairs 1981: 83
117	Stairs n.d.: no. 310
124	Stairs n.d.: no. 529
125	Thaeler n.d.: 38
126	Thaeler n.d.: 45
127	Thaeler n.d.: 15
128	Thaeler n.d.: 15
129	Thaeler n.d.: 48
130	Thaeler n.d.: 17
131	Thaeler n.d.: 44
132	Thaeler n.d.: 44
133	Thaeler n.d.: 36

REFERENCES

The best general bibliographical source is Bright 1967; it is selective and excellently organized; see also McClaran 1973. Other general sources are Parra and Jiménez Moreno 1954, Marino Flores 1957, Parodi 1981. The last edition of the bibliography of work done by members of the Summer Institute of Linguistics is Wares 1979. The *Handbook of Latin American Studies* (Gainsville: University of Florida Press) includes a section on Latin American Indian languages with brief comments; the *Proceedings of the Modern Language Association* carries a bibliography on American languages. The *International Journal of American Linguistics* includes, irregularly, a section of abstracts in which references to Mesoamerican languages can be found; volume 31 (1965) has an index of abstracts by author and languages for volumes 27–30. Bibliographies for language families are: Campbell, Ventur, Stewart and Gardner 1978 (Mayan); Hopkins and Josserand (eds.) 1979: 71–146 (Otomanguean); Langacker 1977 has an extensive bibliography on Uto-Aztecan. For individual languages see León-Portilla, A. 1972 (Nahuatl); Waterhouse 1962 (Coastal and Highland Chontal); Wonderly 1951a (Zoque).

Acuña, R. 1975. *Introducción al estudio del Rabinal Achí*. Instituto de Investigaciones Filológicas. Centro de Estudios Mayas, Cuaderno 12. México: Universidad Nacional Autónoma de México

Adams, R. N. 1967. Nationalization. In Wauchope and Nash (1967). Pp. 469–89

Adelung, J. C. and J. S. Vater 1816. *Mithridates oder allgemeine Sprachenkunde mit dem Vater unser als Sprachprobe in bey nahe fünf hundert Sprachen und Mundarten*. Dritter Theil. Dritte Abtheilung. Berlin: Vossischen Buchhandlung

Albores, B. A. 1976. Trilingüismo y prestigio en un pueblo náhuatl del Estado de México. *Anuario de Letras* (Universidad Nacional Autónoma de México) 14: 239–54

Amador Hernández, M. 1976. *Gramática del mazahua de San Antonio Pueblo Nuevo*. Tesis profesional. Escuela Nacional de Antropología e Historia. México, D. F.

Amador Hernández, M. and P. Casasa García 1979. Un análisis de juegos léxicos reconstruidos del protootomangue. In Hopkins and Josserand (1979). Pp. 13–19

Anderson, A. J. O., F. Berdan and J. Lockhart 1976. *Beyond the codices. The Nahua view of Colonial Mexico*. With a linguistic essay by R. W. Langacker. Berkeley and Los Angeles: University of California Press

Andrews, H. 1949. Phonemes and morphophonemes of Temoayan Otomi. *International Journal of American Linguistics* 15: 213–22

Andrews, J. R. 1975. *Introduction to Classical Nahuatl*. Austin: University of Texas Press

Angulo, J. de 1933. The Chichimeco language (Central Mexico). *International Journal of American Linguistics* 7: 152–94

Arana Osnaya, E. 1955. El idioma de los señores de Tepozcolula. *Anales del Instituto Nacional de Antropología e Historia* (México) 13: 217–30

Arana, E. and M. Swadesh 1965. *Los elementos del mixteco antiguo*. México: Instituto Nacional Indigenista e Instituto Nacional de Antropología e Historia

Aschmann, H. P. 1956. Totonaco phonemes. *International Journal of American Linguistics* 12: 34–43

Aschmann, H. P. 1973. *Diccionario totonaco de Papantla, Veracruz*. Serie de Vocabularios y Diccionarios Indígenas 'Mariano Silva y Aceves' 16. México, D. F.: Instituto Lingüístico de Verano

Aulie, H. W. and E. W. de Aulie 1978. *Diccionario chol–español, español–chol*. Serie de Vocabularios y Diccionarios Indígenas 'Mariano Silva y Aceves' 21. México D. F.: Instituto

177

Lingüístico de Verano

Austin, J. and V. B. Pickett 1974. Popoloca clause and sentence. *Summer Institute of Linguistics – Mexico Workpapers* 1: 59–92

Barreda, N. de la 1960. *Doctrina christiana en lengua chinanteca* (1730). Edición facsímil. Introducción por Howard F. Cline. Papeles de la Chinantla II. Serie Científica 6. México: Museo Nacional de Antropología

Barrera, B. and K. Dakin 1978. *Vocabulario popoloca de San Vicente Coyotepec.* Cuadernos de la Casa Chata 11 (México): Centro de Investigaciones Superiores del Instituto Nacional de Antropología e Historia

Barrera Vásquez, A. (ed.) 1980. *Diccionario maya Cordemex.* Maya–español, español–maya. México: Ediciones Cordemex

Bartholomew, D. A. 1965. *The reconstruction of Otopamean.* University of Chicago Dissertation. (Unpublished)

Bartholomew, D. and E. Brockway 1974. The use of tenses in North Puebla Aztec texts. Paper read at the XLI International Congress of Americanists

Basalenque, D. 1975. *Arte y vocabulario de la lengua matlatzinga vuelto a la castellana* (1642). Versión paleografica de María Elena Bribiescas S., con un estudio preliminar de Leonardo Manrique C. (XIII–XLVI). Biblioteca Enciclopédica del Estado de México No. 23. México

Bascom, B. 1959. Tonomechanics of Northern Tepehuan. *Phonetica* 4: 71–88

Bauernschmidt, A. 1965. Amuzgo syllable dynamics. *Language* 41: 471–83

Beals, R. 1967. Acculturation. In Wauchope and Nash (1967). Pp. 449–68

Beebe, A. 1974. Eastern Popoloca verb stems with person markers. *Summer Institute of Linguistics – Mexico Workpapers* 1: 15–29

Beller, R. and P. 1979. Huasteca Nahuatl. In Langacker (1979). Pp. 199–306

Belmar, F. 1897. *Ensayo sobre lengua trique.* Oaxaca: Imprenta de Lorenzo San Germán

Belmar, F. 1905. *Lenguas indígenas de México. Familia mixteco-zapoteca y sus relaciones con el otomí. Familia zoque-mixe, chontal, huave y mexicano.* México

Benson, E. (ed.) 1968. *Dumbarton Oaks conference on the Olmec, October 28th and 29th 1967.* Dumbarton Oaks, Washington D.C.

Berlin, B. 1968. *Tzeltal numeral classifiers: a study in ethnographic semantics.* The Hague: Mouton

Bernard, H. R. 1974. Otomi tones in discourse. *International Journal of American Linguistics* 40: 141–50

Blair, R. W. 1979. *Yucatec Maya noun and verb morpho-syntax.* Indiana University Ph.D. dissertation 1964. Ann Arbor: University Microfilms, Inc.

Blight, R. C. and E. V. Pike 1976. The phonology of Tenago Otomi. *International Journal of American Linguistics* 42: 51–7

Boas, F. 1913. Phonetics of the Mexican language. *International Congress of Americanists* 18: 107–8. London

Bower, B. and B. Erickson Hollenbach 1967. Tepehua sentences. *Anthropological Linguistics* 9.9: 25–37

Bradley, C. H. 1970. *A linguistic sketch of Jicaltepec Mixtec.* Summer Institute of Linguistics Publications 25. Norman, Oklahoma: Summer Institute of Linguistics and University of Oklahoma

Bradley, C. H. and J. K. Josserand 1980. El protomixteco y sus descendientes. México. (Mimeographed)

Brand, D. D. et al. 1960. *Coalcoman and Motines del Oro. An Ex-Distrito of Michoacan, Mexico.* The Hague: Published for the Institute of Latin American Studies, The University of Texas by Martinus Nijhoff

Bravo Ahuja, G. 1977. *Los materiales didácticos para la enseñanza del español a los indígenas mexicanos.* México: El Colegio de Mexico

Brend, R. M. (ed.) 1974. *Advances in tagmemics.* Amsterdam: North-Holland Publishing Company

Brend, R. M. (ed.) 1975. *Studies in tone and intonation by members of the Summer Institute of Linguistics.* Basel: S. Karger

Bright, W. 1967. Inventory of descriptive materials. In Wauchope and McQuown 1967: 9–62

Bright, W. 1979. Notes on Hispanisms. *International Journal of American Linguistics* 45: 267–71

Brockway, E. 1979. North Puebla Nahuatl. In Langacker (1979). Pp. 141–98

Brown, C. H. and S. R. Witkowski 1979. Aspects of the phonological history of Mayan-Zoquean. *International Journal of American Linguistics* 45: 34–47

Buchler, I. R. and R. Freeze 1962. The distinctive features of pronominal systems. *Anthropological Linguistics* 8.8: 78–105

Burgess, D. and D. Fox 1966. Quiché. In K. Mayers (ed.) *Languages of Guatemala.* Pp. 49–86. London: Mouton and Co

Butler, H. I. M. 1980. *Gramática zapoteca. Zapoteco de Yatzachi el Bajo.* Serie de Gramáticas de Lenguas Indígenas de México vol. 4. México: Instituto Lingüístico de Verano

Campbell, L. 1972. Mayan loan words in Xinca. *International Journal of American Linguistics* 38: 187–90

Campbell, L. 1976a. The last Lenca. *International Journal of American Linguistics* 42: 73–8

Campbell, L. 1976b. The linguistic prehistory of the Southern Mesoamerican periphery. *XIV Mesa Redonda de la Sociedad Mexicana de Antropología. (Tegucigalpa, 1975) vol. 1.* Pp. 157–83. México

Campbell, L. 1977. *Quichean linguistic prehistory.* University of California Publications in Linguistics 81. Berkeley and Los Angeles: University of California Press

Campbell, L. R. 1979. Middle American languages. In L. R. Campbell and M. Mithun (eds.), *The Languages of Native America: Historical and Comparative Assessment.* Pp. 902–1000. Austin and London: University of Texas Press

Campbell, L. and T. Kaufman 1976. A linguistic look at the Olmecs. *American Antiquity* 41: 80–9

Campbell, L. and R. W. Langacker 1978. Proto-Aztecan vowels: Part II. *International Journal of American Linguistics* 44: 197–210

Campbell, L., P. Ventur, R. Stewart and B. Gardner 1978. *Bibliography of Mayan languages and linguistics.* Institute for Mesoamerican Studies. Publication No. 3. Albany: State University of New York

Canger, U. R. 1969. *Analysis in outline of Mam, a Mayan language.* University of California, Berkeley Ph.D. Dissertation. Ann Arbor: University Microfilms, Inc.

Carmack, R. 1973. *Quichean civilization.* Los Angeles: University of California Press

Carochi, H. 1892. *Arte de la lengua mexicana con la declaración de los adverbios della.* México (1645). Reprinted in Colección de Gramáticas de la Lengua Mexicana vol. I: 395–538. México; Museo Nacional

Carrasco, P. 1950. *Los otomies: cultura e historia prehispánica de los pueblos mesoamericanos de habla otomiana.* Publicaciones del Instituto de Historia 1a series No. 15. México, D. F.: Universidad Nacional Autónoma de México e Instituto Nacional de Antropología e Historia

Carrasco, P. 1971a. Social organization of Ancient Mexico. In Wauchope, Ekholm and Bernal (1971). Pp. 349–75

Carrasco, P. 1971b. The peoples of Central Mexico and their historical traditions. In Wauchope, Ekholm and Bernal (1971). Pp. 459–73

Casad, E. H. 1974. *Dialect intelligibility testing.* Norman, Oklahoma: Summer Institute of Linguistics

Casad, Eugene H. 1977. Location and direction in Cora discourse. *Anthropological*

Linguistics 19.5: 216–41

Cazés, D. 1967. *El pueblo matlatzinca de San Francisco Oxtotilpan y su lengua.* Acta Antropológica, 2a. época 3(2). México: Escuela Nacional de Antropología e Historia, Sociedad de Alumnos

Clark, L. (E.) 1961. Sayula Popoloca texts with grammatical outline. Norman, Oklahoma: Summer Institute of Linguistics

Clark, L. E. 1962. Sayula Popoluca morpho-syntax. *International Journal of American Linguistics* 28: 183–98

Clark, L. E. 1977. Linguistic acculturation in Sayula Popoluca. *International Journal of American Linguistics* 43: 128–38

Clements, G. N. 1979. The description of terraced-level tone languages. *Language* 55: 536–58

Cline, H. F. 1972. The Relaciones Geográficas of the Spanish Indies, 1577–1648. In Wauchope and Cline (1972). Pp. 183–242

Cline, H. F. 1973. Sahagún materials and studies. In Wauchope and Cline (1973). Pp. 218–39

Coe, M. D. 1965. *The Jaguar's children: Pre-Classic Central Mexico.* New York Museum of Primitive Art

Coe, M. D. 1968. San Lorenzo and the Olmec civilization. In Benson (1968). Pp. 41–78

Córdova, J. de 1886. *Arte de la lengua zapoteca* (1578). Reprinted as *Arte del idioma zapoteco* . . . Morelia: Imprenta del Gobierno

Coronado Suzán, G., I. Fernandez Areu and S. Cuevas Suárez 1974. Esbozo de una fonología generativa del matlatzinca. In Hopkins and Josserand (1979). Pp. 51–5

Cowan, G. M. 1948. Mazateco whistle speech. *Language* 24: 280–6. Reprinted in Brend (1975). Pp. 108–17

Cowan, G. M. 1952. El idioma silbado entre los Mazatecos de Oaxaca y los tepehuas de Hildago, México. *Tlatoani* 1 (no. 3–4): 31–3

Cowan, M. 1969. *Tzotzil grammar.* Summer Institute of Linguistics Publications 18. Norman, Oklahoma: Summer Institute of Linguistics and University of Oklahoma

Craig, C. G. 1977. *The structure of Jacaltec.* Austin and London: University of Texas Press

Crawford, J. C. 1963. *Totontepec Mixe phonotagmemics.* Summer Institute of Linguistics Publications 8. Norman, Oklahoma: Summer Institute of Linguistics and University of Oklahoma

Dahlgren de Jordán, B. 1954. *La mixteca: su cultura e historia prehispánica.* Cultura Mexicana 11. México: Imprenta Universitaria

Daly, J. P. 1973. *A generative syntax of Peñoles Mixtec.* Summer Institute of Linguistics Publications 42. Norman, Oklahoma: Summer Institute of Linguistics and University of Oklahoma

[Daly, J. P. 1977] *Mixteco de Santa María Peñoles.* Archivo de Lenguas Indígenas de México 3. México: Centro de Investigación para la Integración Social

Day, C. 1973a. *The Jacaltec language.* Language Science Monographs, vol. 12. Bloomington: Indiana University

Day, C. 1973b. The semantics of social categories in a transformational grammar of Jacaltec. In M. S. Edmonson (ed.) *Meaning in Mayan languages.* Pp. 85–105. The Hague: Mouton

Dibble, C. E. 1971. Writing in Central Mexico. In Wauchope, Ekholm and Bernal (1971). Pp. 322–32

Diebold, Jr, A. R. 1960. Determining the centers of dispersal of language groups. *International Journal of American Linguistics* 26: 1–10

Dixon, R. M. W. 1979. Ergativity. *Language* 55: 59–138

Earl, R. 1968. Rincon Zapotec clauses. *International Journal of American Linguistics* 34: 269–74

[Echegoyen Gleason, A. et al.] 1979. *Luces contemporáneas del otomí. Gramática del otomí de la Sierra.* México, D. F.: Instituto Lingüístico de Verano y Secretaría de Educación Pública a través de la Dirección General de Educación a Grupos Marginados

Edmonson, M. S. 1965. *Quiché–English dictionary.* Middle American Research Institute, Publication 30. New Orleans: Tulane University

Edmonson, M. S. 1967a. Classical Quiché. In Wauchope and McQuown (1967). Pp. 249–68

Edmonson, M. S. 1967b. Narrative folklore. In Wauchope and Nash (1967). Pp. 357–68

Edmonson, M. S. 1970. *The book of counsel: The Popol Vuh of the Quiche Maya of Guatemala.* Middle American Research Institute Publication (New Orleans)

Egland, S. and D. Bartholomew 1978. *La inteligibilidad interdialectal en México: Resultados de algunos sondeos.* México, D. F.: Instituto Lingüístico de Verano

Elson, B. F. 1960. *Gramática del popoluca de la Sierra.* Biblioteca de la Facultad de Filosofía y Letras No. 6. Jalapa: Universidad Veracruzana

Elson, B. F. 1967. Sierra Popoluca. In Wauchope and McQuown (1967). Pp. 269–90

[Elson, B. F. and J. Comas 1961]. *A William Cameron Townsend en el vigésimoquinto aniversario del Instituto Lingüístico de Verano.* México

Engel, R. and R. E. Longacre 1963. Syntactic matrices in Ostuacan Zoque. *International Journal of American Linguistics* 29: 331–44

England, N. C. 1976. Mam directionals and verb semantics. In M. McClaran (ed.) *Mayan Linguistics I*: 202–11. University of California 1, Los Angeles: American Indian Studies Center

Escalante (Hernández), R. 1962. *El cuitlateco.* Instituto Nacional de Antropología e Historia, Departamento de Investigaciones Antropológicas, Publicación 9. México

Escalante (H.), R. 1975. Tipología de las lenguas de México. In Arana de Swadesh et al. *Las lenguas de México I.* Pp. 92–127. México: Instituto Nacional de Antropología e Historia

Escalante (Hernández), R. 1977. Función gramatical del tono en matlatzinca. Paper presented at the meeting on Las lenguas otomangues y sus vecinas. Instituto Nacional de Antropología e Historia, Departamento de Lingüística, México. (Unpublished)

Ewald, R. H. 1967. Directed change. In Wauchope and Nash (1967). Pp. 490–511

Finck, F. N. 1909. *Die Hauptypen des Sprachbaues.* Leipzig und Berlin: B. G. Teubner

Flannery, K. V. 1968. The Olmec and the Valley of Oaxaca: A model of inter-regional interaction in formative times. In Benson (1968). Pp. 79–118

Fleming, I. and R. K. Dennis 1977. Tol (Jicaque) phonology. *International Journal of American Linguistics* 43: 121–27

Foris, C. 1978. Verbs of motion in Sochiapan Chinantec. *Anthropological Linguistics* 20.8: 353–8

Foris, D. 1973. Sochiapan Chinantec syllable structure. *International Journal of American Linguistics* 39: 232–5

Foster, M. L. C. 1969. *The Tarascan language.* University of California Publications in Linguistics 56. Berkeley and Los Angeles: University of California Press

Friedrich, Paul 1969. *On the meaning of the Tarascan suffixes of space.* Indiana University Publications in Anthropology and Linguistics, Memoirs 23 and 24 (= *International Journal of American Linguistics* vol. 35 no. 4). Pp. 1–48. Baltimore

Friedrich, P. 1970. Shape in grammar. *Language* 46: 379–407

Friedrich, P. 1971a. Dialectal variation in Tarascan phonology. *International Journal of American Linguistics* 37: 164–87

Friedrich, P. 1971b. Distinctive features and functional groups in Tarascan phonology. *Language* 47: 849–65

Friedrich, P. 1971c. *The Tarascan suffixes of locative space: meaning and morphotactics.* Language Science Monographs Vol. 9. Bloomington: Indiana University

Fries, C. C. and K. L. Pike 1949. Coexistent phonemic systems. *Language* 25: 29–50. Reprinted in R. M. Brend (ed.) *Kenneth Pike, Selected Writings*. Pp. 51–73. The Hague: Mouton, 1972

Fromkin, V. A. (ed.) 1978. *Tone. A linguistic survey*. New York: Academic Press

Furbee-Losee, N. L. 1976. *The correct language, Tojolabal: A grammar with ethnographic notes*. New York: Garland

García de León, A. 1976. *Pajapan: un dialecto mexicano del Golfo*. Colección científica 43. México: Instituto Nacional de Antropología e Historia

Garibay, K. A. M. 1965–8. *Poesía náhuatl II, III. Cantares mexicanos*. Fuentes Indígenas de la Cultura Náhuatl. Instituto de Investigaciones Históricas. Mexico: Universidad Nacional Autónoma de México

Gibson, C. 1966. *Spain in America*. New York: Harper and Row

Gibson, C. 1971. Structure of the Aztec Empire. In Wauchope, Ekholm and Bernal (1971). Pp. 376–94

Gibson, L. 1956. Pame (Otomi) phonemics and morphophonemics. *International Journal of American Linguistics* 22: 242–65

Gibson, L. and D. Bartholomew 1979. Pame noun inflection. *International Journal of American Linguistics* 45: 309–22

Gilberti, M. 1898. *Arte de la lengua tarasca o de Michoacán*. México (1558) ... Reprinted in México: Tipografía de la Oficina Impresora del Timbre

Gilberti, M. 1901. *Diccionario de la lengua tarasca de Michoacán* (1559). México: Tipografía de la Oficina Impresora de Estampillas

González Casanova, P. 1922. El mexicano de Teotihuacán. In M. Gamio (ed.) *La población del Valle de Teotihuacán* vol. 2. Pp. 595–648. México: Dirección de Talleres Gráficos

Goode, C. 1978. *Diccionario triqui de Chicahuaxtla*. Serie de Vocabularios Indígenas 'Mariano Silva y Aceves' 20. México, D. F.: Summer Institute of Linguistics

Gossen, G. H. 1971. Chamula genres of verbal behavior. *Journal of American Folklore* 84: 145–67

Gossen, G. H. 1973. Chamula Tzotzil proverbs: neither fish nor fowl. In M. S. Edmonson (ed.) *Meaning in Mayan Languages*. Pp. 205–33. The Hague: Mouton

Goubaud Carrera, A. 1946. Distribución de las lenguas indígenas actuales de Guatemala. *Boletín del Instituto Indigenista Nacional* (Guatemala) 1: 63–76

Greenberg, J. H. 1978. Some generalizations concerning initial and final consonant clusters. In J. H. Greenberg, C. A. Ferguson and E. A. Moravcsik (eds.) *Universals of human languages, vol. 2: Phonology*. Pp. 243–79. Stanford, California: Stanford University Press

Grimes, J. E. 1955. Style in Huichol structure. *Language* 31: 31–5

Grimes, J. E. 1959. Huichol tone and intonation. *International Journal of American Linguistics* 25: 221–32

Grimes, J. E. 1964. *Huichol syntax*. The Hague: Mouton

Grimes, J. E. 1968. Descriptive linguistics. In Sebeok (1968). Pp. 302–9

Grimes, J. E. 1974. Dialects as optimal communication networks. *Language* 50: 260–9

Grimes, L. 1968. *Cakchiquel-tzutujil: estudio sobre su unidad lingüística*. Estudios Centroamericanos, 4. Guatemala: Editorial del Ministerio de Educación Pública

Gudschinsky, S. C. 1958. Mazatec dialect history: a study in miniature. *Language* 34: 469–81

Gudschinsky, S. C. 1959. Mazatec kernel constructions and transformations. *International Journal of American Linguistics* 25: 81–9

Hale, K. 1958. Internal diversity in Uto-Aztecan: I. *International Journal of American Linguistics* 24: 101–7

Hamp, E. P. 1958. Proto-Popolocan internal relationships. *International Journal of American Linguistics* 24: 150–3

Hart, H. L. 1957. Hierarchical structuring of Amuzgo grammar. *International Journal of American Linguistics* 23: 141–64

Harvey, H. R. 1971. Ethnohistory of Guerrero. In Wauchope, Ekholm and Bernal (1971). Pp. 603–18

Harvey, H. R. 1972. The Relaciones Geográficas 1579–1586: Native languages. In Wauchope and Cline (1972). Pp. 279–323

Heath, G. R. 1913. Notes on Miskito grammar and on other Indian languages of Eastern Nicaragua. *American Anthropologist* n.s. 15: 48–62

Heath, S. B. 1972. *Telling tongues. Language policy in Mexico. Colony to nation*. New York and London: Teachers College Press, Columbia University

Hervás y Panduro, L. 1800–5. *Catálogo de las lenguas de las naciones conocidas y numeración division y clases de éstas según la diversidad de sus idiomas y dialectos*. 6 vols. Madrid: Imprenta de la Administración del Real Arbitrio de Beneficencia. (vol. 1: Lenguas y naciones americanas)

Hess, H. H. 1968. *The syntactic structure of Mezquital Otomi*. The Hague: Mouton

Hill, J. H. and K. C. Hill 1977. Language death and relexification in Tlaxcalan Nahuatl. *International Journal of the Sociology of Language* 12: 55–70

Hill, J. H. and K. C. Hill 1978. Honorific usage in modern Nahuatl. The expression of social distance and respect in the Nahuatl of the Malinche Volcano area. *Language* 54: 123–55

Hills, R. A. and W. R. Merrifield 1974. Ayutla Mixtec, just in case. *International Journal of American Linguistics* 40: 283–91

Hockett, C. F. 1955. *A manual of phonology*. Indiana University Publications in Anthropology and Linguistics, Memoir 11 (= *International Journal of American Linguistics* vol. 21 no. 4). Baltimore

Hockett, C. F. 1958. *A course in modern linguistics*. New York: Macmillan

Hoijer, H. et al. 1946. *Linguistic structures of native America*. Viking Fund Publications in Anthropology 6. New York

Hollenbach, B. E. 1976. Tense-negation interplay in Copala Trique. *International Journal of American Linguistics* 42: 126–32

Hollenbach, B. E. 1977. Phonetic vs. phonemic correspondence in two Trique dialects. In Merrifield (1977). Pp. 35–68

Hollenbach, B. E. 1978. Some syntactic dissimilarities between Huave and Otomanguean. Paper presented at the 77th Annual Meeting of the American Anthropological Association. Los Angeles

[Hollenbach, F. and (B.) E. De Hollenbach 1975]. *Trique de San Juan Copala*. Archivo de lenguas indígenas del Estado de Oaxaca (= Archivo de Lenguas Indígenas de México) 2. México: Instituto de Investigación e Integración Social del Estado de Oaxaca

Holt, D. 1976. La lengua paya y las fronteras lingüísticas de Mesoamérica. *XIV Mesa Redonda de la Sociedad Mexicana de Antropología (Tegucigalpa, 1975) vol. 1*. Pp. 149–56. México

Hoogshagen, S. 1959. Three contrastive vowel lengths in Mixe. *Zeitschrift für Phonetik, Sprachwissenschaft und Kommunikationsforschung* 12: 111–15

Hoogshagen, S. S. 1974. Estructura de la cláusula en mixe de Coatlán. *Summer Institute of Linguistics – Mexico Workpapers* 1: 31–44

Hopkins, N. A. 1970. Estudio preliminar de los dialectos del tzeltal y del tzotzil. In N. A. McQuown and J. Pitt-Rivers (eds.) *Ensayos de Antropología en la Zona Central de Chiapas*. Pp. 185–214. México: Instituto Nacional Indigenista

Hopkins, N. A. 1977. Prehistoria lingüística de Oaxaca. Paper presented at the Congreso de Evaluación de la Antropología en Oaxaca. (Unpublished)

Hopkins, N. A. and J. K. Josserand (eds.) 1979. *Estudios lingüísticos en lenguas otomangues*.

Colección científica 68. México: Instituto Nacional de Antropología e Historia

Horcasitas, F. 1974. *El teatro Náhuatl. Épocas novohispana y moderna.* Serie de Cultura Náhuatl, Monografías 17. Instituto de Investigaciones históricas. México: Universidad Nacional Autónoma de México

Horcasitas de Barros, M. L. and A. M. Crespo 1979. *Hablantes de lenguas indígenas en México.* Colección científica 81. México: Instituto Nacional de Antropología e Historia

Horne, K. M. 1966. *Language typology. 19th and 20th century views.* Washington D. C.: Georgetown University Press

Humboldt, W. v. 1960. *Ueber die Verschiedenheit des menschlichen Sprachbaues und ihre Einfluss auf die geistige Entwicklung des Menschengeschlechtes.* Berlin (1836). Reprinted Bonn: Ferd. Dümmlers Verlag

Instituto de Investigaciones Antropológicas 1980. *Indigenismo y Lingüística: Documentos del foro 'La Política del Lenguaje en México'.* México: Universidad Nacional Autónoma de México

Jacobs, K. and R. E. Longacre 1967. Patterns and rules in Tzotzil grammar. *Foundations of Language* 3: 325–89

Jamieson, A. R. 1977a. Chiquihuitlan Mazatec tone. In Merrifield (1977). Pp. 107–36

Jamieson, A. R. 1977b. Chiquihuitlan Mazatec phonology. In Merrifield (1977). Pp. 93–106

[Jamieson, A. and E. Tejeda 1978]. *Mazateco de Chiquihuitlan.* Archivo de Lenguas Indígenas de México. México: Centro de Investigación para la Integración Social

Jamieson, C. 1976. Chiquitlan Mazatec verbs. *Summer Institute of Linguistics–Mexico Workpapers* 2: 85–107

Jiménez Moreno, W. 1942. El enigma de los olmecas. *Cuadernos Americanos* 1: 113–45

Jiménez Moreno, W. 1954–5. Síntesis de la historia precolonial del Valle de México. *Revista Mexicana de Estudios Antropológicos* 14: 219–36

Jiménez Moreno, W. 1959. Síntesis de la historia pretolteca de Mesoamérica. In C. Cook de Leonard (ed.) *El esplendor del México antiguo* vol. 2. Pp. 1019–1108. México, D. F.: Centro de Investigaciones Antropológicas de México

Jiménez Moreno, W. 1969. Los estudios lingüísticos en México. In *El simposio de México, enero de 1968. Actas, informes y comunicaciones.* Pp. 14–22. México: Universidad Nacional Autónoma de México

Johnson, F. 1940. The linguistic map of Mexico and Central America. In *The Maya and their neighbors.* New York: Appleton-Century

Jones, L. K. and R. E. Longacre 1979. *Discourse studies in Mesoamerican languages.* 2 vols. Summer Institute of Linguistic Publications 58. Dallas: Summer Institute of Linguistics and University of Texas at Arlington

Jones, T. E. and L. M. Knudson 1977. Guelavía Zapotec phonemes. In Merrifield (1977). Pp. 163–80

Karstrom, M. R. and E. V. Pike 1968. Stress in the phonological system of Eastern Popoloca. *Phonetica* 18: 16–30

Karttunen, F. and J. Lockhart 1976. *Nahuatl in the middle years. Language contact phenomena in texts of the Colonial period.* University of California Publications in Linguistics 85. Berkeley: University of California Press

Karttunen, F. and J. Lockhart 1980. La estructura de la poesía náhuatl vista por sus variantes. *Estudios de Cultura Náhuatl* 14: 15–64

Kaufman, T. S. 1964. Mixe-Zoque subgroups and the position of Tapachulteco. *XXXV Congreso Internacional de Americanistas. México 1962. Actas y Memorias vol. II.* Pp. 403–11. México

Kaufman, T. 1969. Teco, a new Mayan language. *International Journal of American Linguistics* 35: 154–74

Kaufman, T. 1971a. Materiales lingüísticos para el estudio de las relaciones y internas y externas de la familia de idiomas mayanos. In Vogt and Ruz L. 1971: 81–136

Kaufman, T. 1971b. *Tzeltal phonology and morphology*. University of California Publications in Linguistics 61. Berkeley and Los Angeles: University of California Press

Kaufman, T. S. 1973. Areal linguistics in Middle America. In Sebeok (1977). Vol. 2, 63–87

Kaufman, T. 1974a. *Idiomas de Mesoamerica*. Seminario de Integración Social Guatemalteca, Publicación No. 33. Guatemala, C. A.: Editorial José de Pomada Ibarra (A shorter version is Kaufman 1974b.)

Kaufman, T. 1974b. Meso-American Indian Languages. *Encyclopaedia Britannica 15th edn*, vol. 11: 956–63

Kaufman, T. 1978. Archeological and linguistic correlations in Mayaland and associated areas of Meso-America. *World Archeology* 8: 101–18

Keller, K. C. 1955. The Chontal (Mayan) numeral system. *International Journal of American Linguistics* 21: 258–75

Kelley, D. H. 1976. *Deciphering the Maya script*. Austin: University of Texas Press

Kiemele Muro, M. 1975. *Vocabulario mazahua–español y español–mazahua*. Edición preparada por Mario Colín. Biblioteca Enciclopedica del Estado de México. No. 35. México

[Knudson, L.] 1980. *Zoque de Chimalapa*. Archivo de Lenguas Indígenas de México 6. Mexico: Centro de Investigación para la Integración Social

Konetzke, R. 1964. Die Bedeutung der Sprachenfrage in der Spanischen Kolonisation Amerikas. *Jahrbuch für Geschichte von Staat, Wirtschaft und Gesellschaft Lateinamerika I.* Pp. 72–116. Köln

Konetzke, R. 1965. *Süd- und Mittelamerika I. Die Indianerkulturen Altamerikas und die Spanisch–portugiesische Kolonialherrschaft*. Fischer Weltgeschichte Band 22. Frankfurt am Main: Fischer Bücherei

Kuiper, A. and W. R. Merrifield 1975. Diuxi Mixtec verbs of motion and arrival. *International Journal of American Linguistics* 41: 32–45

Kuiper, A. and V. B. Pickett 1974. Personal pronouns in Diuxi Mixtec. *Summer Institute of Linguistics–Mexico Workpapers* 1: 53–8

Lamb, S. M. 1964. The classification of the Uto-Aztecan languages: A historical survey. In W. Bright (ed.) *Studies in Californian Linguistics*. Pp. 106–25. University of California Publications in Linguistics 34. Berkeley and Los Angeles: University of California Press

Langacker, R. W. 1976. *Non-distinct arguments in Uto-Aztecan*. University of California Publications in Linguistics 82. Berkeley and Los Angeles: University of California Press

Langacker, R. W. 1977. *An overview of Uto-Aztecan grammar. Studies in Uto-Aztecan grammar volume 1*. Summer Institute of Linguistics Publications 56. Arlington: Summer Institute of Linguistics and University of Texas at Arlington

Langacker, R. W. (ed.) 1979. *Modern Aztec grammatical sketches. Studies in Uto-Aztecan grammar volume 2*. Summer Institute of Linguistics Publications 56. Arlington: Summer Institute of Linguistics and University of Texas at Arlington

Larsen, R. and E. V. Pike 1949. Huasteco intonations and phonemes. *Language* 25: 268–77

Lastra (de Suárez), Y. 1973. Panorama de los estudios de lenguas yutoaztecas. *Anales de Antropología* (Universidad Nacional Autónoma de México) 10: 337–86

Lastra de Suárez, Y. 1978. Bilingualism in Mexico. In J. E. Alatis (ed.) *Georgetown University Round Table on Languages and Linguistics 1978*. Pp. 202–13. Washington, D. C.: Georgetown University Press

Lastra de Suárez, Y. 1980a. *El náhuatl de Tetzcoco en la actualidad*. México, D. F.: Universidad Nacional Autónoma de México

Lastra de Suárez, Y. 1980b. Náhuatl de Acaxochitlán Archivo de Lenguas Indígenas de México 10. Mexico: Centro de Investigación para la Integración Social

Law, H. W. 1955. The phonemes of Isthmus Nahuatl. *El México Antiguo* 8: 267–78

Law, H. W. 1958. Morphological structure of Isthmus Nahuat. *International Journal of American Linguistics* 24: 108–29

Law, H. W. 1961. Linguistic acculturation in Isthmus Nahuat. In Elson and Comas (1961). Pp. 555–61

Law, H. W. 1966. *Obligatory constructions of Isthmus Nahuat grammar.* The Hague: Mouton

Lehmann, W. 1920. *Zentral-Amerika. Erster Teil: Die Sprachen Zentral-Amerikas in ihren Beziehungen zueinander sowie zu Süd-Amerika und Mexiko.* 2 vols. Berlin: D. Reimer

León, N. 1900. Familias lingüísticas de México. *Memorias de la Sociedad Científica Antonio Alzate* 15: 274–84

León, N. 1903. Familias lingüísticas de México. *Anales del Museo Nacional, época 1* 7: 279–309

León-Portilla, A. H. de 1972. Bibliografía lingüística nahua. *Estudios de Cultura Náhuatl* 10: 404–41

León-Portilla, M. 1969. *Pre-Columbian literatures of Mexico.* Norman, Oklahoma: University of Oklahoma Press

Lind, J. O. 1964. Clause and sentence syntagmemes in Sierra Popoluca. *International Journal of American Linguistics* 30: 341–54

Lindenfeld, J. 1973. *Yaqui syntax.* University of California Publications in Linguistics 76. Berkeley and Los Angeles: University of California Press

Longacre, R. E. 1952. Five phonemic pitch levels in Trique. *Acta Linguistica* 7: 62–81

Longacre, R. E. 1959. Trique tone morphemics. *Anthropological Linguistics* 1.4: 5–42

Longacre, R. E. 1964. Progress in Otomanguean reconstruction. In H. G. Lunt (ed.) *Proceedings of the Ninth International Congress of Linguists, Cambridge, Mass. August 27–31, 1962.* Pp. 1016–25. London: Mouton and Co.

Longacre, R. E. 1966. Trique clause and sentence: a study in contrast, variation and distribution. *International Journal of American Linguistics* 32: 242–52

Longacre, R. E. 1967. Systemic comparison and reconstruction. In Wauchope and McQuown (1967). Pp. 118–59

Longacre, R. E. 1968. Comparative reconstruction of indigenous languages. In Sebeok et al. (1968). Pp. 320–60. Reprinted in Sebeok (1977) II. Pp. 99–139

Longacre, R. E. and R. Millon 1961. Proto-Mixtecan and Proto-Amuzgo-Mixtecan vocabularies. *Anthropological Linguistics* 3.4: 1–44

Lyman, L. 1964. The verb syntagmemes of Choapan Zapotec. *Linguistics* 7: 16–41

Lyman, L. and R. Lyman 1977. Choapan Zapotec phonology. In Merrifield (1977). Pp. 137–62

Lyon, D. D. 1967. Tlahuitoltepec Mixe verb syntagmemes. *International Journal of American Linguistics* 33: 34–45

[Lyon, D.] 1980. *Mixe de Tlahuitoltepec.* Archivo de Lenguas Indígenas de México 8. México: Centro de Investigación para la Integración Social.

Lyon, S. 1967. Tlahuitoltepec Mixe clause structure. *International Journal of American Linguistics* 33: 25–33

McArthur, H. S. and L. McArthur 1956. Aguacatec (Mayan) phonemes within the stress group. *International Journal of American Linguistics* 22: 72–6

McClaran, M. 1973. Mexico. In T. A. Sebeok (ed.) *Current Trends in Linguistics* 10. Pp. 1079–99. The Hague: Mouton. Reprinted in Sebeok (1977). II. Pp. 141–61

McKaughan, H. 1954. Chatino formulas and phonemes. *International Journal of American Linguistics* 20: 23–7

McLaughlin, R. M. 1975. *The great Tzotzil dictionary of San Lorenzo Zinacantán.* Smithsonian Contributions to Anthropology 19. Washington D.C.

McMahon, A. 1967. Phonemes and phonemic units of Cora (Mexico). *International Journal of American Linguistics* 33: 128–34

McQuown, N. A. 1940. *A grammar of the Totonac language.* Yale University Ph.D. dissertation. (Revised 1950.) (Unpublished)

McQuown, N. A. 1955. The indigenous languages of Latin America. *American Anthropologist* 57: 501–70

McQuown, N. A. 1960a. American Indian and general linguistics. *American Anthropologist* n.s. 62: 318–26

McQuown, N. A. 1960b. (Middle American linguistics: 1955. *Middle American Anthropology* vol. 2. Special Symposium of the American Anthropological Association. Washington D.C.: Pan American Union) *Social Science Monographs* 10: 12–32

McQuown, N. A. 1962. Indian and ladino bilingualism: sociocultural contrasts in Chiapas, Mexico. *Monograph Series on Languages and Linguistics* 15: 85–106. Washington, D.C.: Georgetown University Press

McQuown, N. A. 1967a. Classical Yucatec (Maya). In Wauchope and McQuown (1967). Pp. 201–47

McQuown, N. A. 1967b. History of studies in Middle American linguistics. In Wauchope and McQuown (1967). Pp. 3–6

McQuown, N. A. 1971. Los orígenes y diferenciación de los mayas según se infiere del estudio comparativo de las lenguas mayanas. In Vogt and Ruz L. (1971). Pp. 49–80

McQuown, N. A. 1976. *American Indian Linguistics in New Spain.* Lisse, The Netherlands: The Peter de Ridder Press (Reprinted from *American Indian Languages and American Linguistics* edited by W. L. Chafe, pp. 105–27. Lisse: the Peter de Ridder Press 1976)

Mak, C. 1953. A comparison of two tonemic systems. *International Journal of American Linguistics* 19: 85–100

Manrique, C. L. 1967. Jiliapan Pame. In Wauchope and McQuown (1967). Pp. 331–48

Manrique, C. L. 1975. Relaciones entre las áreas lingüísticas y las áreas culturales. *XIII Mesa Redonda de la Sociedad Mexicana de Antropología* vol. 3. Pp. 137–60. México

Marino Flores, A. 1957. *Bibliografía lingüística de la República Mexicana.* México, D.F.: Instituto Indigenista Interamericano

Marino Flores, A. 1967. Indian population and its identification. In Wauchope and Nash (1967). Pp. 12–25

Martínez Hernández, J. (ed.) 1929. *Diccionario de Motul maya–español atribuido a Fray Antonio de Ciudad Real y Arte de la lengua maya por Fray Juan Coronel.* Mérida: Compañía Tipográfica Yucateca

Matthews, P. H. 1972. Huave verb morphology: some comments from a non-tagmemic standpoint. *International Journal of American Linguistics* 38: 96–118

Mayer, E. and E. Masferrer 1979. La población indígena de América en 1978. *América Indígena* 39: 217–37

Mayers, M. K. 1960. The phonemes of Pocomchí. *Anthropological Linguistics* 2.9: 1–39

Mendizabal, M. O. de and W. Jiménez Moreno n.d. *Distribución prehispánica de las lenguas indígenas de México.* (Map) México: Instituto Panamericano de Geografía e Historia, Instituto Mexicano de Investigaciones Lingüísticas and Museo Nacional

Mendizabal, M. O. de and W. Jiménez Moreno 1937. *Mapa lingüístico de Norte- y Centro-América.* México: Instituto Panamericano de Geografía e Historia and Instituto Mexicano de Investigaciones Lingüísticas

Merrifield, W. R. 1963. Palantla Chinantec syllable types. *Anthropological Linguistics* 5.5: 1–16

Merrifield, W. R. 1968. *Palantla Chinantec grammar.* Papeles de la Chinantla 5, Serie científica 5. México: Museo Nacional de Antropología

Merrifield, W. R. (ed.) 1977. *Studies in Otomanguean phonology.* Arlington: Summer Institute of Linguistics and University of Texas at Arlington

Miles, S. W. 1965. Summary of preconquest ethnology of the Guatemala-Chiapas Highlands and the Pacific Slopes. In Wauchope and Willey (1965a). Pp. 276–87

Miller, W. R. 1967. *Uto-Aztecan cognate sets.* University of California Publications in Linguistics 48. Berkeley and Los Angeles: University of California Press

Miller, W. R. 1977. *Preliminary description of Varohío.* (Mimeographed)

Misteli, F. 1893. *Charakteristik der hauptsächlichsten Typen des Sprachbaues. Neubearbeitung des Werkes von Prof. H. Steinthal (1861).* Berlin: Ferd. Dümmlers Verlagsbuchhandlung

[Mock, C.] 1977. *Chocho de Santa María Ocotlán, Oaxaca.* Archivo de Lenguas Indígenas de México. México: Centro de Investigación para la Integración Social

Molina, A. de 1970. *Vocabulario en lengua castellana y mexicana y mexicana y castellana* (1571), edición facsimilar. México: Editorial Porrúa

Mörner, M. 1967a. *Race mixture in the history of Latin America.* Boston: Little, Brown

Mörner, M. 1967b. La difusión del castellano y el aislamiento de los indios. Dos aspiraciones contradictorias de la Corona española. *Homenaje a Vicens Vives* vol. 2. Pp. 435–46. Barcelona: Universidad de Barcelona

Mörner, M. 1974. *Estado, razas y cambio social en la Hispanoamérica colonial.* Sep Setentas 128. México, D.F.: Secretaría de Educación Pública

Müller, F. 1882. *Grundriss der Sprachwissenschaft II. Band: Die Sprachen der schlichthaarigen Rassen.* Wien: Alfred Hölder

Needham, D. and M. Davis 1946. Cuicateco phonology. *International Journal of American Linguistics* 12: 139–46

Newman, S. 1967. Classical Nahuatl. In Wauchope and McQuown (1967). Pp. 179–99

Nicholson, H. B. 1973. Sahagun's 'Primeros memoriales', Tepepulco. In Wauchope and Cline (1973). Pp. 207–18

Nicolau d'Olwer, L. and H. F. Cline 1973. Sahagún and his works. In Wauchope and Cline (1973). Pp. 186–207

Nolasco Armas, M. 1972. *Oaxaca indígena (Problemas de aculturación en el Estado de Oaxaca y subáreas culturales).* México: Instituto de Investigación e Integración Social del Estado de Oaxaca

Nordell, N. 1962. On the status of Popoluca in Zoque-Mixe. *International Journal of American Linguistics.* 28: 146–9

Olivera, M., M. I. Ortiz and C. Valverde n.d. *Distribución de las lenguas indígenas de México por lengua predominante a nivel municipal según el censo de 1970.* (Map) México: Universidad Nacional Autónoma de México. (In press)

Olmos, A. de 1972. *Arte para aprender la lengua mexicana.* (México 1547) Publicado con notas, aclaraciones etc. por Rémi Siméon. Reimpresión con prólogo y versión al castellano de la introducción para esta edición por Miguel León Portilla. Guadalajara: Edmundo Aviña Levy

Oltrogge, D. 1977. Proto-Jicaque–Subtiaba–Tequistlateco: A comparative reconstruction. In Oltrogge and Rensch (1977). Pp. 1–52

Oltrogge, D. and C. R. Rensch 1977. *Two studies in Middle American comparative linguistics.* Arlington: Summer Institute of Linguistics and University of Texas at Arlington

Orozco y Berra, M. 1864. *Geografía de las lenguas y carta etnográfica de México.* México, D.F.: Imprenta de S. M. Andrade y E. Escalante

Pankratz, L. and E. V. Pike 1967. Phonology and morphophonemics of Ayutla Mixtec. *International Journal of American Linguistics* 33: 287–99. Reprinted in Brend (1975). Pp. 131–51

Parodi, C. 1981. La investigación lingüística en México 1970–1980. México: Universidad Nacional Autònoma de México

Parra, G. M. and W. Jiménez Moreno 1954. *Bibliografía indigenista de México y Centroamérica 1850–1950.* Memorias del Instituto Nacional Indigenista IV. México

Parry, J. H. 1966. *The Spanish seaborne empire.* London: Hutchinson

Paulín, G. 1971. *Monolingües y bilingües en la población de México en 1960.* México: Universidad Nacional Autónoma de México

Paulín de Siade, G. 1974. Los indígenas de México frente a la castellanización. Mexico: Universidad Nacional Autónoma de México

Pickett, V. B. 1953. Isthmus Zapotec verb analysis I. *International Journal of American Linguistics* 19: 292–6

Pickett, V. B. 1955. Isthmus Zapotec verb analysis II. *International Journal of American Linguistics* 21: 217–32

Pickett, V. B. 1960. *The grammatical hierarchy of Isthmus Zapotec. Language* 36(1), pt 2. Language Dissertation 56. Baltimore

Pickett, V. B. 1967. Isthmus Zapotec. In Wauchope and McQuown (1967). Pp. 291–310

[Pickett, V. B. 1974]. *Zapoteco del Istmo.* Archivo de Lenguas Indígenas del Estado de Oaxaca l. México: Instituto de Investigación para la Integración Social del Estado de Oaxaca

Pickett, V. B. 1976. Further comments on Zapotec motion verbs. *International Journal of American Linguistics* 42: 162–4

Pickett, V. B. 1978. Los idiomas de México y los universales sintácticos de Greenberg. Paper read at the V Congreso de la Asociación de Lingüística y Filología de América Latina, Caracas, Venezuela. (Unpublished)

Pickett, V. B. et al. 1965. *Castellano–zapoteco, zapoteco–castellano.* Vocabularios indígenas 'Mariano Silva y Aceves' 3. 2nd edn. México: Instituto Lingüístico de Verano

Pike, E. V. 1951. Tonemic–intonemic correlation in Mazahua (Otomi). *International Journal of American Linguistics* 17: 37–71. Reprinted in Brend (1975). Pp. 100–7

Pike, E. V. 1956. Tonally differentiated allomorphs in Soyaltepec Mazatec. *International Journal of American Linguistics* 22: 57–71

Pike, E. V. 1967. Huautla de Jiménez Mazatec. In Wauchope and McQuown (1967). Pp. 311–30

Pike, E. V. 1974a. A multiple stress system versus a tone system. *International Journal of American Linguistics* 40: 169–75

Pike, E. V. 1974b. Los idiomas tonales de México. Paper presented at the XLI International Congress of Americanists (Mexico). (Unpublished)

Pike, E. V. 1976. Phonology. In R. M. Brend and K. L. Pike (eds.) *Tagmemics, volume 1: Aspects of the field.* Pp. 45–83. Trends in Linguistics. Studies and Monographs 1. The Hague: Mouton

Pike, E. V. and P. Small 1974. Downstepping terrace tone in Coatzospan Mixtec. In Brend (1974). Pp. 105–34

Pike, E. V. and K. Wistrand 1974. Step-up terrace tone in Acatlán Mixtec. In Brend (1974). Pp. 81–104

Pike, K. L. 1946. Phonemic pitch in Maya. *International Journal of American Linguistics* 12: 82–8

Pike, K. L. 1947. *Phonemics. A technique for reducing languages to writing.* Ann Arbor: The University of Michigan Press

Pike, K. L. 1948. *Tone languages, a technique for determining the number and type of pitch contrasts in a language, with studies in tonemic substitution and fusion.* University of Michigan Publications, Linguistics, vol. 4. Ann Arbor: The University of Michigan Press

Pike, K. L. 1949. A problem in morphology–syntax division. *Acta Linguistica* 5: 125–38. Reprinted in R. M. Brend (ed.). *Kenneth Pike, Selected writings,* pp. 74–84. The Hague – Paris: Mouton 1972

Pike, K. L. 1970. *Tagmemic and matrix linguistics applied to selected African languages.* Summer Institute of Linguistics Publications 23. Norman, Oklahoma: Summer Institute of Linguistics and University of Oklahoma

Pike, K. L. and E. V. Pike 1947. Immediate constituents of Mazateco syllables. *International*

Journal of American Linguistics 13: 78–91. Reprinted in Brend (1975). Pp. 62–83

Pike, K. L. and M. Warkentin 1961. Huave: a study in syntactic tone with low lexical functional load. In Elson and Comas (1961). Pp. 627–42. Reprinted in Brend (1975). Pp. 155–72

Pimentel, F. 1874–5. *Cuadro descriptivo y comparativo de las lenguas indígenas de México, o tratado de filología mexicana.* 2nd edn. 3 vols. México D.F.: Tipografía de I. Epstein

Pittman, R. S. 1954. *A grammar of Tetelcingo (Morelos) Nahuatl.* Language dissertation 50. (Supplement to *Language* vol. 30 no. 1, pt 2.) Baltimore: Linguistic Society of America

Pozas, I. de and R. Pozas 1956. *Del monolingüismo indígena al bilingüismo en lengua nacional.* Oaxaca: Nuevo Paso Nacional

Pozas, R. and I. H. de Pozas 1972. *Los indios en las clases sociales de México.* 2nd edn. México: Siglo XXI

Preuss, K. T. 1912. *Die Nayarit-Expedition: Text-Aufnahmen und Beobachtungen unter Mexikanischen Indianern. Erster Band, Die Religion des Cora-Indianer in Texten nebst Wörterbuch.* Leipzig: B. G. Tuebner

Preuss, K. T. 1932. Grammatik der Cora-Sprache. *International Journal of American Linguistics* 7: 1–84

Pride, K. 1965. *Chatino Syntax.* Summer Institute of Linguistics Publications 12. Norman, Oklahoma: Summer Institute of Linguistics and University of Oklahoma

Pride, L. 1963. Chatino tonal structure. *Anthropological Linguistics* 5.2: 19–28

Reid, A. A. and R. G. Bishop 1974. *Diccionario totonaco de Xicotepec de Juárez, Puebla.* Serie de Vocabularios y Diccionarios Indígenas 'Mariano Silva y Aceves' 17. México, D.F.: Summer Institute of Linguistics

Reid, A. A., R. G. Bishop, E. M. Button and R. E. Longacre 1968. *Totonac: from clause to discourse.* Summer Institute of Linguistics Publications 17. Norman, Oklahoma: Summer Institute of Linguistics and University of Oklahoma

Rensch, C. 1963. Some aspects of Chinantec grammar: a tagmemic view. *XIV Annual Round Table Meeting on Linguistics and Language Studies.* Pp. 81–90. Washington, D.C.: Georgetown University Press

Rensch, C. R. 1973. Otomanguean isoglosses. In T. Sebeok (ed.) *Current trends in linguistics, vol. 11: Diachronic, areal and typological linguistics.* Pp. 259–316. The Hague: Mouton. Reprinted in Sebeok (1977) II. Pp. 163–84

Rensch, C. R. 1976. *Comparative Otomanguean phonology.* Indiana University Publications, Language Science Monographs No. 14. Bloomington: Indiana University

Rensch, C. R. 1977. Classification of the Otomanguean languages and the position of Tlapanec. In Oltrogge and Rensch (1977). Pp. 58–108

Rensch, C. and C. M. Rensch 1966. The Lalana Chinantec syllable. In A. Pompa y Pompa (ed.) *Summa Anthropologica: en homenaje a Roberto J. Weitlaner.* Pp. 455–63. México: Instituto Nacional de Antropología e Historia

Reyes, A. de los 1890. *Arte en lengua mixteca.* México en casa de Pedro Belli 1593. Publié par le Comte H. de Charencey. Paris: Klincksieck

Ricard, R. 1933. *Conquête Spirituelle du Mexique.* Travaux et Mémoires de l'Institut d'Ethnologie vol. XX, Université de Paris. (English translation by Lesley Bird Simpson, *The spiritual conquest of Mexico. An Essay on the Apostolate and the Evangelizing Methods of the Mendicant Orders in New Spain: 1523–1572.* Berkeley and Los Angeles: University of California Press, 1966)

Robbins, F. E. 1961. Quiotepec Chinantec syllable patterning. *International Journal of American Linguistics* 27: 237–50

Robbins, F. E. 1968. *Quiotepec Chinantec grammar.* Papeles de la Chinantla 4, Serie Científica 8. México: Museo Nacional de Antropología

Robbins, F. E. 1975. Nasal words without phonetic vowels in Quiotepec Chinantec. In Brend (1975). Pp. 126–30

Robertson, J. S. 1977. A proposed revision in Mayan subgrouping. *International Journal of American Linguistics* 43: 105–20

Robinson, D. F. (ed.) 1969. *Aztec studies I: Phonological and grammatical studies in modern Nahuatl dialects.* Summer Institute of Linguistics Publications 19. Norman, Oklahoma: Summer Institute of Linguistics and University of Oklahoma

Robinson, D. F. 1969. Puebla (Sierra) Nahuat prosodies. In Robinson (ed.) (1969). Pp. 17–32

Robinson, D. F. 1970. *Aztec studies II: Sierra Nahuat word structure.* Summer Institute of Linguistics Publications 22. Norman, Oklahoma: Summer Institute of Linguistics and University of Oklahoma

Robinson, D. F. and W. Sischo 1969. Michoacán (Pómaro) Nahual clause structure. In Robinson (ed.) (1969). Pp. 53–74

Romero Castillo, M. 1961. Morfemas clasificadores del maya-yucateco. In Elson and Comas (1961). Pp. 657–62

Ros Romero, M. del C. 1979. Un análisis comparativo de sistemas pronominales en lenguas otomangues. In Hopkins and Josserand (1979). Pp. 20–4

[Rupp, J.] 1980. *Chinanteco. San Juan Lealao.* Archivo de Lenguas Indigenas de México 9. México: Centro de Investigación para la Integración Social

Sahagún, B. de 1950–63. *Florentine codex. General history of the things of New Spain.* Translated from the Aztec into English, with notes and illustrations, by A. J. O. Anderson and C. E. Dibble. 12 vols. Santa Fe, New Mexico: University of Utah

Sanders, W. T. and Barbara J. Price 1968. *Mesoamerica. The evolution of a civilization.* New York: Random House

Sapir, E. 1911. The problem of noun incorporation in American languages. *American Anthropologist,* n.s. 73: 250–82

Sapir, E. 1913. Southern Paiute and Nahuatl, a study in Uto-Aztecan Part I. *Journal de la Société des Américanistes,* Paris, n.s. 10: 379–425

Sapir, E. 1914–19. Southern Paiute and Nahuatl, a study in Uto-Aztecan Part II. *Journal de la Société des Américanistes* Paris, n.s. 11: 443–88

Sapir, E. 1915. Southern Paiute and Nahuatl, a study in Uto-Aztecan Part II. *American Anthropologist* n.s. 17: 98–120, 306–28

Schoembs, J. 1949. *Aztekische Schriftsprache.* Heidelberg: Carl Winter. Universitätsverlag

Schoenhals, A. and L. Schoenhals 1965. *Vocabulario mixe de Totontepec.* Vocabularios indígenas 'Mariano Silva y Aceves' 14. México: Instituto Lingüístico de Verano

Scholes, F. V. and D. Warren 1965. The Olmec region at Spanish contact. In Wauchope and Willey (1965b). Pp. 776–87

Schultze-Jena, L. 1933. *Indiana I: Leben, Glaube und Sprache der Quiché von Guatemala.* Jena: Gustav Fischer

Schultze-Jena. L. 1935. *Indiana II: Mythen in der Muttersprache der Pipil von Izalco in El Salvador.* Jena: Gustav Fischer

Schultze-Jena, L. 1938. *Indiana III: Bei den Azteken, Mixteken und Tlapaneken der Sierra Madre del Sur von Mexiko.* Jena: Gustav Fischer

Schultze-Jena, L. 1944. *Popol Vuh. Das heilige Buch der Quiché Indianer von Guatemala.* Quellenwerke zur alten Geschichte Amerikas 2. Stuttgart: W. Kohlhammer Verlag

Schultze-Jena, L. 1957. *Alt-Aztekische Gesänge.* Quellenwerke zur alten Geschichte Amerikas 6. Stuttgart: W. Kohlhammer Verlag

Sebeok, T. A. 1977. *Native languages of the Americas.* 2 vols. New York and London: Plenum Press

Sebeok, T. A. (ed.) 1968. *Current Trends in Linguistics IV: Ibero-American and Caribbean*

Linguistics. The Hague: Mouton

Sischo, W. R. 1979. Michoacán Nahual. In Langacker (1979). Pp. 307–80

Skinner, L. E. 1962. Usila Chinantec syllable structure. *International Journal of American Linguistics* 28: 251–5

Small, P. C. 1974. Coatzospan Mixtec pronouns. *Summer Institute of Linguistics – Mexico Workpapers* 1: 9–14

Speck, C. H. 1978. *The phonology of Texmelucan Zapotec verb irregularity.* University of North Dakota Master of Arts Thesis (Unpublished)

Speck, C. and V. B. Pickett 1976. Some properties of the Texmelucan Zapotec verbs *go, come,* and *arrive. International Journal of American Linguistics* 42: 58–64

Spicer, E. H. 1962. *Cycles of conquest. The impact of Spain, Mexico, and the United States on the Indians of the Southwest 1533–1960.* Tucson: The University of Arizona Press

Spores, R. 1965. The Zapotec and Mixtec at Spanish contact. In Wauchope and Willey (1965b). Pp. 962–87

Spores, R. 1967. *The Mixtec kings and their people.* Norman, Oklahoma: University of Oklahoma Press

Spotts, H. 1953. Vowel harmony and consonant sequences in Mazahua (Otomi). *International Journal of American Linguistics* 19: 253–8

[Stairs, E. F.] n.d. *Huave de San Mateo del Mar.* Archivo de Lenguas Indígenas de Mexico. Mexico: Centro de Investigación para la Integración Social. (In press)

Stairs, E. F. and B. E. Hollenbach 1969. Huave verb morphology. *International Journal of American Linguistics* 35: 38–53

Stairs Kreger, G. A. and E. F. Scharfe de Stairs 1981. *Diccionario Huave de San Mateo del Mar.* Vocabularios y diccionarios indigenas 'Mariano Silva y Aceves' 24. México, D.F.: Instituto Linguística de Verano

Stark, Sharon 1976. The verb word of Northern Popoloca. *Summer Institute of Linguistics – Mexico Workpapers* 2: 1–73

Stark, S. and P. Machin 1977. Stress and tone in Tlacoyalco Popoloca. In Merrifield (1977). Pp. 69–92

Stoll, O. 1884. *Zur Ethnographie der Republik Guatemala.* Zürich: Druck von Orell Füssli

Suárez, J. A. 1968. Classical languages. In Sebeok (1968). Pp. 254–74. Reprinted with additions in Sebeok (1977) II. Pp. 3–25

Suárez, J. A. 1972. La clasificación del papabuco y del solteco. *Anuario de Letras* (Universidad Nacional Autónoma de México) 10: 219–32

Suárez, J. A. 1975. *Estudios huaves.* Colección científica 22. México: Instituto Nacional de Antropología e Historia

Suárez, J. A. 1977a. La clasificación de las lenguas zapotecas. Paper presented at the Congreso de Evaluación de la Antropología en Oaxaca. Instituto Nacional de Antropología e Historia, Centro Regional de Oaxaca. (Unpublished)

Suárez, J. A. 1977b. La influencia del español en la estructura gramatical del náhuatl. *Anuario de Letras* (Universidad Nacional Autónoma de México) 15: 115–64

Suárez, J. A. 1979. Observaciones sobre la evolución fonológica del tlapaneco. *Anales de Antropología* (Universidad Nacional Autónoma de México) 16: 371–86

Suárez, J. A. n.d. La lengua Tlapaneca de Malinaltepec. México: Universidad Nacional Autónoma de México. (In press)

Swadesh, M. 1967. Lexicostatistic classification. In Wauchope and McQuown (1967). Pp. 79–115

Swadesh, M. 1969. *Elementos del tarasco antiguo.* Instituto de Investigaciones Históricas, Serie Antropológica 11. México: Universidad Nacional Autónoma de México

Swadesh, M. and M. Sancho 1966. *Los mil elementos del mexicano clásico. Base analítica de la lengua nahua.* Instituto de Investigaciones Históricas, Serie de Cultura Náhuatl, Monografías 9. México: Universidad Nacional Autónoma de México

Tapia Zenteno, C. de 1885. *Arte novísima de la lengua mexicana*. México. Reprinted in Colección de Gramáticas de la Lengua Mexicana vol. 3: 1–42. México: Museo Nacional (Imprenta de Ignacio Escalante)

Thaeler, M. D. and A. D. n.d. *Miskito Grammar*. Published by the Board of Christian Education in Nicaragua

Thomas, C. and J. R. Swanton 1911. *Indian languages of Mexico and Central America and their geographical distribution*. Bureau of American Ethnology, Bulletin 44. Washington, D.C.

Thompson, J. E. S. 1943. *Pitfalls and stimuli in the interpretation of history through loanwords*. Middle American Research Institute. The Tulane University of Louisiana, Publication 11. Philological and Documentary Studies Vol. 1 No. 2. New Orleans 1943

Tuggy, D. H. 1979. Tetelcingo Nahuatl. In Langacker (1979). Pp. 3–140

Turner, P. 1967a. Highland Chontal phonemics. *Anthropological Linguistics* 9.4: 26–32

Turner, P. 1967b. Highland Chontal phrase syntagmemes. *International Journal of American Linguistics* 33: 282–6

Turner, P. 1968a. Highland Chontal clause syntagmemes. *Linguistics* 38: 77–83

Turner, P. 1968b. Highland Chontal sentence syntagmemes. *Linguistics* 42: 117–25

Turner, P. and S. 1971. *Chontal to Spanish–English Dictionary. Spanish to Chontal*. Tucson, Arizona: The University of Arizona Press 1971

Uribe Villegas, O. 1970. *Un mapa del monolingüismo y el bilingüismo de los indígenas de México en 1960*. México: Universidad Nacional Autónoma de México

Van Haitsma, J. D. and W. Van Haitsma 1976. *A hierarchical sketch of Mixe as spoken in San José El Paraíso*. Summer Institute of Linguistics Publications 44. Norman, Oklahoma: Summer Institute of Linguistics and University of Oklahoma

Vivó, J. A. 1941. *Razas y lenguas indígenas de México; su distribución geográfica*. Publicaciones del Instituto Panamericano de Geografía e Historia No. 52. México

Voegelin, C. F. and F. M. and K. Hale 1962. *Typological and comparative grammar of Uto-Aztecan: I (Phonology)*. Indiana University Publications in Anthropology and Linguistics, Memoir 17 (= *International Journal of American Linguistics* vol. 28 no. 1)

Vogt, E. Z. and A. Ruz L. (eds.) 1971. *Desarrollo cultural de los mayas*. México: Universidad Nacional Autónoma de México

Wallis, E. E. 1956. Simulfixation in aspect markers of Mezquital Otomi. *Language* 32: 453–9

Wallis, E. E. 1964. Mezquital Otomi verb fusion. *Language* 40: 75–82

Wallis, E. E. 1968. The word and the phonological hierarchy of Mezquital Otomí. *Language* 44: 76–90

Wares, A. C. 1974. Tarascan verb inflection. *Summer Institute of Linguistics – Mexico Workpapers* 1: 93–100

Wares, A. C. 1979. *Bibliography of the Summer Institute of Linguistics 1935–1975*. Dallas: Summer Institute of Linguistics

Waterhouse, V. 1962. *The grammatical structure of Oaxaca Chontal*. *International Journal of American Linguistics* 28(2), pt II. Indiana Research Center in Anthropology, Folklore, and Linguistics, Publication 19. Bloomington, Indiana

Waterhouse, V. 1967. Huamelultec Chontal. In Wauchope and McQuown (1967). Pp. 349–67

[Waterhouse, V.] 1980. *Chontal de la Sierra*. Archivo de lenguas indígenas de México 7. México: Centro de Investigación para la Integración Social.

Waterhouse, V. and M. Morrison 1950. Chontal phonemes. *International Journal of American Linguistics* 16: 35–9

Wauchope, R. and H. F. Cline (eds.) 1972. *Handbook of Middle American Indians. Vol. 12: Guide to ethnohistorical sources, Part one*. Austin: University of Texas Press

Wauchope R. and H. F. Cline (eds.) 1973. *Handbook of Middle American Indians. Vol. 13: Guide to ethnohistorical sources, Part two*. Austin: University of Texas Press

Wauchope, R. and N. A. McQuown (eds.) 1967. *Handbook of Middle American Indians*.

Vol. 5: Linguistics. Austin: University of Texas Press

Wauchope, R. and M. Nash (eds.) 1967. *Handbook of Middle American Indians. Vol. 6: Social Anthropology.* Austin: University of Texas Press

Wauchope, R. and E. Z. Vogt (eds.) 1969. *Handbook of Middle American Indians. Vols. 7, 8: Ethnology.* Austin: University of Texas Press

Wauchope, R. and G. R. Willey (eds.) 1965a. *Handbook of Middle American Indians. Vol. 2: Archeology of Southern Mesoamerica, Part one.* Austin: University of Texas Press

Wauchope, R. and G. R. Willey (eds.) 1965b. *Handbook of Middle American Indians. Vol. 3: Archeology of Southern Mesoamerica, Part two.* Austin: University of Texas Press

Wauchope, R., G. F. Ekholm, and I. Bernal (eds.) 1971. *Handbook of Middle American Indians. Vol. 11: Archeology of Northern Mesoamerica, Part two.* Austin: University of Texas Press

Westley, D. O. 1971. The Tepetotutla Chinantec stressed syllable. *International Journal of American Linguistics* 37: 160–3

Whetten, N. L. 1961. *Guatemala: the land and the people.* New Haven: Yale University Press

Whorf, B. L. 1946. The Milpa Alta dialect of Aztec with notes on the Classical and the Tepoztlan dialects. In Hoijer et al. (1946). Pp. 367–97

Willet, T. L. 1978. The southeastern Tepehuan verb. *Anthropological Linguistics* 20.6: 272–94

Willey, G. R. 1966. *An introduction to American archeology. Vol. 1 North and Middle America.* Englewood Cliffs, New Jersey: Prentice-Hall

Willey, G. R. 1971. An archeological frame of reference for Maya culture history. In Vogt and Ruz L. (1971). Pp. 137–86

Willey, G. R., G. F. Ekholm, and R. F. Millon 1964. The patterns of farming life and civilization. In Wauchope, R. and R. C. West (eds.) 1964. *Handbook of Middle American Indians. Vol. 1: Natural environment and early cultures.* Pp. 446–98. Austin: University of Texas Press

Williams, A. F. and R. F. Longacre 1967. Popoluca clause types. *Acta Linguistica Hafniensia* 10: 161–86

Wolf, E. 1959. *Sons of the shaking earth.* Chicago and London: The University of Chicago Press

Wonderly, W. L. 1946. Phonemic acculturation in Zoque. *International Journal of American Linguistics* 12: 92–5

Wonderly, W. L. 1949. Some Zoquean phonemic and morphophonemic correspondences. *International Journal of American Linguistics* 15: 1–11

Wonderly, W. L. 1951a. Zoque I: introduction and bibliography. *International Journal of American Linguistics* 17: 1–9

Wonderly, W. L. 1951b. Zoque II: phonemes and morphophonemes. *International Journal of American Linguistics* 17: 105–23

Wonderly, W. L. 1951c. Zoque III: morphological classes, affix list, and verbs. *International Journal of American Linguistics* 17: 137–62

Wonderly, W. L. 1951d. Zoque IV: auxiliaries and nouns. *International Journal of American Linguistics* 17: 235–51

Wonderly, W. L. 1952a. Zoque V: other stem and word classes. *International Journal of American Linguistics* 18: 35–48

Wonderly, W. L. 1952b. Zoque VI: text. *International Journal of American Linguistics* 18: 189–202

Zavala, S. 1977a. *'¿EL castellano lengua obligatoria?' Discurso de ingreso a la Academia Mexicana Correspondiente de la Española.* México: Condumex, S. A.

Zavala, S. 1977b. '¿EL castellano lengua obligatoria?' Adiciones. *Memorias de El Colegio Nacional* 8: 141–62

LANGUAGE INDEX

This index contains names of languages and language groups that occur in the main text including tables and figures, but not those that occur in the sections on Sources, Further Reading, and References. Most names that consist of a phrase are entered by the last component, that is *San Antonio Ocotlan Zapotec* is entered within parentheses (*San Antonio Ocotlan*) in the *Zapotec* entry after references common to Zapotec, if any. In some cases, e.g. *Otomi*, a name occurs twice as a main entry: as the name of a group of languages, and as the name of a language or language complex. The classification is given according to the symbols in table 1, within brackets after the name of the language or language group. The location of each language is also given; but it is indicated in different ways according to the possibilities that map 1 offers to locate the language: (a) for a language which has its own number, for example *Quiché* or *Northern Tepehuán*, only the country is indicated if the language is located outside Mexico, but the country and state(s) if the language is located in Mexico; (b) the same procedure is followed for language complexes (see p. 18 and table 13) which have a compact distribution, for example *Chinantec* or *Mazatec*; (c) for those language complexes (all of them in Mexico) that have an extensive or scattered distribution, under the common name of the complex the location is given by state(s), and under each individual language name the location is given in terms of state and, if necessary, of cardinal points. When no page, figure or table is indicated it means that the name only occurs in table 1.

Acatec [IX.D.b.α.68. Guatemala]

Aguacatec [IX.E.b.73. Guatemala] phonemic system, 35, table 9; stress, 35

Amuzgo [III.D]

Amuzgo (*Guerrero* [III.D.27. Mexico: Guerrero]) bilabial trill, 46; consonants, 39; palatalized stops, 44; stop series, 45; syllables, 39; tones, 51; vowels, 46. (*Oaxaca* [III.D.28. Mexico: Oaxaca])

Arahuacan [XIII]

Aztecan [I.H.]

Black Carib [XIII.86. Belize; Honduras] 13

Cahitic [I.F.b]

Cakchiquel [IX.F.a.75. Guatemala] consonants, 35; speakers, 170

Chatino [III.F.a.33. Mexico: Oaxaca] borrowings, 158; infixes, 67; pronouns, 83; vowels, 40; vs. Zapotec, 21. (*Yaitepec*) coordination vs. subordination, 128; laterals, 46; tones, 51, 52

Chatino-Zapotec [III.F] internal classification, 25

Chiapanec [III.H.36. Mexico: Chiapas]

Chiapanec-Mangue [III.H] migration, 149

Chibchan [XII] migrations, 153

Chichimec [III.A.a.16. Mexico: Guanajuato] negation and tense, 75; tense system, 72; verbal phrase, 126; word order, 96, table 22

Chicomuceltec [IX.A.54. Mexico: Chiapas] migration, 150

Chinantec [III.G.35. Mexico: Oaxaca] (*Lalana*) clusters, 40; stops, 45; tones, 51. (*Lealao*) comparative constructions, 129; locative verbs, 126; tones, 51. (*Palantla*) affixing, 67; nasal vowels, 47; pronouns, 81, 83; questions, 125; syllables, 40; tones, 51, 52; verb, 60. (*Quiotepec*) emphasis, 124; possession in nouns, 85–6; syllabic nasals, 45; verbal phrase, 126; voice contrast, 45; vowels, 40, 46. (*Sochiapan*) tones, 51. (*Tepetotutla*) tones, 51. (*Usila*) syllables, 40; tones, 51

Chinantec(an) [III.G] categories in verbs, 80; infixes, 67; tones, 51; whistled speech, 54

Chocho [III.B.a.22. Mexico: Oaxaca] consonants, 39; person, 77; possessive clauses, 126; pronouns, 82, table 17; questions, 125; relative clauses, 128; stops, 45

SUBJECT INDEX

This index list subjects, geographical names, and personal names but not those in the sections on sources, further reading and references. For language names and subjects in reference to languages the Language Index should be consulted.

actor, 94, 99, 106, 111, 113, 117, 118, 130, 135; in passive clauses 102; indefinite 99, 102, 118, 130
Adelung, J. C., 5–6
adjectival clauses, 102, 108, 118, 125, 131, 133
adjectives, 64, 131
agent, 99, 106, 113, 117, 122–3, 123–4, 130; indefinite 106
alternations: of consonants, 68; of vowels, 67
Alvarado Tezozomoc, F., 141
Angulo, J. de, 8
Annals of Quauhtitlan, 140
Annals of the Cakchiquels, 143
Annals of Tlatelolco, 140
antipassive, 118
archaeological periods, table 26; Classic, 147; Early Formative, 146; Late Classic, 147; Middle Formative, 146; Postclassic, 147
area traits, 159–62; criteria for, 160–1; due to Spanish influence, 161; grammatical, 161; mechanisms responsible for, 159–60; phonological, 160; semantic, 161
article, 86, 120, 128
aspect, 72f
assimilation, 42, 43
association, as participant, 98
auxiliary verbs, 94, 108–9, 111, 120, 126, 131, 134
Azcapozalco, 148
Aztecs, 140, 148, 149, 153, map 3

baby talk, 48
Basalenque, D., 3
Belmar, F., 7–8
beneficiary, 94, 106, 111, 113, 117, 123, 130, 133
bicultural education, 173
bilingual education, 168
bilingualism: and communication, 172; and Indian social classes, 159; and number of

speakers, 170; trends, 171
Boas, F., 8
books, pictorial, 139
borrowing, 129; among Indian languages, 154–9; and area traits, 159–60; criteria for, 155; for glosses in the basic list, 155; mechanism for incorporating Spanish verbs, 115, 126, 131; of animal names, 155; of Spanish grammatical particles, 100, 104, 105, 108, 109, 111, 115, 121, 135–6, table 23; seeming, 155, 156; *see also* calque
breathy phonation, 48

Cakchiquel kingdom, 148, map 3
calendar, 140, 158
calque, 120, 132, 137, 161
Carochi, H., 3, 4, 6
case, 83, 87, 108, 111
causative, 81, 122–3, 125, 130
Cempoala, 150
Chichén Itzá, 147, map 2
Chichimec History, 140
Chilam Balam, Books of, 142
Chimalpahin, D., 141
classification of languages, 13
classificatory verbs, 89–91, tables 19, 20, 21
classifiers, 87–9, 128, table 18
clauses, 101, 108, 117
clitics, 57, 59, 66, 79, 80, 131
Colima, 163
comparative constructions, 101, 105, 110, 112, 115, 129, 133, 135
compounding, 62, 66
consonant loss, 42
consonants: affricates, 44–5; aspirated stops, 45; bilabial trill, 46; contrast of obstruents, 45; dental vs. alveolar, 44; fortes vs. lenes, 39; fricatives, 45; glottal stop, 45; glottalized, 36; glottalized nasals, 45; labials, 38, 39, 44; labials with rounding, 44; labiovelars, 44; laterals, 46; nasals, 45; palatalized, 32, 33, 44; pre-